1988

W9-AXJ-295

3 0301 00056068 6

Harvard Business Review

The Business of Ethics and Business

© Contents of this book copyrighted
1957, 1959, 1960, 1961, 1968, 1970, 1973,
1975, 1977, 1981, 1982, 1983, 1986
by the President and Fellows
of Harvard College.
All rights reserved.
No part of this publication may be
reproduced or transmitted in any form or
by any means, electronic or mechanical,
including photocopy, recording, or any
information storage and retrieval system,
without permission in writing from the
publishers.
Printed in U.S.A.

ISBN 0-86735-239-6

Editor's note

Many of the articles we include in this
series were written before women started
to play an important role in management
in impressive numbers. For this reason,
the authors of certain pieces assumed all
readers were men and that the typical
manager was a "he" instead of a "he or
she." In planning this series, we wanted to
correct our older articles but found that
the expense of resetting them would
increase the price of the series and thus
limit its distribution.

The editors ask that whenever you read
the words "he," "him," or "his" in an
article, you take it to mean "she," "her," or
"hers" as well. Whenever you see "man"
either alone or as part of a word, think of a
person of either gender. We hope that the
archaic use of the masculine gender does
not undermine the effectiveness of the
articles.

174.4
H339b

Table of contents

129,634

LIBRARY
College of St. Francis
JOLIET, ILLINOIS

Biographical update

Some of the articles in this series were written a number of years ago. Although many of the authors' professional activities have remained the same, here are a few changes to the biographical sketches that precede each article (information current as of January 1987).

Kenneth R. Andrews
("Can the Best Corporations Be Made Moral?") is professor emeritus at the Harvard Business School.

Arch R. Doolley
(coauthor, "Personal Values and Business Decisions") is the Jesse Philips Professor of Manufacturing at the Harvard Business School.

David W. Ewing
("Case of the Rogue Division"), formerly managing editor of HBR, is now engaged in research at the Harvard Business School.

Saul W. Gellerman
("Why 'Good' Managers Make Bad Ethical Choices") is dean of the graduate school of management at the University of Dallas.

Edmund P. Learned
(coauthor, "Personal Values and Business Decisions") is professor emeritus at the Harvard Business School, where he served on the faculty from 1927 to 1967.

Theodore Levitt
("The Morality(?) of Advertising") is editor of HBR and the Edward W. Carter Professor of Business Administration at the Harvard Business School.

1 The ethical corporation

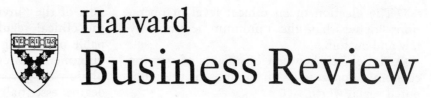

Harvard Business Review

Kenneth R. Andrews

Can the best corporations be made moral?

*Not by heroic management action,
but by maturity and breadth of perspective in
the design of measurement systems*

Foreword

"The overriding master problem now impeding the further progress of corporate responsibility is the difficulty of making credible and effective, throughout a large organization, the social component of a corporate strategy originating in the moral convictions and values of the chief executive." So asserts this author, who then adds that the source of the difficulty is the nature and impact of narrowly designed measurement and reward-and-penalty systems. In this article, he discusses the issue of public responsibility in a private corporation, and suggests the outlines of a management program of action.

Mr. Andrews is Donald K. David Professor of Business Administration, Harvard Business School; Member of the Faculty of Arts and Sciences of Harvard University; and Master of Leverett House. In addition, he is Chairman of the Editorial Board of HBR and a director of four corporations.

Reprint 73301

The concept of corporate social responsibility has made steady progress during the past 40 years. The words mean in part voluntary restraint of profit maximization. More positively, they mean sensitivity to the social costs of economic activity and to the opportunity to focus corporate power on objectives that are possible but sometimes less economically attractive than socially desirable. The term includes:

○ The determination of a corporation to reduce its profit by voluntary contributions to education and other charities.

○ The election of an ethical level of operations higher than the minimum required by law and custom.

○ The choice between businesses of varying economic opportunity on grounds of their imputed social worth.

○ The investment for reasons other than (but obviously still related to) economic return in the quality of life within the corporation itself.

This doctrine of corporate social responsibility is vigorously opposed honestly and openly by conservative lawyers and economists and covertly by the adherents of business as usual. Milton Friedman, the conservative economist of the University of Chicago, denounces the concern for responsibility as "fundamentally subversive" to a free society. He argues that "there is one and only one social responsibility of business— to use its resources and engage in activities designed to increase its profits so long as it . . . engages in open and free competition without deception or fraud." [1]

Thus, for example, the manager who makes decisions affecting immediate profit by reducing pollution and increasing minority employment more than present law requires is in effect imposing taxes upon his stockholders and acting without authority as a public legislative body.

Other critics of the doctrine like to point out:

○ How much easier are the platitudes of virtue than the effective combination of profitable and socially responsive corporate action.

○ How little experience with social questions businessmen immersed in their narrow ambitions and technology can be expected to have.

○ How urgent are the pressures of survival in hard times and against competition.

○ How coercive of individual opinion in an organization is a position on social issues dictated by its management.

○ How infrequently in the entire population occur the intelligence, compassion, knowledge of issues, and morality required of the manager presumptuous enough to factor social responsibility into his economic decisions.

Given the slow rate at which verbalized good intentions are being converted into action, many critics of the large corporation suspect that for every chief executive announcing pious objectives there are a hundred closet rascals quietly conducting business in the old ways and taking immoral comfort in Friedman's moral support. The interventionists question the effective-

ness of the "invisible hand" of competition as the ethical regulator of great corporations capable of shaping in significant degree their environments. Interventionists think also that regulation by government, while always to some degree essential under imperfect competition, is not sufficiently knowledgeable, subtle, or timely to reconcile the self-interest of corporate entrepreneurship and the needs of the society being sore-tried and well served by economic activity.

The advocates of public responsibility for a so-called "private" enterprise assert that, in an industrial society, corporate power, vast in potential strength, must be brought to bear on certain social problems if the latter are to be solved at all. They argue that corporate executives of the integrity, intelligence, and humanity required to run companies whose revenues often exceed the gross national product of whole nations cannot be expected to confine themselves to economic activity and ignore its consequences, and that henceforth able young men and women coming into business will be sensitive to the social worth of corporate activity.

To reassure those uneasy about the dangers of corporate participation in public affairs, the social interventionists say to the economic isolationists that these hazards can be contained through professional education, government control, and self-regulation.

This is not the place to argue further against Friedman's simplistic faith in the powers of the market to purify self-interest. We must observe, however, that the argument for the active participation of corporations in public affairs, for responsible assessment of the impact of economic activity, and for concern with the quality of corporate purposes is gaining ground, even as uneasiness increases about the existence of corporate power in the hands of managers who (except in cases of crisis) are answerable only to themselves or to boards of directors they have themselves selected.

Criticism of corporate activity is manifest currently in consumerism, in the movement to in-

1. *Capitalism and Freedom* (Chicago, University of Chicago Press, 1962), p. 133.

troduce social legislation into stockholder meetings and to reform board memberships, and (more dangerously) in apathy or antipathy among the young. The most practicable response to this criticism by those holding corporate power is to seek to justify limited government by using power responsibly—the ultimate obligation of free persons in any relatively free society.

We need the large corporation, not for its size but for its capability. Even the vivisectionists of the Justice Department who seek a way to divide IBM into smaller parts presumably have no illusion that the large corporation can or should be eliminated from the world as we know it.

On the assumption, then, that corporate social responsibility is not only here to stay, but must increase in scope and complexity as corporate power increases, I suggest that we look forward to the administrative and organizational consequences of the incursion of private corporations into public responsibility.

Nature of the problem

Among the many considerations confronting the executive who would make social responsibility effective, there are some so well known that we can quickly pass them by. Hypocrisy, insincerity, and hollow piety are not really dangerous, for they are easily detected.

In fact, it is much more likely that genuinely good intentions will be thought insincere than that hypocritical protestations of idealism will be mistaken for truth. "Mr. Ford (or Mr. Kaiser or Mr. Rockefeller) doesn't really mean what he says," as an organization refrain is more Mr. Ford's or Mr. Kaiser's or Mr. Rockefeller's problem than what he should say. Cynicism, the by-product of impersonal bureaucracy, remains one of the principal impediments to the communication of corporate social policy.

I would like to set aside also the problem of choice of what social contribution should be attempted—a problem which disparity between the infinite range of social need and the limits of available corporate resources always brings to mind.

Self-consistent strategy

The formulation of specific corporate social policy is as much a function of strategic planning as the choice of product and market combina-tions, the establishment of profit and growth objectives, or the choice of organization structure and systems for accomplishing corporate purposes.

Rather than wholly personal or idiosyncratic contributions (like supporting the museum one's wife is devoted to) or safe and sound contributions like the standard charities, or faddist entry into fashionable areas, corporate strategic response to societal needs and expectations makes sense when it is closely related to the economic functions of the company or to the peculiar problems of the community in which it operates.

For a paper company, it would seem a strategic necessity to give first priority to eliminating the poisonous effluents from its mills rather than, for example, to support cultural institutions like traveling art exhibits. Similarly, for an oil company it would seem a strategic necessity to look at its refinery stacks, at spillage, and at automobile exhaust.

The fortunate company that is paying the full social cost of its production function can make contributions to problems it does not cause—like juvenile delinquency, illiteracy, and so on—or to other forms of environmental improvement more appropriate to corporate citizenship than directly related to its production processes.

As leaders of business move beyond conventional philanthropic contributions to strategy-

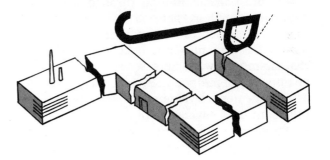

related investments in social betterment, they begin to combine the long-run economic interests of their companies with the priorities (as for pollution) becoming evident in public concern, seeking those points where indeed what is good for the country is good for General Motors.

Once the conscious planning which a fully developed corporate strategy requires is understood, the practical alternatives before any company are not impossibly difficult to identify and to rank according to relevance to economic strategy or to organization needs and resources.

The outcome is an integrated self-consistent strategy embodying defined obligations to society relevant to but not confined to its economic purposes. The top management of a large company, once it elects to, can be expected to have less difficulty in articulating such a strategy than in dealing with the problems of organization behavior to which I now turn.

Organization behavior

The advance of the doctrine of corporate social responsibility has been the apparent conversion of more and more chief executive officers. Change toward responsible behavior and the formulation of strategic intentions are obviously not possible without their concern, compassion, and conviction.

So long as the organization remains small enough to be directly influenced by the chief executive's leadership, certain results can be traced to his determination that they occur—as in centrally decided investments, specific new ventures, cash contributions to charity, and compensation, promotion, and other personnel policies.

But as an organization grows larger and as operations become more decentralized, the power and influence of the chief executive are reinterpreted and diffused. For example:

If a large company is to be sufficiently decentralized to make worldwide operations feasible, power must be distributed throughout a hierarchy inhabited by persons (a) who may not share their chief executive's determination or fervor, (b) who may not believe (more often) that he means what he says, and (c) who may be impelled to postpone action on such problems as management development, pollution, or employment and advancement of minority representatives.

At this point, the overriding master problem now impeding the further progress of corporate responsibility is the difficulty of making credible and effective, throughout a large organization, the social component of a corporate strategy originating in the moral convictions and values of the chief executive.

Quantifiable results: The source of the difficulty is the nature and impact of our systematic planning processes, forms of control, systems of measurement, and pattern of incentives, and the impersonal way all these are administered. The essence of the systematic rational planning

we know most about is quantitative information furnished to the process and quantitative measures of results coming out.

Once plans are put into effect, managers are measured, evaluated, promoted, shelved, or discharged according to the relation of their accomplishments against the plan. In the conventions of accounting and the time scale of exact quantification, performance becomes short-run economic or technical results inside the corporation. Evaluation typically gives full marks for current accomplishment, with no estimate of the charges against the future which may have been made in the effort to accomplish the plan.

Since progress in career, dependent on favorable judgments of quantifiable performance, is the central motivation in a large organization, general and functional managers at divisional, regional, district, and local levels are motivated to do well what is best and most measured, to do it now, and to focus their attention on the internal problems that affect immediate results.

In short, the more quantification and the more supervision of variance, the less attention there will be to such intangible topics as the social role of Plant X in Community Y or the quality of corporate life in the office at Sioux City.

The leaner the central staff of a large organization is kept, the more stress there will be on numbers; and, more importantly, the more difficulty there will be in making qualitative evaluation of such long-term processes as individual and management development, the steady augmentation of organizational competence, and the progress of programs for making work meaningful and exciting, and for making more than economic contributions to society.

The small headquarters group supervising the operations of a conglomerate of autonomous organizations hitherto measured by ranking them with respect to return on equity would not expect to have before it proposals from the subsidiaries for important investments in social responsibility. Such investments could only be made by the corporate headquarters, which would not itself be knowledgeable about or much motivated to take action on opportunities existing throughout the subsidiaries.

Corporate amorality: One colleague of mine, Joseph L. Bower, has examined the process by which corporate resources are allocated in large organizations.[2] Another, Robert W. Ackerman, has documented through field studies the dilemmas which a financially oriented and present-

2. *Managing the Resource Allocation Process* (Boston, Division of Research, Harvard Business School, 1969).

tense accounting system pose for the forward progress of specific social action, like pollution abatement and provision of minority opportunity.[3] Still a third, Malcolm S. Salter, has studied the impact of compensation systems in multinational corporations.[4]

It appears that the outcome of these and other research studies will establish what we have long suspected—that good works, the results of which are long term and hard to quantify, do not have a chance in an organization using conventional incentives and controls and exerting pressure for ever more impressive results.

It is quite possible then, and indeed quite usual, for a highly moral and humane chief executive to preside over an "amoral organization"[5]—one made so by processes developed before the liberalization of traditional corporate economic objectives. The internal force which stubbornly resists efforts to make the corporation compassionate (and exacting) toward its own people and responsible (as well as economically efficient) in its external relationships is the incentive system forcing attention to short-term quantifiable results.

The sensitivity of upward-oriented career executives at lower and middle levels to what quantitative measures say about them is part of their ambition, their interest in their compensation, and their desire for the recognition and approval of their superiors. When, as they usually do, they learn how to beat the system, the margin of capacity they reserve for a rainy day is hoarded for survival, not expended in strengthening their suborganization's future capability or in part-time participation in corporate good works or responsible citizenship on their own time.

With individuals, as with organizations, survival takes precedence over social concern. All we need do to keep even experienced, capable, and profit-producing managers on the ropes of survival is to focus the spotlight on their day-to-day activities and exhaust their ingenuity in outwitting the system by increasing the level of short-term results they are asked to attain.

The isolationists should be quite content with the amorality of an organization motivated by career-oriented responsiveness to narrowly

3. "Managing Corporate Responsibility," scheduled for publication in HBR July-August 1973.

4. "Tailor Incentive Compensation to Strategy," HBR March-April 1973, p. 94.

5. The phrase is Joseph L. Bower's, from *Technology, the Corporation, and the State*, edited by R. Maris and E.J. Mesthene, to be published by the Program on Technology and Society at Harvard University.

designed measurement and reward-and-penalty systems. The interventionists are not. They look for solutions in the experience, observation, and research I have been drawing on in describing the set of problems a new breadth of vision reveals to us.

Thus the art of using the two-edged sword of contribution to society and of stimulation to creative achievement within the corporation becomes even more sophisticated when that institution must not only relate to the societies of different countries and cultures but also attract and keep the dedication of men and women with values and desires not typically American.

Program of action

Inquiry into the nature of the problem suggests the outlines of a program of action. It begins with the incorporation into strategic and operating plans—of subsidiaries, country or area organizations, or profit centers—of specific objectives in areas of social concerns strategically related to the economic activity and community environment of the organization unit.

Since the executive in New York cannot specify the appropriate social strategy for the company in Brazil or the branch in Oregon, or even know what the people there want to work on, intermediate managers who are aware of the social and organization policy of the company, must elicit (with staff help if necessary) pro-

posals for investment of money, energy, time, or concern in these areas.

The review of plans submitted may result in reduction or increase in commitments in all areas; it is essential that the negotiation include attention to social and organization objectives, with as much quantification as reasonable but with qualitative objectives where appropriate.

The development of such strategic and operating plans turns critically on the initiative of responsible corporate individuals, who must be competent enough to accomplish demanding economic and social tasks and have time as well for their families and private affairs.

Financial, production, and sales requirements may be transmitted down rather than drawn upward in an efficient (though often sterilizing) compaction of the planning process. The top-down promulgation of an imaginative and community-centered social and organization strategy, except in terms so general as to be ineffective, is not only similarly unwise in stifling creativity and commitment but also virtually impossible.

Qualitative attention

Once targets and plans have been defined (in the negotiation between organization levels), the measurement system must incorporate in appropriate proportion quantitative and qualitative measures. The bias to short-term results can be corrected by qualitative attention to social and organization programs. The transfer and promotion of managers successful in achieving short-term results is a gamble until their competence in balancing short- and long-term objectives is demonstrated.

Incidentally, rapid rotation virtually guarantees a low level of interest in the particular city through which the manager is following his career; one day it will be seen to be as wasteful as an organization-building and management-development device as it is useful in staffing a growing organization. The alternative—to remain in a given place, to develop fully the company's business in a given city assisted by knowledge and love of the region—needs to become open to executives who do not wish to become president of their companies.

When young middle managers fall short of their targets, inquiry into the reasons and ways to help them achieve assigned goals should precede adverse judgment and penalty. Whenever measurement and control can be directed toward ways to correct problems observed, the shriveling effects of over-emphatic evaluation are postponed. In addition, managers learn that something is important to their superiors other than a single numerical indicator of little significance when detached from the future results to which it relates.

Internal audit: The curse of unquantifiability which hangs over executive action in the areas of corporate responsibility may someday be lifted by the "social audit," now in very early stages of development.[6] In its simplest form, this is a kind of balance sheet and operating state-ment. On it are listed the dollar values of such corporate investments as training programs, individual development activities, time devoted by individuals to community projects, contributions to pollution abatement, transportation, taxes, and the'like. All of these investments call the attention of a company and community to the cumulative dollar worth of corporate functions ancillary to production and sales.

But the further evolvement of the social audit, which one day may develop the conventions that make comparison possible, is not essential to immediate qualitative attention to progress being made by managers at all organizational levels toward their noneconomic goals. Consider, for example:

◊ Internal audit groups, necessarily oriented to examining what the public accounting firm must ultimately certify, can be supplemented by adding to their auditors and accountants permanent or temporary personnel, public relations, or general management persons who are qualified to examine, make comment on, and counsel with managers on their success and difficulties in the areas of social contribution and organization morale.

◊ The role in the community of a local branch office, the morale of the work force, clerical and functional staffs, and the expertise and enthusiasm of the salesmen are all capable of assessment, not in hard numbers but nevertheless in valid and useful judgments.

◊ The public relations and personnel staffs of organizations are all too often assigned to superficial and trivial tasks. The employment of such persons in the internal audit function, especially if they have—without necessarily the qualifications or temperament of high-spirited doers—the experience, perspective, and judgment of long service in the organization, would raise the importance of these functions by increasing their usefulness.

Maturity of judgment: Every large corporation develops unintentionally a group of highly experienced but, after a time, uncompulsive managers who are better assigned to jobs requiring maturity of judgment rather than the ability to sprint. The internal qualitative audit, combined with a parallel inquiry by a committee of outside directors, to which I shall allude in a moment, could be an internal counseling, review, and support function epitomizing effective staff

6. See Raymond A. Bauer and Dan H. Fenn, Jr., "What *Is* a Corporate Social Audit?" HBR January-February 1973, p. 37.

support of line operations. It could also provide opportunity for the cadre of older managers no longer motivated by primitive incentives.

Men with executive responsibility, including accountants and controllers, often exercise judgment only distantly affected by numbers; this is not a new requirement or experience. To the extent that managers in the hierarchy are capable of interpreting numbers intelligently, they must be capable of relating results produced to those in gestation and of judging the significance of a profit figure (not to be found in the figure itself) at a given point of time.

Incentive modification: If measurement of performance is to be broad and knowledgeable enough to encompass progress under a strategy containing social and organizational objectives, then the incentive system in a company or organization unit must reward and penalize accomplishments other than those related to economic efficiency.

Moreover, it must become well known in such an organization that persons can be demoted or discharged for failure to behave responsibly toward their subordinates, for example, even if they are successful in economic terms. Career-oriented middle managers must learn, from the response that their organization leadership and community activities receive, how to appreciate the intrinsic worth and how to estimate the value to their own future of demonstrated responsibility.

Management development

Besides liberating the evaluation process by adding qualitative judgment to numbers, the activity which needs expansion in making an organization socially effective and internally healthy is management development—not so much in terms of formal training programs (although I should be the last person to demean the importance of these) as in planned careers.

If organizations elect, as interesting organizations will, high standards of profit and social contribution to be achieved simultaneously, then much is required of the character, general education, and professional competence of managers who must show themselves—whatever their schooling—as liberally educated.

It follows from the argument I am making that, in moderating the amorality of organizations, we must expect executive mid-career education to include exposure to the issues of

responsibility raised here and to the invaluable experience of participating in nonprofit community or government organizations. Under short-term pressures, attention to development

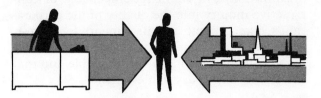

is easily postponed, either as a cost that should be avoided for now or as a process requiring more attention to persons than is convenient or possible.

The management action so far suggested does not constitute innovation so much as reemphasis: it requires not heroic action but maturity and breadth of perspective. Once the aspiration to reach beyond economic to social and human objectives is seen to require extending conventional incentive and performance measurement systems, it is not difficult to avoid imbalance and the unintended organizational consequences of which I have spoken. Awareness of the problem generates its solution.

Audit by directors

But the current move toward revitalization of the board of directors does provide a formal resource to the chief executive who is secure enough and interested enough to avail himself of it. Committees of outside directors are now being formed in a number of companies to meet regularly with the internal audit and outside audit staffs to look closely at the thoroughness and adequacy of the procedures used to ensure that the true condition of the company is reflected in its published accounting statements.

The Penn Central debacle, in the midst of which the board of directors was apparently unaware of approaching disaster, has given considerable impetus to this trend.

If internal audit teams were to extend their counsel, nonpunitive inspection, and recommendations for improvement to social performance and to the quality of organization life as felt by its members, the information they would gather and the problems they would encounter could be summarized for the board committee in the same way as the more conventional subjects of their scrutiny.

In any case, the pervasiveness of the chief executive's posture on social responsibility can be inquired into, and the quality of the management across the organization can be reported on. The board of directors, supposed to provide judgment and experience not available inside the organization, can be—in its proper role of constructive inquiry into the quality of the corporation's management and its support for investment in improving it—a potent force in moderating the management's understandable internal interest in day-to-day achievement.

Conclusion

Nothing will happen, either inward or outward, to further advance the doctrine of social responsibility unless those in charge of the corporation want it to happen and unless their associates share their values and put their backs into solving the organization's master problem. There must be desire and determination first. It must be embodied in a strategy that makes a consistent whole of private economic opportunity and public social responsibility, planned to be implemented in an organization which will be humanely and challengingly led and developed.

A few good guys cannot change the course of a large corporation by their personal influence, but they can arrange that the systems of implementation are appropriate in scope to the breadth of corporate economic and social purpose. Now that enlightened chief executives have made this commitment, it would be tragic to have their will subverted, their determination doubted, and their energy dissipated by bureaucratic organization.

The giant corporation, which in small numbers does half the work of our economic system, is here to stay. It is the dominant force of our industrial society. In its multinational forms it has no higher sovereignty to which it reports; in its national forms it is granted wide latitude. Thus it is important to all of us that its affairs be responsibly conducted and that limited knowledge of the art of managing a large organization not be permitted to thwart us.

If organizations cannot be made moral, the future of capitalism will be unattractive—to all of us and especially to those young people whose talents we need. It is not the attack of the muckrakers we should fear but the apathy of our corporate citizenry.

Douglas S. Sherwin

The ethical roots of the business system

*For business leaders,
ethical action is tied
into the purpose of business
and the nature of the
institution itself*

What does it mean to say that someone acts ethically? For most of us, it means that someone acts according to certain standards of behavior. But what are the standards of behavior for business? The author of this article, who has been a businessman all his working life, ponders what it means to be an ethical business person. He begins his inquiry by exploring the nature of business. He maintains it is a system of interdependent members that can thrive only when all its members are given equal emphasis. To act ethically, then, a manager has to ensure that the owners, employees, and customers all share fairly in the business's gain. The author also contends that the leaders' values that guide the conduct of business must be the same values that have led society to leave a place for business among its institutions.

During his 40-year career with Phillips Petroleum Company, Mr. Sherwin held a variety of staff and line management positions and until recently was president of Phillips Products Company, Inc., a Phillips subsidiary that he and others acquired from Phillips in 1982. Now retired from Phillips, he is chairman of the board of directors of that company (renamed Duraco Products, Inc.), serves on the boards of two other corporations, and is managing partner of Sherwin, Davison, and Associates, an investment and acquisition partnership. This is his fourth article for HBR, the last one being "Management of Objectives" (May-June 1976).

Illustrations by Karen Watson.

Reprint 83616

In George Bernard Shaw's play *Major Barbara*, Undershaft, the old munitions maker, talks with his 24-year-old son about a career. Undershaft asks his son if he is interested in literature, and the young man replies, "No, I have nothing of the artist about me."

"Philosophy then?" his father asks. And the son replies, "Oh, I make no such ridiculous pretension." His father queries him about the army, the church, and the bar. The son disclaims any knowledge of or interest in any of these.

Finally Undershaft asks, "Well come, is there anything you know or care for?" To which the son replies, "I know the difference between right and wrong." "You don't say so!" exclaims Undershaft. "What, no capacity for business, no knowledge of law, no sympathy with art, no pretension to philosophy, only a simple knowledge of the secret that has puzzled all the philosophers, baffled all the lawyers, muddled all the men of business, and ruined most of the artists? The secret of right and wrong—at 24, too."

Probably you have to be 24 to enjoy such certainty. No longer 24, I won't offer any absolute answers, just a point of view.

For many years now, people have argued the question of right and wrong for business. For a long time, they couched the question in terms of social responsibility. More recently, they have asked whether the corporation can or should have a conscience.

Unhappily, the long debate hasn't improved the public's perception of business and business people. Business is criticized for its behavior at almost every interface with the rest of society: for being unresponsive to consumers, employees, its own shareholders, and the public; for enjoying a symbiotic relationship with a government that gives it inordinate power to serve its own interests; for failing to provide employment for all who want to work; for promoting a biased distribution of income; and for plundering the planet with its voracious appetite for resources, which it then dissipates in trivial products.

In these criticisms the implied remedy for such perceived evils is for the corporation to be socially responsible, behave ethically, and have a conscience. If only business people weren't wholly preoccupied with profits, the argument goes, the necessity for these criticisms would disappear.

Unfortunately, what is meant by social responsibility or ethical behavior remains unclear. But if both business and public leaders could come to some accord on what these concepts mean in the context of business, then possibly business performance and the public's expectations for business performance could converge at a higher level of satisfaction for society. So in this article, I will offer a view of what the social responsibility and ethical behavior of business consist of and consider whether the corporation can have a conscience.

A concept of business

Because accepting my view depends on accepting certain premises concerning the purpose of business and the nature of business, I need to describe these ideas first.

Business as a system

At its core, business is a feedback system.[1] Capital owners, employees, and consumers are the members of the system. They coproduce its output. In the ideal, each member contributes value to the system's processes and requires in return a share of the system's output in proportion to the value of the contribution. Owners risk capital and expect to be paid fair profit. Employees supply energy, knowledge, and imagination in exchange for appropriate monetary and psychological income. Consumers supply the essential revenues out of which come wages and profits. If the system's members don't get what they expect, they reduce the quality or quantity of their contributions.

What is ofttimes not appreciated, even by the members themselves, is that the system's members are *interdependent.* Together, and *only* together, can they produce the output they subsequently share. What each member receives is constrained by what other members require, and no member can in the long run enjoy a disproportionate share.

Besides being interdependent, the members of the system are entirely equal in importance.

Business people often claim primacy for capital, perceiving it as the fuel of enterprise, while consumers tend to assume that the whole point of business is to provide them with goods and services. But no member of a system can be primary. Since the contribution of every member is necessary and no contribution is sufficient, the members are equal.

The purpose of business

To the owners of a company, the purpose of business is to yield them profits and appreciation of capital. To employees, its purpose is to afford them a living. Consumers see its purpose as furnishing them goods and services. But like the blind men of Indostan examining the elephant, their points of view do not account for the whole animal.

Public policy circumscribes the activities of the business system. Its rules govern the relationships among the members of the system and between the business system and the rest of society. But society could go further and replace the private, competitive business institution as we know it with a different arrangement altogether—such as socialism, communism, or any centralized and supervised economy. If we aren't convinced of that, we have only to recall Justice Holmes's chilling observation that "it would not be argued today that the power to regulate does not include the power to prohibit."

So business exists at the pleasure of society. But while society has set limits to business's operations, it has also very consciously left a great deal of room among the nation's institutions for these operations to take place. The question is, Why?

The answer tells us what the purpose of business is from society's point of view.

Our society sees potentials in private, competitive business that justify it over alternative methods for producing and distributing goods and services. Society perceives that, because the future is uncertain, the risks to which capital is exposed in production and distribution are unavoidable regardless of the political form. But we believe that the *costs* of risk will be minimized in private, competitive businesses because the persons undertaking the risk, in order to have something left over for profit, will pay more attention to costs than the state would in using someone else's money.

Our society expects that to satisfy customers, competitive enterprise will produce a greater quantity, quality, and variety of goods than a government or another monopoly would. And because profits are what is left after employees, suppliers, creditors, and governments have been paid, we assume that competitive businesses will strive to maximize the productivity of resources and conserve their use. We expect that this conserving of resources and maximizing of productivity will result in lower cost of goods and services for consumers and higher real income for workers than other political production systems would yield.

Society sees these potentials as benefiting the public at large too. Because the risks are borne by volunteers, society is spared the higher costs of collective risk taking and the indiscriminate spread of these costs to the taxpaying public.

The discipline that runs through society's justification for the business system is economy. Lionel Robbins identified the essence of economics in a definition almost all economists now accept. Economic behavior, he wrote, consists of the allocation of scarce means with alternative uses to deserving, competing ends. "The criterion of economy...is the securing of given ends with least means."[2]

The sphere of business

Clearly, U.S. public policy did not by mere accident leave a place for private business among the nation's institutions. The decision reflects the pragmatic strategy to define a sphere in which to secure economic efficiency as a social good.

But besides thus implementing society's value that economic efficiency is good, public policy expresses society's sentiment about the value of this social good in relation to that of the many other social goods our society recognizes—equality, justice, health, and quality of life, for example. When society prefers the economic results of business to other social goods, or vice versa, public policy adjusts.

The business institution is society's principal mechanism for producing and distributing economic goods. Since public policy has assigned this realm to business to secure behavior that is uniquely economic, the purpose of business must be to deliver economic performance to society. Economic performance is both the means and the end of the business system: it is the means business uses to conduct its internal affairs, and it is the end society seeks in assigning a sphere to the business system.

Business executives do not usually describe their jobs in economic terms. Fletcher Byrom, retiring CEO of Koppers Company, Inc., does, however. "My function as leader," he said recently in an inter-

1 See C. West Churchman,
The Design of Inquiring Systems
(New York: Basic Books, 1971).
He identifies nine conditions
something has to meet
to be considered a system.

2 Lionel Robbins,
*An Essay on the Nature and
Significance of Economic Science*
(London: Macmillan, 1947), p. 145.

view, "is fundamentally to make decisions on the basis of economic criteria."[3]

Values & leadership

I have described business as essentially an economic institution. Must it therefore operate without values? It operates according to the values of its leaders.

As citizens we are vitally interested in what the business institution does. What it does is determined by its leaders. And what leaders cause it to do is determined by their values. Deciding what values are "good" is, therefore, the first responsibility of business leadership.

The values that govern the conduct of business must be conditioned by "the why" of the business institution. They must therefore flow from the purpose of business, carry out that purpose, and be constrained by it. If that logic holds, then business leaders have the responsibility of running the businesses in their charge to realize the potential economic performance of each business.

Business leaders' values must rest also on an adequate conception of the nature of the business organism. If, as I have suggested, business can be fairly described as a system of equal, necessary, and interdependent members, then the leaders' values and their management of business operations must faithfully reflect that conception.

They don't always. Understandably, managers identify with the owners of a business and tend to give priority to the owners' profit objectives. But the concept of business as a system of equal, necessary, and interdependent members suggests that this unilateral orientation can be self-defeating. Profit is the purpose the owners have in risking their capital. It is the reward for bearing risk. And the owners' requirement for profit supplies one of the great disciplines that makes business an economic system. But profit is not the purpose of business.

Giving profits priority endangers them, for, ironically, only by giving equal regard to the requirements of all the system's members can a manager in fact maximize profits and the company's market value for the owners. If a manager rewards capital owners at the expense of employees or consumers, those members will reduce the quantity or quality of their contribution and jeopardize future returns to capital.

In a system, managers are driven by the requirements of their task to distribute to the system's members benefits that are commensurate with the members' contributions. And managers must do that even if, say, the owners whose agents they are have no interest in the rewards being distributed to consumers and workers, or if those members care nothing about whether capital owners get adequate returns for risking their capital. On the other hand, if managers do not manage business as a system, some members of the system will reduce the value of their contributions, economic performance will suffer, and society's purpose for the business institution will be compromised.

Management's values govern how the business is run. They must pervade all its operations. It is a key responsibility of business leadership, therefore, to manage these values throughout the organization so that they are effective in every action. This is the hard conclusion that follows: if in any of the business's operations managers do not realize potential economic performance, either the values of the leadership are not congruent with society's value (that economic performance is the good desired from business) or the leadership is failing to extend its own value system throughout the organization.

The reach of ethics

In conversation, when people use the term *ethics,* they mean a set of moral principles or values to guide behavior. Ethical behavior is, then, behavior that conforms to these values.

But *ethics* also has a more fundamental meaning. Ethics is the discipline that considers the justifications people offer for the principles and values they hold.

I am using the term both ways. My main concern in this article is with ethics in the latter sense: to offer a justification for particular values that should govern business behavior. That justification attempts to draw a straight line from the purpose of business and its systemic nature to the values business leaders should adopt. When business behavior violates values that connect with the purpose and nature of business, I call that behavior unethical.

The ethics of a company's leadership (in the first sense) consists of the set of values the leadership holds. But among these many values, business leaders must hold those particular values that are rooted in society's purpose for business. These values are controlling, for they imply a kind of contract

---

3 See
"Manager's Journal,"
Wall Street Journal,
June 1, 1982.

between business and society for managers to deliver the benefits for which society justifies the existence of the business system. These values identify economic performance as a good that society desires. And because they do, they impose requirements and set limits on leaders in their conduct of business.

Some people claim that the values of business people are on a par with the general values in American culture – no better and no worse. If that is true, it's too bad. Business leaders, it seems to me, should have more strongly held values than the rest of society because they have a fiduciary responsibility – a position of trust with employees, stockholders, and customers – in short, with society.

Many of the decisions business leaders make under their stewardship reflect a resolution of the different values they hold. Very often, then, this creates a tension between a person's values and the decision taken or contemplated. Sometimes the leader's cultural values and the controlling values society imposes that are rooted in the purpose of business reinforce each other in opposing an action. Other times they may be in opposition – in which case the controlling values have to be those rooted in business's purpose. In either case, though, the greater the pull of values, the more intense will be the leader's search for solutions – and the greater the likelihood of good decisions.

If business leaders hold strong cultural values onto which are superimposed the values rooted in the purpose of business, what guidance do they give to deal with the dilemmas that beset a company? For such leaders, ethical considerations must perforce reach more deeply into a company's internal affairs than perhaps many people realize and will also sometimes require business to do less in its external relationships than its critics ask of it. The following examples illustrate both these situations.

Within the company itself

Setting annual objectives for return on investment and appraising employee performance are of course two common practices in U.S. industry. I have chosen them as examples to discuss in relation to values for three reasons – first, because they are common practices; second, because both examples illustrate the structural, and sometimes obscure, ways in which management can hamper economic performance; and third, because, having faced firsthand some of the problems in these programs, I think they can be made more effective if we take their limitations into account.

Annual ROI objectives

Return on investment is usually the primary annual objective for profit center managers. But many activities affecting ROI take time to complete: developing new products, redesigning products, restructuring the organization, broadening sales coverage, expanding capacity, and so forth. In the meantime, such programs penalize current earnings and may increase investment. But profit center managers are often fast-track executives being tested for advancement in short-term assignments. Given this incentive, profit center managers may forgo the very developments on which the sustained economic performance of the business depends.

This tension presents an obvious challenge to the leadership's values. Is it fair to employees to make them choose between the benefits to themselves and to their families, which would follow from a string of short-term successes, and the long-term performance of the company? But even beyond this, is it ethical for the leadership to *institutionalize* an organizational practice that compromises the economic purpose for which society justifies a place for the business system?

Clearly, we need to monitor business performance regularly and to test and measure employee performance. But the conflict of interest inherent in this method threatens long-term economic performance.

In the Phillips Petroleum subsidiary that I headed, the tension between these divergent pulls led us to look for a way to enhance long-term economic performance while still meeting the need for testing managers in short-term assignments. To counter the short-term bias, we adopted an internal audit to assess whether managers of the profit centers had strengthened the fundamentals of the business over the year. Stronger fundamentals, of course, increase the potential for future satisfactory return on investment.

We based the audit on the assumption that the fundamentals of a business unit would be strengthened if certain conditions were met: if the workplace climate improved; if the quality of production machinery approached state-of-the-art; if structure and staffing were strengthened; and so on up to a dozen or so criteria. In this way, we tried to introduce a long-term component into short-term assignments and to convey to profit center managers the necessity for increasing the ability of the business unit to produce future return on investment.

Performance appraisals & MBO

An employee contracts with his supervisor to achieve certain objectives; at the end of a period the supervisor compares the results with the objectives and rates and counsels the employee. Perfor-

mance appraisals and management by objectives are thus inextricably bound together.

When introduced, MBO looked promising. It seemed to meet two clear organizational needs: to move the company toward its business objectives and to evaluate employees' performance fairly and objectively for salary administration. My observations have persuaded me that MBO meets neither need as well as it might. I have struggled to understand why such a simple commonsense notion hasn't fulfilled its great promise and offer these thoughts.[4]

First, as it has evolved, management by objectives has embraced the wrong purpose. When Peter Drucker presented us with this concept 30 years ago, the objectives he referred to were the objectives of the *business.* The objectives in current MBO programs, however, are the objectives managers and employees agree on as the basis for appraising employee performance. Personnel administrators have captured the concept for their own good purposes and made MBO an adjunct to salary administration.

The employee's objectives are either identical with the business's objectives or not. If they are not, an MBO program is not the instrument to move the company toward its objectives and management will have to provide a different instrument for that purpose.

On the other hand, if the objectives assigned to the employee are the business's objectives, MBO programs as currently designed won't accomplish them either. No employee working alone can attain any significant business objective. Reaching a business objective requires the contribution of several cooperating functions. Take a quality control manager. In a typical MBO program, one of his objectives might be to achieve a certain level of rejects or of returns and allowances for the manufacturing unit. He cannot do this by himself. The training and the performance of operators, the design of the product, the condition of the tools and machinery, and factors other functions control come into play.

The false premise that an employee can by himself achieve a company objective has two unsatisfactory consequences. It may result in an employee being rated as having successfully achieved an objective when it would have been impossible without the effective contribution of the other necessary functions. Or the employee may be rated as not meeting the objective when the necessary contributions of others were lacking through no fault of his own. But even more important, the company's objective is not reached and economic performance suffers.

Ethical considerations enter the situation this way. If MBO programs as now practiced cannot properly appraise employee performance, do not advance the company toward its objectives, and thus cause economic performance to suffer, then a business leader's accepting such programs violates both the fairness principle in his set of values and the values rooted in society's purpose for the business institution.

In this case, the leader's cultural values reinforce and are reinforced by the controlling values rooted in business's purpose to create a tension between what is being done and what can possibly be done better. And this tension can motivate managers to seek a way to appraise performance more fairly and at the same time to accomplish the company's objectives.

A way becomes evident as soon as we acknowledge the distinction between the objectives of the business (or business unit) and the contributions employees make toward these objectives. If achieving a business objective requires the functional contributions of several employees, the manager has a fundamental responsibility to identify the functional contributions needed for a given objective and to organize into a team the particular employees who will make those contributions.

That step taken, it becomes possible for managers to appraise what employees are actually doing—and can realistically do. Performance appraisal then becomes a judgment of the employees' effectiveness in making their contributions to the various teams they are members of and, through these teams, of their effectiveness in contributing to the objectives of the business.

Managers face many other seemingly intractable problems. For example, providing for succession to leadership is clearly a condition for the survival of a business, but it is rarely possible without making challenging assignments available to younger executives when older ones are better qualified. Public policy, of course, makes such discrimination unlawful. Managers, trying to make the best of what they regard as impossible situations, may consciously or unconsciously rate the older employees' performance lower and classify them as unpromotable. Discrimination still occurs, but documentation now lets the company do as it needs to without challenge from the EEOC.

Perhaps, though, if the problem is viewed as an ethical issue rather than as a dilemma between a legal solution and an expedient one, a more creative solution might emerge. A leadership determined to hold to its values might even find a way to use the better qualified older employees to help the younger ones.

If viewed from the perspective of values, other problems might yield better solutions: Do we tell the employees of newly acquired companies that

---

4 See my article,
"Management *of* Objectives,"
HBR May-June 1976, p. 149.

there will be no changes? Is there a net justification for "golden parachutes" for top executives when the company is threatened by unfriendly takeovers, or are these executives simply feathering their own nests? When we cut back employment or shut down facilities in a faltering economy, are we just doing what has to be done, or are we correcting mistakes we made earlier? Most business problems seldom have easy answers. What should be sought in such situations is solutions that resist the compromise of leadership values. The resulting tension offers a challenge to creativity and imagination that can produce superior solutions.

Beyond the company

Besides having ethical considerations that reach deep into everyday operations, business has critics who require that it take broad social action. Let's see how leadership's values might influence decisions in two cases.

Conflicting demands on business

How might management's values prevent the following problem?

"This year's annual stockholders' meeting of Midton [not its real name], one of the largest companies producing baked goods, has just ended with a dramatic confrontation. A group of stockholders, the Whole Life Sisters of Faith, holding 30 of Midton's 66 million shares of common stock, has formally submitted a request to the Midton board that the company establish a corporate policy drastically restricting advertising to children."[5]

Midton's business generated by advertising directly to children has been very profitable. The advertising is not illegal, and the sisters cannot make the company do anything because they cannot possibly get a majority of the stockholders to support their proposal.

Here, rather than considering what Midton's management should do now, let's go back to the strategic planning that resulted in Midton's predicament and ask how, if it had appealed to strongly held values, the leadership might have avoided the dilemma and at the same time added to the economic performance of the business.

Executives in the strategy meeting would probably all have agreed that advertising to children would be effective in increasing sales and profits. They would also undoubtedly have recognized that this strategy would work by making it difficult for parents to deny gratification to their children. Valuing fairness, Midton's leadership might have looked for another course.

But at a more sophisticated level, the strategy they chose rested on an inadequate concept of the nature of business. In the business system it isn't possible to reward one group at the expense of another without diminishing the economic performance of the whole. In this case, the Whole Life Sisters, acting as surrogates of the company's customers, have caused the company to expend resources to deal with them and then more resources to devise a new strategy to accommodate the changed situation. Later on, the company might also lose customers and revenues if parents, sensitized by the sisters to what the company has done, resolve to patronize other bakers.

Had Midton's leaders felt a tension between its business values and the strategy it was contemplating, they might have conceived a better strategy. Of course I am not qualified to say what that strategy might have been. Midton might have allocated resources to advertising frankly to parents that Midton's products taste good. Children, after all, do not live by bread alone either. And Midton might have followed the lead of its successful small competitor, Sunlite Foods, and, by applying greater resources than Sunlite, catered with new products to the nationwide interest in health and nutrition.

And what of Midton's competitors who advertise directly to children? Would they gain or lose market share against Midton's different strategy? We cannot know. But we can be reasonably sure that they would have the Whole Life Sisters of Faith over there and waste resources dealing with them.

Business's responsibility to the public

How should business respond to some of the concerns and demands of its critics?

Business is asked to cure many of society's ills. Its critics ask it in the cause of social action, for example, to hire less qualified persons when better qualified workers are available, to provide workers with psychological income from their work, to desist from doing business in apartheid South Africa, to internalize the costs of doing business, and so forth.

When, for example, its critics demand that business internalize the costs of damaging the environment, their reasoning seems only straightforward and just: business laid the costs on the public; business ought to pay.

But the issue is not as straightforward as it first seems. Society's purpose for the business system and its public policy implementing this purpose have to be taken into account. Public policy determines

5 See Douglas N. Dickson,
"Sugar Babies and the Sisterhood—
A Business Case Study,"
Across the Board,
January 1982, p. 41;
and "Sugar Babies Revisited,"

Across the Board,
June 1982, p. 36.

6 See Kenneth E. Goodpaster and
John B. Matthews, Jr.,
"Can a Corporation Have a Conscience?"
HBR January-February 1982, p. 132.

whether in a given case the environment needs protection beyond the present standards. If it does, public policy also determines the form the protection will take. Whatever public policy requires of business, business, of course, must do: reduce pollutants to meet the new standards, repair the damage afterwards, or pay higher taxes to compensate for the damage done.

But if business is already conforming to the requirements of public policy, one can infer that, for that case and for the time being at least, society prefers the social good of economic performance from business to the social good of reduced pollution and accepts the existing degree of pollution. If the business system nevertheless voluntarily internalizes the cost, it is depriving its members of value and altruistically conferring that value on a public that isn't directly a part of the system. If society wants economic performance from business in a sphere it has defined by public policy, such a gift from management thwarts society's strategy.

One can hardly discuss what managers should and should not do without thinking of Milton Friedman's arguments. Friedman categorically disqualifies managers' taking social action on two grounds: first, in complex situations, business managers will probably not know the correct action to take to achieve the "desired" result and, second, by taking social action, managers would be acting as unauthorized civil servants. Because evidence all around us demonstrates that not even the specialists know what actions produce what effects, agreeing with the first reason is easy enough. But because in a sense all citizens are public servants, the second reason is not so easy to accept. It is arguable that, in allowing and even nurturing the business institution, society commissions leaders to achieve its purpose.

Friedman was right to disqualify managers from social action but not, I think, for the right reason. The right reason is simply that social action falls outside the economic sphere that society's public policy has assigned to the business system.

What we managers do, then, when confronted by demands for social action beyond the requirements of public policy is at root an ethical matter for us. If in order to escape visibility managers yield to the pressures of social action interest groups and stray from the system's mission to deliver economic performance, they circumvent society's value that economic performance is good and desired in the given sphere.

There is, nevertheless, a very important counterpoise to these strictures on the behavior of business leaders. Executives must not only lead their businesses; they must accept the responsibility of leading the business institution. The economic results that society seeks from the business system require maximum benefits from minimum consumption of resources. But the operation of the business system unavoidably imposes costs on society that add to the resources consumed and subtract from other social goods. Society, of course, is concerned with the overall good. By adjusting public policy, society continually strives to optimize the balance between the net economic goods the business system delivers and the other social goods it desires.

Business leaders must be concerned about whatever concerns society. And while they should not, in my view, make de facto public policy by unilaterally altering boundaries that public policy has set between economic and other social goods, their responsibility as leaders requires them to join with other social leaders in a dialogue to make public policy affecting business more reflective of the needs and desires of American society.

Can the corporation have a conscience?

Many students of business have asked whether the corporation can have a conscience and whether it can be made moral, and they usually offer affirmative answers.[6] Society surely has the right to expect moral behavior from business. But the underlying question remains: What is right conduct for the business corporation? We are back to Undershaft's problem. I do not think that the consciences of either business executives or business's critics are dependable guides. The reasoning to support this opinion applies to both parts of the question, since conscience and moral behavior are opposite sides of the same coin.

Moral behavior is behavior conforming to a standard of what is right and good. Conscience is the sense a person has of the moral goodness or blameworthiness of his or her own behavior, together with a feeling of obligation to do right and be good. We want our corporations to do right, but the question whether a corporation can have a conscience seems an empty one to secure that objective for three reasons.

First, a corporation is a construct of the mind and the law; it is a juristic, not a real, person. Society has to look to the corporation's leaders for whatever behavior it wants from the corporation.

Second, asking the wrong question diverts society's attention from its real concern—that is, what business leaders should cause their corporations to do in particular cases and why. Advocates of the idea of corporate conscience generally argue that the responsibilities of real persons and of artificial persons like corporations are not separate; they hold that corporations and real persons should be equally morally responsible, hence that they should do the same right thing. What real persons do depends on their values. But when the real persons are also leaders of a business corporation, the values that must be controlling for them are the values that connect with the purpose for which society justifies a place for private business among its institutions. Private persons do not have this obligation.

And third, conscience, without a justification acceptable to society for the "right conduct" that conscience would enjoin, is too variable, open-ended, and undisciplined for society to depend on. Just as in other people, the conscience of business people can vary from zero to the other extreme where it can also defeat society's aims. So it is the *justification* for right conduct by business leaders that should be the object of scholars' attention rather than conscience, which varies from person to person.

The means are the ends

What I have attempted to do in this essay is to suggest a justification for a kind of business leadership that is rooted in the purpose of business. American society has purposefully left a place for business among its institutions to secure economic performance in the production and distribution of goods and services. It follows, for me, that business leaders have the responsibility to try to deliver the benefits society seeks through this strategy. The values that govern our leadership must therefore be grounded in this purpose, must implement it, and must be constrained by it.

Society's choice of this strategy expresses the value that in a circumscribed sphere economic efficiency is good. But society always has this strategy on trial; it continually compares it with alternative strategies for securing economic good and monitors it for negative effects that business's economic behavior might have on other social goods it values. The signs are that society is nowhere near satisfied with business performance, governance, leadership, or values. Our society's perception of business seems to parallel Winston Churchill's description of democracy: as "the worst system in the world, excepting all others."

Fortunately, business is not a static institution: it evolves and develops. Public policy governing its operations sometimes fails to translate society's desires and doesn't always reflect the public interest. But, surely, if business leaders and the critics of business behavior agree on the purpose of business and on the values that are rooted in that purpose, by listening to one another, they ought to be able to make business a better instrument for achieving its purpose.

Moral mazes: bureaucracy and managerial work

Robert Jackall

With moral choices tied to personal fates, how does bureaucracy shape managerial morality?

Generations of Americans have been taught that the way to move up in corporate management is to work hard and make sound decisions. Has the bureaucratic world changed all that? Has the connection between work and reward become more capricious? The author of this study believes that the answer to both questions is yes. Interviewing more than 100 managers, he sought answers to such questions as: What kind of ethic does bureaucracy produce in middle and upper middle managers? Why does one person rise to the top while another doesn't? The managers interviewed offer many provocative answers to questions like these. They describe the experiences of themselves and their acquaintances. They speak freely—and sometimes humorously—of how they see credit for accomplishments being awarded, the role of loyalties and alliances, the meaning of team play, the significance of patrons, the ambiguities of "hitting your numbers," the part played by luck, "blame time," outrunning one's mistakes, the subtleties of bureaucratic language, and other elements of their work. While the impressions reported are unlikely to gratify top management, they may lead the HBR reader to rethink the unintended consequences of working for large-scale enterprises and to see the problems of executive development in a new light.

Mr. Jackall is associate professor of sociology at Williams College. He is the author of Workers in a Labyrinth: Jobs and Survival in a Bank Bureaucracy *(Allanheld, Osmun and Co., 1978), and the co-editor (with Henry M. Levin) of* Worker Cooperatives in America *(University of California Press, 1984). He is also working on a book about managerial work to be published by Oxford University Press.*

Illustrations by Christopher Bing.

Reprint 83507

Corporate leaders often tell their charges that hard work will lead to success. Indeed, this theory of reward being commensurate with effort has been an enduring belief in our society, one central to our self-image as a people where the "main chance" is available to anyone of ability who has the gumption and the persistence to seize it. Hard work, it is also frequently asserted, builds character. This notion carries less conviction because businessmen, and our society as a whole, have little patience with those who make a habit of finishing out of the money. In the end, it is success that matters, that legitimates striving, and that makes work worthwhile.

What if, however, men and women in the big corporation no longer see success as necessarily connected to hard work? What becomes of the social morality of the corporation—I mean the everyday rules in use that people play by—when there is thought to be no "objective" standard of excellence to explain how and why winners are separated from also-rans, how and why some people succeed and others fail?

This is the puzzle that confronted me while doing a great many extensive interviews with managers and executives in several large corporations, particularly in a large chemical company and a large textile firm. (See the insert for more details.) I went into these corporations to study how bureaucracy—the prevailing organizational form of our society and economy—shapes moral consciousness. I came to see that managers' rules for success are at the heart of what may be called the bureaucratic ethic.

This article suggests no changes and offers no programs for reform. It is, rather, simply an

Author's note: I presented an earlier version of this paper in the Faculty Lecture Series at Williams College on March 18, 1982. The intensive field work done during 1980 and 1981 was made possible by a Fellowship for Independent Research from the National Endowment for the Humanities and by a Junior Faculty Leave and small research grant from Williams College.

Editor's note: All references are listed at the end of the article.

interpretive sociological analysis of the moral dimensions of managers' work. Some readers may find the essay sharp-edged, others familiar. For both groups, it is important to note at the outset that my materials are managers' own descriptions of their experiences.[1] In listening to managers, I have had the decided advantages of being unencumbered with business responsibilities and also of being free from the taken-for-granted views and vocabularies of the business world. As it happens, my own research in a variety of other settings suggests that managers' experiences are by no means unique; indeed they have a deep resonance with those of other occupational groups.

What happened to the Protestant Ethic?

To grasp managers' experiences and the more general implications they contain, one must see them against the background of the great historical transformations, both social and cultural, that produced managers as an occupational group. Since the concern here is with the moral significance of work in business, it is important to begin with an understanding of the original Protestant Ethic, the world view of the rising bourgeois class that spearheaded the emergence of capitalism.

The Protestant Ethic was a set of beliefs that counseled "secular asceticism"–the methodical, rational subjection of human impulse and desire to God's will through "restless, continuous, systematic work in a worldly calling."[2] This ethic of ceaseless work and ceaseless renunciation of the fruits of one's toil provided both the economic and the moral foundations for modern capitalism.

On one hand, secular asceticism was a ready-made prescription for building economic capital; on the other, it became for the upward-moving bourgeois class–self-made industrialists, farmers, and enterprising artisans–the ideology that justified their attention to this world, their accumulation of wealth, and indeed the social inequities that inevitably followed such accumulation. This bourgeois ethic, with its imperatives for self-reliance, hard work, frugality, and rational planning, and its clear definition of success and failure, came to dominate a whole historical epoch in the West.

But the ethic came under assault from two directions. First, the very accumulation of wealth that the old Protestant Ethic made possible gradually stripped away the religious basis of the ethic, especially among the rising middle class that benefited from it. There were, of course, periodic reassertions of the religious context of the ethic, as in the case of John D. Rockefeller and his turn toward Baptism. But on the whole, by the late 1800s the religious roots of the ethic survived principally among independent farmers and proprietors of small businesses in rural areas and towns across America.

In the mainstream of an emerging urban America, the ethic had become secularized into the "work ethic," "rugged individualism," and especially the "success ethic." By the beginning of this century, among most of the economically successful, frugality had become an aberration, conspicuous consumption the norm. And with the shaping of the mass consumer society later in this century, the sanctification of consumption became widespread, indeed crucial to the maintenance of the economic order.

Affluence and the emergence of the consumer society were responsible, however, for the demise of only aspects of the old ethic–namely, the imperatives for saving and investment. The core of the ethic, even in its later, secularized form–self-reliance, unremitting devotion to work, and a morality that postulated just rewards for work well done–was undermined by the complete transformation of the organizational form of work itself. The hallmarks of the emerging modern production and distribution systems were administrative hierarchies, standardized work procedures, regularized timetables, uniform policies, and centralized control–in a word, the bureaucratization of the economy.

This bureaucratization was heralded at first by a very small class of salaried managers, who were later joined by legions of clerks and still later by technicians and professionals of every stripe. In this century, the process spilled over from the private to the public sector and government bureaucracies came to rival those of industry. This great transformation produced the decline of the old middle class of entrepreneurs, free professionals, independent farmers, and small independent businessmen–the traditional carriers of the old Protestant Ethic–and the ascendance of a new middle class of salaried employees whose chief common characteristic was and is their dependence on the big organization.

Any understanding of what happened to the original Protestant Ethic and to the old morality and social character it embodied–and therefore any understanding of the moral significance of work today–is inextricably tied to an analysis of bureaucracy. More specifically, it is, in my view, tied to an analysis of the work and occupational cultures of managerial groups within bureaucracies. Managers are the quintessential bureaucratic work group; they not only fashion bureaucratic rules, but they are also bound by them. Typically, they are not just *in* the organization; they are *of* the organization. As such, managers represent the prototype of the white-collar salaried employee. By analyzing the kind of ethic bureaucracy produces in managers, one can begin to understand how bureaucracy shapes morality in our society as a whole.

Pyramidal politics

American businesses typically both centralize and decentralize authority. Power is concentrated at the top in the person of the chief executive officer and is simultaneously decentralized; that is, responsibility for decisions and profits is pushed as far down the organizational line as possible. For example, the chemical company that I studied—and its structure is typical of other organizations I examined—is one of several operating companies of a large and growing conglomerate. Like the other operating companies, the chemical concern has its own president, executive vice presidents, vice presidents, other executive officers, business area managers, entire staff divisions, and operating plants. Each company is, in effect, a self-sufficient organization, though they are all coordinated by the corporation, and each president reports directly to the corporate CEO.

Now, the key interlocking mechanism of this structure is its reporting system. Each manager gathers up the profit targets or other objectives of his or her subordinates, and with these formulates his commitments to his boss; this boss takes these commitments, and those of his other subordinates, and in turn makes a commitment to *his* boss. (Note: henceforth only "he" or "his" will be used to allow for easier reading.) At the top of the line, the president of each company makes his commitment to the CEO of the corporation, based on the stated objectives given to him by his vice presidents. There is always pressure from the top to set higher goals.

This management-by-objectives system, as it is usually called, creates a chain of commitments from the CEO down to the lowliest product manager. In practice, it also shapes a patrimonial authority arrangement which is crucial to defining both the immediate experiences and the long-run career chances of individual managers. In this world, a subordinate owes fealty principally to his immediate boss. A subordinate must not overcommit his boss; he must keep the boss from making mistakes, particularly public ones; he must not circumvent the boss. On a social level, even though an easy, breezy informality is the prevalent style of American business, the subordinate must extend to the boss a certain ritual deference: for instance, he must follow the boss's lead in conversation, must not speak out of turn at meetings, and must laugh at the boss's jokes while not making jokes of his own.

In short, the subordinate must not exhibit any behavior which symbolizes parity. In return, he can hope to be elevated when and if the boss is elevated, although other important criteria also intervene here. He can also expect protection for mistakes made up to a point. However, that point is never exactly defined and always depends on the complicated politics of each situation.

Who gets credit?

It is characteristic of this authority system that details are pushed down and credit is pushed up. Superiors do not like to give detailed instructions to subordinates. The official reason for this is to maximize subordinates' autonomy; the underlying reason seems to be to get rid of tedious details and to protect the privilege of authority to declare that a mistake has been made.

It is not at all uncommon for very bald and extremely general edicts to emerge from on high. For example, "Sell the plant in St. Louis. Let me know when you've struck a deal." This pushing down of details has important consequences:

1   Because they are unfamiliar with entangling details, corporate higher echelons tend to expect highly successful results without complications. This is central to top executives' well-known aversion to bad news and to the resulting tendency to "kill the messenger" who bears that news.

2   The pushing down of detail creates great pressure on middle managers not only to transmit good news but to protect their corporations, their bosses, and themselves in the process. They become the "point men" of a given strategy and the potential "fall guys" when things go wrong.

Credit flows up in this structure and usually is appropriated by the highest ranking officer involved in a decision. This person redistributes credit as he chooses, bound essentially by a sensitivity to public perceptions of his fairness. At the middle level, credit for a particular success is always a type of refracted social honor; one cannot claim credit even if it is earned. Credit has to be given, and acceptance of the gift implicitly involves a reaffirmation and strengthening of fealty. A superior may share some credit with subordinates in order to deepen fealty relationships and induce greater future efforts on his behalf. Of course, a different system is involved in the allocation of blame, a point I shall discuss later.

Fealty to the 'king'

Because of the interlocking character of the commitment system, a CEO carries enormous influence in his corporation. If, for a moment, one thinks of the presidents of individual operating companies as barons, then the CEO of the parent company is the king. His word is law; even the CEO's wishes and whims are taken as commands by close subordinates on the corporate staff, who zealously turn them into policies and directives.

A typical example occurred in the textile company last year when the CEO, new at the time, expressed mild concern about the rising operating costs of the company's fleet of rented cars. The following day, a stringent system for monitoring mileage replaced the previous casual practice.

Great efforts are made to please the CEO. For example, when the CEO of the large conglomerate that includes the chemical company visits a plant, the most important order of business for local management is a fresh paint job, even when, as in several cases last year, the cost of paint alone exceeds $100,000. I am told that similar anecdotes from other organizations have been in circulation since 1910; this suggests a certain historical continuity of behavior toward top bosses.

The second order of business for the plant management is to produce a complete book describing the plant and its operations, replete with photographs and illustrations, for presentation to the CEO; such a book costs about $10,000 for the single copy. By any standards of budgetary stringency, such expenditures are irrational. But by the social standards of the corportion, they make perfect sense. It is far more important to please the king today than to worry about the future economic state of one's fief, since if one does not please the king, there may not be a fief to worry about or indeed any vassals to do the worrying.

By the same token, all of this leads to an intense interest in everything the CEO does and says. In both the chemical and the textile companies, the most common topic of conversation among managers up and down the line is speculation about their respective CEOs' plans, intentions, strategies, actions, styles, and public images.

Such speculation is more than idle gossip. Because he stands at the apex of the corporation's bureaucratic and patrimonial structures and locks the intricate system of commitments between bosses and subordinates into place, it is the CEO who ultimately decides whether those commitments have been satisfactorily met. Moreover, the CEO and his trusted associates determine the fate of whole business areas of a corporation.

Field work details

The field work during 1980 to 1981 encompassed four companies – a large chemical company, one of several operating companies of a diversified conglomerate; a large textile company; a medium-sized chemical company; and a large defense contractor. My access to the latter two businesses was limited to a series of interviews with top executive officers, some observation, and some access to internal company documents. Although many of the themes treated in this article emerged in my work in these two companies, I have for the most part treated these materials as preliminary data.

It is also important to note that I was denied access to 36 companies, an instructive experience in itself. In about half these cases, access was denied after lengthy negotiations involving interviews with various company officials; these materials are also treated as preliminary. In this article, when I claim that something occurs in all the companies that I studied, I mean to include these preliminary materials as well as the more substantive data described here.

I concentrated most of my substantive work in the two companies where my access was broadest – in the large textile company and particularly in the large chemical company. I pursued the research in these companies until mid-1982 and mid-1983, respectively. I draw my analysis principally from these two organizations. My materials from both are rich and detailed; moreover, their size and complexity make them representative of important sectors of American industry. Further, the kinds of problems managers face in these companies – organizational, regulatory, and personal – are, I think, typical of those confronted more generally.

My methodology in this research was intensive semi-structured interviews with managers and executives at every level of management. The interviews usually lasted between two and three hours but, sometimes, especially with reinterviews, went much longer. I interviewed more than 100 people in these two companies alone.

In addition, I gathered material in a number of more informal ways – for example, through nonparticipant observation, over meals, and in attendance at various management seminars. I also had extensive access to internal company documents and publications.

Shake-ups & contingency

One must appreciate the simultaneously monocratic and patrimonial character of business bureaucracies in order to grasp what we might call their contingency. One has only to read the *Wall Street Journal* or the *New York Times* to realize that, despite their carefully constructed "eternal" public image, corporations are quite unstable organizations. Mergers, buy-outs, divestitures, and especially "organizational restructuring" are commonplace aspects of business life. I shall discuss only organizational shake-ups here.

Usually, shake-ups occur because of the appointment of a new CEO and/or division president, or because of some failure that is adjudged to demand retribution; sometimes these occurrences work together. The first action of most new CEOs is some form of organizational change. On the one hand, this prevents the inheritance of blame for past mistakes; on the other, it projects an image of bareknuckled aggressiveness much appreciated on Wall Street. Perhaps most important, a shake-up rearranges the fealty structure of the corporation, placing in power those barons whose style and public image mesh closely with that of the new CEO.

A shake-up has reverberations throughout an organization. Shortly after the new CEO of the conglomerate was named, he reorganized the whole business and selected new presidents to head each of the five newly formed companies of the corporation. He mandated that the presidents carry out a thorough reorganization of their separate companies complete with extensive "census reduction"—that is, firing as many people as possible.

The new president of the chemical company, one of these five, had risen from a small but important specialty chemicals division in the former company. Upon promotion to president, he reached back into his former division, indeed back to his own past work in a particular product line, and systematically elevated many of his former colleagues, friends, and allies. Powerful managers in other divisions, particularly in a rival process chemicals division, were: (1) forced to take big demotions in the new power structure; (2) put on "special assignment"—the corporate euphemism for Siberia (the saying is: "No one ever comes back from special assignment"); (3) fired; or (4) given "early retirement," a graceful way of doing the same thing.

Up and down the chemical company, former associates of the president now hold virtually every important position. Managers in the company view all of this as an inevitable fact of life. In their view, the whole reorganization could easily have gone in a completely different direction had another CEO been named or had the one selected picked a different president for the chemical company, or had the president come from a different work group in the old organization. Similarly, there is the abiding feeling that another significant change in top management could trigger yet another sweeping reorganization.

Fealty is the mortar of the corporate hierarchy, but the removal of one well-placed stone loosens the mortar throughout the pyramid and can cause things to fall apart. And no one is ever quite sure, until after the fact, just how the pyramid will be put back together.

12 9,634

Success & failure

It is within this complicated and ambiguous authority structure, always subject to upheaval, that success and failure are meted out to those in the middle and upper middle managerial ranks. Managers rarely spoke to me of objective criteria for achieving success because once certain crucial points in one's career are passed, success and failure seem to have little to do with one's accomplishments. Rather, success is socially defined and distributed. Corporations do demand, of course, a basic competence and sometimes specified training and experience; hiring patterns usually ensure these. A weeding-out process takes place, however, among the lower ranks of managers during the first several years of their experience. By the time a manager reaches a certain numbered grade in the ordered hierarchy—in the chemical company this is Grade 13 out of 25, defining the top 8 1/2% of management in the company—managerial competence as such is taken for granted and assumed not to differ greatly from one manager to the next. The focus then switches to social factors, which are determined by authority and political alignments—the fealty structure—and by the ethos and style of the corporation.

Moving to the top

In the chemical and textile companies as well as the other concerns I studied, five criteria seem to control a person's ability to rise in middle and upper middle management. In ascending order they are:

1   **Appearance and dress.** This criterion is so familiar that I shall mention it only briefly. Managers have to look the part, and it is sufficient to say that corporations are filled with attractive, well-groomed, and conventionally well-dressed men and women.

2   **Self-control.** Managers stress the need to exercise iron self-control and to have the ability to mask all emotion and intention behind bland, smiling, and agreeable public faces. They believe it is a fatal weakness to lose control of oneself, in any way, in a public forum. Similarly, to betray valuable secret knowledge (for instance, a confidential reorganization plan) or intentions through some relaxation of self-control—for example, an indiscreet comment or a lack of adroitness in turning aside a query—can not only jeopardize a manager's immediate position but can undermine others' trust in him.

College of St. Francis Library
Joliet, Illinois

3   **Perception as a team player.** While being a team player has many meanings, one of the most important is to appear to be interchangeable with other managers near one's level. Corporations discourage narrow specialization more strongly as one goes higher. They also discourage the expression of moral or political qualms. One might object, for example, to working with chemicals used in nuclear power, and most corporations today would honor that objection. The public statement of such objections, however, would end any realistic aspirations for higher posts because one's usefulness to the organization depends on versatility. As one manager in the chemical company commented: "Well, we'd go along with his request but we'd always wonder about the guy. And in the back of our minds, we'd be thinking that he'll soon object to working in the soda ash division because he doesn't like glass."

Another important meaning of team play is putting in long hours at the office. This requires a certain amount of sheer physical energy, even though a great deal of this time is spent not in actual work but in social rituals—like reading and discussing newspaper articles, taking coffee breaks, or having informal conversations. These rituals, readily observable in every corporation that I studied, forge the social bonds that make real managerial work—that is, group work of various sorts—possible. One must participate in the rituals to be considered effective in the work.

4   **Style.** Managers emphasize the importance of "being fast on your feet"; always being well organized; giving slick presentations complete with color slides; giving the appearance of knowledge even in its absence; and possessing a subtle, almost indefinable sophistication, marked especially by an urbane, witty, graceful, engaging, and friendly demeanor.

I want to pause for a moment to note that some observers have interpreted such conformity, team playing, affability, and urbanity as evidence of the decline of the individualism of the old Protestant Ethic.[3] To the extent that commentators take the public images that managers project at face value, I think they miss the main point. Managers up and down the corporate ladder adopt the public faces that they wear quite consciously; they are, in fact, the masks behind which the real struggles and moral issues of the corporation can be found.

Karl Mannheim's conception of self-rationalization or self-streamlining is useful in understanding what is one of the central social psychological processes of organizational life.[4] In a world where appearances—in the broadest sense—mean everything, the wise and ambitious person learns to cultivate assiduously the proper, prescribed modes of appearing. He dispassionately takes stock of himself, treating himself as an object. He analyzes his strengths and weaknesses, and decides what he needs to change in order to survive and flourish in his organization. And then he systematically undertakes a program to reconstruct his image. Self-rationalization curiously parallels the methodical subjection of self to God's will that the old Protestant Ethic counseled; the difference, of course, is that one acquires not moral virtues but a masterful ability to manipulate personae.

5   **Patron power.** To advance, a manager must have a patron, also called a mentor, a sponsor, a rabbi, or a godfather. Without a powerful patron in the higher echelons of management, one's prospects are poor in most corporations. The patron might be the manager's immediate boss or someone several levels higher in the chain of command. In either case the manager is still bound by the immediate, formal authority and fealty patterns of his position; the new – although more ambiguous – fealty relationships with the patron are added.

A patron provides his "client" with opportunities to get visibility, to showcase his abilities, to make connections with those of high status. A patron cues his client to crucial political developments in the corporation, helps arrange lateral moves if the client's upward progress is thwarted by a particular job or a particular boss, applauds his presentations or suggestions at meetings, and promotes the client during an organizational shake-up. One must, of course, be lucky in one's patron. If the patron gets caught in a political crossfire, the arrows are likely to find his clients as well.

motable" by belonging to central political networks. Patrons protect those already selected as rising stars from the negative judgments of others; and only the foolhardy point out even egregious errors of those in power or those destined for it.

Failure is also socially defined. The most damaging failure is, as one middle manager in the chemical company puts it, "when your boss or someone who has the power to determine your fate says: 'You failed.'" Such a godlike pronouncement means, of course, out-and-out personal ruin; one must, at any cost, arrange matters to prevent such an occurrence.

As it happens, things rarely come to such a dramatic point even in the midst of an organizational crisis. The same judgment may be made but it is usually called "nonpromotability." The difference is that those who are publicly labeled as failures normally have no choice but to leave the organization; those adjudged nonpromotable can remain, provided they are willing to accept being shelved or, more colorfully, "mushroomed" – that is, kept in a dark place, fed manure, and left to do nothing but grow fat. Usually, seniors do not tell juniors they are nonpromotable (though the verdict may be common knowledge among senior peer groups). Rather, subordinates are expected to get the message after they have been repeatedly overlooked for promotions. In fact, middle managers interpret staying in the same job for more than two or three years as evidence of a negative judgment. This leads to a mobility panic at the middle levels which, in turn, has crucial consequences for pinpointing responsibility in the organization.

Social definitions of performance

Surely, one might argue, there must be more to success in the corporation than style, personality, team play, chameleonic adaptability, and fortunate connections. What about the bottom line – profits, performance?

Unquestionably, "hitting your numbers" – that is, meeting the profit commitments already discussed – is important, but only within the social context I have described. There are several rules here. First, no one in a line position – that is, with responsibility for profit and loss – who regularly "misses his numbers" will survive, let alone rise. Second, a person who always hits his numbers but who lacks some or all of the required social skills will not rise. Third, a person who sometimes misses his numbers but who has all the desirable social traits will rise.

Performance is thus always subject to a myriad of interpretations. Profits matter, but it is much more important in the long run to be perceived as "pro-

Capriciousness of success

Finally, managers think that there is a tremendous amount of plain luck involved in advancement. It is striking how often managers who pride themselves on being hardheaded rationalists explain their own career patterns and those of others in terms of luck. Various uncertainties shape this perception. One is the sense of organizational contingency. One change at the top can create profound upheaval throughout the entire corporate structure, producing startling reversals of fortune, good or bad, depending on one's connections. Another is the uncertainty of the markets that often makes managerial planning simply elaborate guesswork, causing real economic outcome to depend on factors totally beyond organizational and personal control.

It is interesting to note in this context that a line manager's credibility suffers just as much from missing his numbers on the up side (that is, achieving profits higher than predicted) as from missing them on the down side. Both outcomes undercut the ideology of managerial planning and control, perhaps the only bulwark managers have against market irrationality.

Even managers in staff positions, often quite removed from the market, face uncertainty. Occupational safety specialists, for instance, know that the bad publicity from one serious accident in the workplace can jeopardize years of work and scores of safety awards. As one high-ranking executive in the chemical company says, "In the corporate world, 1,000 'Attaboys!' are wiped away by one 'Oh, shit!'"

Because of such uncertainties, managers in all the companies I studied speak continually of the great importance of being in the right place at the right time and of the catastrophe of being in the wrong place at the wrong time. My interview materials are filled with stories of people who were transferred immediately before a big shake-up and, as a result, found themselves riding the crest of a wave to power; of people in a promising business area who were terminated because top management suddenly decided that the area no longer fit the corporate image desired; of others caught in an unpredictable and fatal political battle among their patrons; of a product manager whose plant accidentally produced an odd color batch of chemicals, who sold them as a premium version of the old product, and who is now thought to be a marketing genius.

The point is that managers have a sharply defined sense of the *capriciousness* of organizational life. Luck seems to be as good an explanation as any of why, after a certain point, some people succeed and others fail. The upshot is that many managers decide that they can do little to influence external events in their favor. One can, however, shamelessly streamline oneself, learn to wear all the right masks, and get to know all the right people. And then sit tight and wait for things to happen.

'Gut decisions'

Authority and advancement patterns come together in the decision-making process. The core of the managerial mystique is decision-making prowess, and the real test of such prowess is what managers call "gut decisions," that is, important decisions involving big money, public exposure, or significant effects on the organization. At all but the highest levels of the chemical and textile companies, the rules for making gut decisions are, in the words of one upper middle manager: "(1) Avoid making any decisions if at all possible; and (2) if a decision has to be made, involve as many people as you can so that, if things go

south, you're able to point in as many directions as possible."

Consider the case of a large coking plant of the chemical company. Coke making requires a gigantic battery to cook the coke slowly and evenly for long periods; the battery is the most important piece of capital equipment in a coking plant. In 1975, the plant's battery showed signs of weakening and certain managers at corporate headquarters had to decide whether to invest $6 million to restore the battery to top form. Clearly, because of the amount of money involved, this was a gut decision.

No decision was made. The CEO had sent the word out to defer all unnecessary capital expenditures to give the corporation cash reserves for other investments. So the managers allocated small amounts of money to patch the battery up until 1979, when it collapsed entirely. This brought the company into a breach of contract with a steel producer and into violation of various Environmental Protection Agency pollution regulations. The total bill, including lawsuits and now federally mandated repairs to the battery, exceeded $100 million. I have heard figures as high as $150 million, but because of "creative accounting," no one is sure of the exact amount.

This simple but very typical example gets to the heart of how decision making is intertwined with a company's authority structure and advancement patterns. As the chemical company managers see it, the decisions facing them in 1975 and 1979 were crucially different. Had they acted decisively in 1975 – in hindsight, the only rational course – they would have salvaged the battery and saved their corporation millions of dollars in the long run.

In the short run, however, since even seemingly rational decisions are subject to widely varying interpretations, particularly decisions which run counter to a CEO's stated objectives, they would have been taking a serious risk in restoring the battery. What is more, their political networks might have unraveled, leaving them vulnerable to attack. They chose short-term safety over long-term gain because they felt they were judged, both by higher authority and by their peers, on their short-term performances. Managers feel that if they do not survive the short run, the long run hardly matters. Even correct decisions can shorten promising careers.

By contrast, in 1979 the decision was simple and posed little risk. The corporation had to meet its legal obligations; also it had to either repair the battery the way the EPA demanded or shut down the plant and lose several hundred million dollars. Since there were no real choices, everyone could agree on a course of action because everyone could appeal to inevitability. Diffusion of responsibility, in this case by procrastinating until total crisis, is intrinsic to organizational life because the real issue in most gut decisions is: Who is going to get blamed if things go wrong?

'Blame time'

There is no more feared hour in the corporate world than "blame time." Blame is quite different from responsibility. There is a cartoon of Richard Nixon declaring: "I accept all of the responsibility, but none of the blame." To blame someone is to injure him verbally in public; in large organizations, where one's image is crucial, this poses the most serious sort of threat. For managers, blame – like failure – has nothing to do with the merits of a case; it is a matter of social definition. As a general rule, it is those who are or who become politically vulnerable or expendable who get "set up" and become blamable. The most feared situation of all is to end up inadvertently in the wrong place at the wrong time and get blamed.

Yet this is exactly what often happens in a structure that systematically diffuses responsibility. It is because managers fear blame time that they diffuse responsibility; however, such diffusion inevitably means that someone, somewhere is going to become a scapegoat when things go wrong. Big corporations encourage this process by their complete lack of any tracking system. Whoever is currently in charge of an area is responsible – that is, potentially blamable – for whatever goes wrong in the area, even if he has inherited others' mistakes. An example from the chemical company illustrates this process.

When the CEO of the large conglomerate took office, he wanted to rid his capital accounts of all serious financial drags. The corporation had been operating a storage depot for natural gas which it bought, stored, and then resold. Some years before the energy crisis, the company had entered into a long-term contract to supply gas to a buyer – call him Jones. At the time, this was a sound deal because it provided a steady market for a stably priced commodity.

When gas prices soared, the corporation was still bound to deliver gas to Jones at 20¢ per unit instead of the going market price of $2. The CEO ordered one of his subordinates to get rid of this albatross as expeditiously as possible. This was done by selling the operation to another party – call him Brown – with the agreement that Brown would continue to meet the contractual obligations to Jones. In return for Brown's assumption of these costly contracts, the corporation agreed to buy gas from Brown at grossly inflated prices to meet some of its own energy needs.

In effect, the CEO transferred the drag on his capital accounts to the company's operating expenses. This enabled him to project an aggressive, asset-reducing image to Wall Street. Several levels down the ladder, however, a new vice president for a particular business found himself saddled with exorbitant operating costs when, during a reorganization, those plants purchasing gas from Brown at inflated prices came under his purview. The high costs helped to undercut the vice president's division earnings and thus to erode his position in the hierarchy. The origin of the situation did not matter. All that counted was that the vice president's division was steadily losing big money. In the end, he resigned to "pursue new opportunities."

One might ask why top management does not institute codes or systems for tracking responsibility. This example provides the clue. An explicit system of accountability for subordinates would probably have to apply to top executives as well and would restrict their freedom. Bureaucracy expands the freedom of those on top by giving them the power to restrict the freedom of those beneath.

On the fast track

Managers see what happened to the vice president as completely capricious, but completely understandable. They take for granted the absence of any tracking of responsibility. If anything, they blame the vice president for not recognizing soon enough the dangers of the situation into which he was being drawn and for not preparing a defense – even perhaps finding a substitute scapegoat. At the same time, they realize that this sort of thing could easily happen to them. They see few defenses against being caught in the wrong place at the wrong time except constant wariness, the diffusion of responsibility, and perhaps being shrewd enough to declare the ineptitude of one's predecessor on first taking a job.

What about avoiding the consequences of their own errors? Here they enjoy more control. They can "outrun" their mistakes so that when blame time arrives, the burden will fall on someone else. The ideal situation, of course, is to be in a position to fire one's successors for one's own previous mistakes.

Some managers, in fact, argue that outrunning mistakes is the real key to managerial success. One way to do this is by manipulating the numbers. Both the chemical and the textile companies place a great premium on a division's or a subsidiary's return on assets. A good way for business managers to increase their ROA is to reduce their assets while maintaining sales. Usually they will do everything they can to hold down expenditures in order to decrease the asset base, particularly at the end of the fiscal year. The most common way of doing this is by deferring capital expenditures, from maintenance to

innovative investments, as long as possible. Done for a short time, this is called "starving" a plant; done over a longer period, it is called "milking" a plant.

Some managers become very adept at milking businesses and showing a consistent record of high returns. They move from one job to another in a company, always upward, rarely staying more than two years in any post. They may leave behind them deteriorating plants and unsafe working conditions, but they know that if they move quickly enough, the blame will fall on others. In this sense, bureaucracies may be thought of as vast systems of organized irresponsibility.

Flexibility & dexterity with symbols

The intense competition among managers takes place not only behind the agreeable public faces I have described but within an extraordinarily indirect and ambiguous linguistic framework. Except at blame time, managers do not publicly criticize or disagree with one another or with company policy. The sanction against such criticism or disagreement is so strong that it constitutes, in managers' view, a suppression of professional debate. The sanction seems to be rooted principally in their acute sense of organizational contingency; the person one criticizes or argues with today could be one's boss tomorrow.

This leads to the use of an elaborate linguistic code marked by emotional neutrality, especially in group settings. The code communicates the meaning one might wish to convey to other managers, but since it is devoid of any significant emotional sentiment, it can be reinterpreted should social relationships or attitudes change. Here, for example, are some typical phrases describing performance appraisals followed by their probable intended meanings:

Stock phrase	Probable intended meaning
Exceptionally well qualified	Has committed no major blunders to date
Tactful in dealing with superiors	Knows when to keep his mouth shut
Quick thinking	Offers plausible excuses for errors
Meticulous attention to detail	A nitpicker
Slightly below average	Stupid
Unusually loyal	Wanted by no one else

For the most part, such neutered language is not used with the intent to deceive; rather, its purpose is to communicate certain meanings within specific contexts with the implicit understanding that, should the context change, a new, more appropriate meaning can be attached to the language already used. In effect, the corporation is a setting where people are not held to their word because it is generally understood that their word is always provisional.

The higher one goes in the corporate world, the more this seems to be the case; in fact, advancement beyond the upper middle level depends greatly on one's ability to manipulate a variety of symbols without becoming tied to or identified with any of them. For example, an amazing variety of organizational improvement programs marks practically every corporation. I am referring here to the myriad ideas generated by corporate staff, business consultants, academics, and a host of others to improve corporate structure; sharpen decision making; raise morale; create a more humanistic workplace; adopt Theory X, Theory Y, or, more recently, Theory Z of management; and so on. These programs become important when they are pushed from the top.

The watchword in the large conglomerate at the moment is productivity and, since this is a pet project of the CEO himself, it is said that no one goes into his presence without wearing a blue *Productivity!* button and talking about "quality circles" and "feedback sessions." The president of another company pushes a series of managerial seminars that endlessly repeats the basic functions of management: (1) planning, (2) organizing, (3) motivating, and (4) controlling. Aspiring young managers attend these sessions and with a seemingly dutiful eagerness learn to repeat the formulas under the watchful eyes of senior officials.

Privately, managers characterize such programs as the "CEO's incantations over the assembled multitude," as "elaborate rituals with no practical effect," or as "waving a magic wand to make things wonderful again." Publicly, of course, managers on the way up adopt the programs with great enthusiasm, participate in or run them very effectively, and then quietly drop them when the time is right.

Playing the game

Such flexibility, as it is called, can be confusing even to those in the inner circles. I was told the following by a highly placed staff member whose work requires him to interact daily with the top figures of his company:

"I get faked out all the time and I'm part of the system. I come from a very different culture. Where I come from, if you give someone your *word*, no one ever questions it. It's the old hard-work-will-lead-to-success ideology. Small community, Protestant, agrarian, small business, merchant-type values. I'm disadvantaged in a system like this."

He goes on to characterize the system more fully and what it takes to succeed within it:

"It's the ability to play this system that determines whether you will rise....And part of the adeptness [required] is determined by how much it bothers people. One thing you have to be able to do is to play the game, but you can't be disturbed by the game. What's the game? It's bringing troops home from Vietnam and declaring peace with honor. It's saying one thing and meaning another.

"It's characterizing the reality of a situation with *any* description that is necessary to make that situation more palatable to some group that matters. It means that you have to come up with a culturally accepted verbalization to explain why you are *not* doing what you are doing....[Or] you say that we had to do what we did because it was inevitable; or because the guys at the [regulatory] agencies were dumb; [you] say we won when we really lost; [you] say we saved money when we squandered it; [you] say something's safe when it's potentially or actually dangerous....Everyone knows that it's bullshit, but it's *accepted.* This is the game."

In addition, then, to the other characteristics that I have described, it seems that a prerequisite for big success in the corporation is a certain adeptness at inconsistency. This premium on inconsistency is particularly evident in the many areas of public controversy that face top-ranking managers. Two things come together to produce this situation. The first is managers' sense of beleaguerment from a wide array of adversaries who, it is thought, want to disrupt or impede management's attempts to further the economic interests of their companies. In every company that I studied, managers see themselves and their traditional prerogatives as being under siege, and they respond with a set of caricatures of their perceived principal adversaries.

For example, government regulators are brash, young, unkempt hippies in blue jeans who know nothing about the businesses for which they make rules; environmental activists—the bird and bunny people—are softheaded idealists who want everybody to live in tents, burn candles, ride horses, and eat berries; workers' compensation lawyers are out-and-out crooks who prey on corporations to appropriate exorbitant fees from unwary clients; labor activists are radical troublemakers who want to disrupt harmonious industrial communities; and the news media consist of rabble-rousers who propagate sensational antibusiness stories to sell papers or advertising time on shows like "60 Minutes."

Second, within this context of perceived harassment, managers must address a multiplicity of audiences, some of whom are considered adversaries. These audiences are the internal corporate hierarchy with its intricate and shifting power and status cliques, key regulators, key local and federal legislators, special publics that vary according to the issues, and the public at large, whose goodwill and favorable opinion are considered essential for a company's free operation.

Managerial adeptness at inconsistency becomes evident in the widely discrepant perspectives, reasons for action, and presentations of fact that explain, excuse, or justify corporate behavior to these diverse audiences.

Adeptness at inconsistency

The cotton dust issue in the textile industry provides a fine illustration of what I mean. Prolonged exposure to cotton dust produces in many textile workers a chronic and eventually disabling pulmonary disease called byssinosis or, colloquially, brown lung. In the early 1970s, the Occupational Safety and Health Administration proposed a ruling to cut workers' exposure to cotton dust sharply by requiring textile companies to invest large amounts of money in cleaning up their plants. The industry fought the regulation fiercely but a final OSHA ruling was made in 1978 requiring full compliance by 1984.

The industry took the case to court. Despite an attempt by Reagan appointees in OSHA to have the case removed from judicial consideration and remanded to the agency they controlled for further cost/benefit analysis, the Supreme Court ruled in 1981 that the 1978 OSHA ruling was fully within the agency's mandate, namely, to protect workers' health and safety as the primary benefit exceeding all cost considerations.

During these proceedings, the textile company was engaged on a variety of fronts and was pursuing a number of actions. For instance, it intensively lobbied regulators and legislators and it prepared court materials for the industry's defense, arguing that the proposed standard would crush the industry and that the problem, if it existed, should be met by increasing workers' use of respirators.

The company also aimed a public relations barrage at special-interest groups as well as at the general public. It argued that there is probably no such thing as byssinosis; workers suffering from pulmonary problems are all heavy smokers and the real culprit is the government-subsidized tobacco industry. How can cotton cause brown lung when cotton is white? Further, if there is a problem, only some workers are afflicted, and therefore the solution is more careful

screening of the work force to detect susceptible people and prevent them from ever reaching the workplace. Finally, the company claimed that if the regulation were imposed, most of the textile industry would move overseas where regulations are less harsh.[5]

In the meantime, the company was actually addressing the problem but in a characteristically indirect way. It invested $20 million in a few plants where it knew such an investment would make money; this investment automated the early stages of handling cotton, traditionally a very slow procedure, and greatly increased productivity. The investment had the side benefit of reducing cotton dust levels to the new standard in precisely those areas of the work process where the dust problem is greatest. Publicly, of course, the company claims that the money was spent entirely to eliminate dust, evidence of its corporate good citizenship. (Privately, executives admit that, without the productive return, they would not have spent the money and they have not done so in several other plants.)

Indeed, the productive return is the only rationale that carries weight within the corporate hierarchy. Executives also admit, somewhat ruefully and only when their office doors are closed, that OSHA's regulation on cotton dust has been the main factor in forcing technological innovation in a centuries-old and somewhat stagnant industry.

Such adeptness at inconsistency, without moral uneasiness, is essential for executive success. It means being able to say, as a very high-ranking official of the textile company said to me without batting an eye, that the industry has never caused the slightest problem in any worker's breathing capacity. It means, in the chemical company, propagating an elaborate hazard/benefit calculus for appraisal of dangerous chemicals while internally conceptualizing "hazards" as business risks. It means publicly extolling the carefulness of testing procedures on toxic chemicals while privately ridiculing animal tests as inapplicable to humans.

It means lobbying intensively in the present to shape government regulations to one's immediate advantage and, ten years later, in the event of a catastrophe, arguing that the company acted strictly in accordance with the standards of the time. It means claiming that the real problem of our society is its unwillingness to take risks, while in the thickets of one's bureaucracy avoiding risks at every turn; it means as well making every effort to socialize the risks of industrial activity while privatizing the benefits.

The bureaucratic ethic

The bureaucratic ethic contrasts sharply with the original Protestant Ethic. The Protestant Ethic was the ideology of a self-confident and independent propertied social class. It was an ideology that extolled the virtues of accumulating wealth in a society organized around property and that accepted the stewardship responsibilities entailed by property. It was an ideology where a person's word was his bond and where the integrity of the handshake was seen as crucial to the maintenance of good business relationships. Perhaps most important, it was connected to a predictable economy of salvation – that is, hard work will lead to success, which is a sign of one's election by God – a notion also containing its own theodicy to explain the misery of those who do not make it in this world.

Bureaucracy, however, breaks apart substance from appearances, action from responsibility, and language from meaning. Most important, it breaks apart the older connection between the meaning of work and salvation. In the bureaucratic world, one's success, one's sign of election, no longer depends on one's own efforts and on an inscrutable God but on the capriciousness of one's superiors and the market; and one achieves economic salvation to the extent that one pleases and submits to one's employer and meets the exigencies of an impersonal market.

In this way, because moral choices are inextricably tied to personal fates, bureaucracy erodes internal and even external standards of morality, not only in matters of individual success and failure but also in all the issues that managers face in their daily work. Bureaucracy makes its own internal rules and social context the principal moral gauges for action. Men and women in bureaucracies turn to each other for moral cues for behavior and come to fashion specific situational moralities for specific significant people in their worlds.

As it happens, the guidance they receive from each other is profoundly ambiguous because what matters in the bureaucratic world is not what a person is but how closely his many personae mesh with the organizational ideal; not his willingness to stand by his actions but his agility in avoiding blame; not what he believes or says but how well he has mastered the ideologies that serve his corporation; not what he stands for but whom he stands with in the labyrinths of his organization.

In short, bureaucracy structures for managers an intricate series of moral mazes. Even the inviting paths out of the puzzle often turn out to be invitations to jeopardy.

References

1 There is a long sociological tradition of work on managers and I am, of course, indebted to that literature. I am particularly indebted to the work, both joint and separate, of Joseph Bensman and Arthur J. Vidich, two of the keenest observers of the new middle class. See especially their *The New American Society: The Revolution of the Middle Class* (Chicago: Quadrangle Books, 1971).

2 See Max Weber, *The Protestant Ethic and the Spirit of Capitalism,* translated by Talcott Parsons (New York: Charles Scribner's Sons, 1958), p. 172.

3 See William H. Whyte, *The Organization Man* (New York: Simon & Schuster, 1956), and David Riesman, in collaboration with Reuel Denney and Nathan Glazer, *The Lonely Crowd: A Study of the Changing American Character* (New Haven: Yale University Press, 1950).

4 Karl Mannheim, *Man and Society in an Age of Reconstruction* [London: Paul (Kegan), Trench, Trubner Ltd. 1940], p. 55.

5 On February 9, 1982, the Occupational Safety and Health Administration issued a notice that it was once again reviewing its 1978 standard on cotton dust for "cost-effectiveness." See *Federal Register,* vol. 47, p. 5906. As of this writing (May 1983), this review has still not been officially completed.

Can a corporation have a conscience?

*In a sense it can,
for its members can make the
corporation act
as a morally
responsible person
would*

When making a profit conflicts with respecting the welfare of the community, corporations do not always choose profit as their only goal. Nor do they always decide that such debates of principle are beyond their domain. They look within to their boards of directors and managers, they take the time to hear community representatives, and they choose courses of action carefully geared to the needs of the community as well as their own. Deciding things this way isn't easy, and it bears all the marks of a person trying to decide the right course in a situation that is fraught with conflict. That is why the authors say that conscience can reside in the organization. This opinion represents a change in perspective, for traditionally the notion of conscience has been associated with the

Kenneth E. Goodpaster
and John B. Matthews, Jr.

notion of person. Sometimes, stepping outside one discipline with the help of another presents a perspective from which to see how to make conflict manageable and goals clear. Such a new orientation is what this article offers those who are trying to cope with the complexities of corporate management in today's society. With some terminology and insight from moral philosophy, the authors think through the confusion surrounding the concept of corporate responsibility and find a way to define it. By looking closely at the realm in which responsibility is usually understood—the individual's action

and intention—and then projecting the light of this understanding onto the company, they hope to help corporations inform their decisions with moral concerns.

Mr. Goodpaster has come from the discipline of philosophy at the University of Notre Dame to the Harvard Business School, where as lecturer on business administration he teaches a popular course on business and ethics. Mr. Matthews has had a long, successful career of teaching business policy at the Harvard Business School, where he is the Joseph C. Wilson Professor of Business Administration. Reprint 82104

During the severe racial tensions of the 1960s, Southern Steel Company (actual case, disguised name) faced considerable pressure from government and the press to explain and modify its policies regarding discrimination both within its plants and in the major city where it was located. SSC was the largest employer in the area (it had nearly 15,000 workers, one-third of whom were black) and had made great strides toward removing barriers to equal job opportunity in its several plants. In addition, its top executives (especially its chief executive officer, James Weston) had distinguished themselves as private citizens for years in community programs for black housing, education, and small business as well as in attempts at desegregating all-white police and local government organizations.

SSC drew the line, however, at using its substantial economic influence in the local area to advance the cause of the civil rights movement by pressuring banks, suppliers, and the local government:

"As individuals we can exercise what influence we may have as citizens," James Weston said, "but for a corporation to attempt to exert any kind of economic compulsion to achieve a particular end in a social area seems to me to be quite beyond what a corporation should do and quite beyond what a corporation can do. I believe that while government may seek to compel social reforms, any attempt by a private organization like SSC to impose its views, its beliefs, and its will upon the community would be repugnant to our American constitutional concepts and that appropriate steps to correct this abuse of corporate power would be universally demanded by public opinion."

Weston could have been speaking in the early 1980s on any issue that corporations around the United States now face. Instead of social justice, his theme might be environmental protection, product safety, marketing practice, or international bribery. His statement for SSC raises the important issue of corporate responsibility. Can a corporation have a conscience?

Weston apparently felt comfortable saying it need not. The responsibilities of ordinary persons and of "artificial persons" like corporations are, in his view, separate. Persons' responsibilities go beyond those of corporations. Persons, he seems to have believed, ought to care not only about themselves but also about the dignity and well-being of those around them—ought not only to care but also to act. Organizations, he evidently thought, are creatures of, and to a degree prisoners of, the systems of economic incentive and political sanction that give them reality and therefore should not be expected to display the same moral attributes that we expect of persons.

Others inside business as well as outside share Weston's perception. One influential philosopher—John Ladd—carries Weston's view a step further:

"It is improper to expect organizational conduct to conform to the ordinary principles of morality," he says. "We cannot and must not expect formal organizations, or their representatives acting in their official capacities, to be honest, courageous, considerate, sympathetic, or to have any kind of moral integrity. Such concepts are not in the vocabulary, so to speak, of the organizational language game."[1]

In our opinion, this line of thought represents a tremendous barrier to the development of business ethics both as a field of inquiry and as a practical force in managerial decision making. This is a matter about which executives must be philosophical and philosophers must be practical. A corporation can and should have a conscience. The language of ethics does have a place in the vocabulary of an organization. There need not be and there should not be a disjunction of the sort attributed to SSC's James Weston. Organizational agents such as corporations should be no more and no less morally responsible (rational, self-interested, altruistic) than ordinary persons.

We take this position because we think an analogy holds between the individual and the corporation. If we analyze the concept of moral responsibility as it applies to persons, we find that projecting it to corporations as agents in society is possible.

1 See John Ladd,
"Morality and the Ideal of
Rationality in
Formal Organizations,"
The Monist,
October 1970,
p. 499.

Defining the responsibility of persons

When we speak of the responsibility of individuals, philosophers say that we mean three things: someone is to blame, something has to be done, or some kind of trustworthiness can be expected. (See the *Exhibit* on page 40.)

Holding accountable

We apply the first meaning, what we shall call the *causal* sense, primarily to legal and moral contexts where what is at issue is praise or blame for a past action. We say of a person that he or she was responsible for what happened, is to blame for it, should be held accountable. In this sense of the word, *responsibility* has to do with tracing the causes of actions and events, of finding out who is answerable in a given situation. Our aim is to determine someone's intention, free will, degree of participation, and appropriate reward or punishment.

Rule following

We apply the second meaning of *responsibility* to rule following, to contexts where individuals are subject to externally imposed norms often associated with some social role that people play. We speak of the responsibilities of parents to children, of doctors to patients, of lawyers to clients, of citizens to the law. What is socially expected and what the party involved is to answer for are at issue here.

Decision making

We use the third meaning of *responsibility* for decision making. With this meaning of the term, we say that individuals are responsible if they are trustworthy and reliable, if they allow appropriate factors to affect their judgment; we refer primarily to a person's independent thought processes and decision making, processes that justify an attitude of trust from those who interact with him or her as a responsible individual.

The distinguishing characteristic of moral responsibility, it seems to us, lies in this third

*For the Confucian—but also for the philosopher of the Western tradition— only **law** can handle the rights and objections of collectives. **Ethics** is always a matter of the person.*

But is this adequate for a "society of organizations" such as ours? This may be the central question for the philosopher of modern society, in which access to livelihood, career and achievement exists primarily in and through organizations—and especially for the highly educated person for whom opportunities outside of organizations are very scarce indeed. In such a society, both the society and the individual increasingly depend on the performance, as well as the "sincerity," of organizations.

But in today's discussion of "business ethics" it is not even seen that there is a problem.

Peter Drucker

"What Is Business Ethics?"
The Public Interest, No. 64,
Spring 1981, p. 18
© 1981
by National Affairs, Inc.

sense of the term. Here the focus is on the intellectual and emotional processes in the individual's moral reasoning. Philosophers call this "taking a moral point of view" and contrast it with such other processes as being financially prudent and attending to legal obligations.

To be sure, characterizing a person as "morally responsible" may seem rather vague. But vagueness is a contextual notion. Everything depends on how we fill in the blank in "vague for _____ purposes."

In some contexts the term "six o'clock-ish" is vague, while in others it is useful and informative. As a response to a space-shuttle pilot who wants to know when to fire the reentry rockets, it will not do, but it might do in response to a spouse who wants to know when one will arrive home at the end of the workday.

We maintain that the processes underlying moral responsibility can be defined and are not themselves vague, even though gaining consensus on specific moral norms and decisions is not always easy.

What, then, characterizes the processes underlying the judgment of a person we call morally responsible? Philosopher William K. Frankena offers the following answer:

"A morality is a normative system in which judgments are made, more or less consciously, [out of a] consideration of the effects of actions…on the lives of persons…including the lives of others besides the person acting.…David Hume took a similar position when he argued that what speaks in a moral judgment is a kind of sympathy.…A little later,…Kant put the matter somewhat better by characterizing morality as the business of respecting persons as ends and not as means or as things.…"[2]

Frankena is pointing to two traits, both rooted in a long and diverse philosophical tradition:

1   Rationality. Taking a moral point of view includes the features we usually attribute to rational decision making, that is, lack of impulsiveness, care in mapping out alternatives and consequences, clarity about goals and purposes, attention to details of implementation.

2   Respect. The moral point of view also includes a special awareness of and concern for the effects of one's decisions and policies on others, special in the sense that it goes beyond the kind of awareness and concern that would ordinarily be part of rationality, that is, beyond seeing others merely as instrumental to accomplishing one's own purposes. This is respect for the lives of others and involves taking their needs and interests seriously, not simply as resources in one's own decision making but as limiting conditions which change the very definition of one's habitat from a self-centered to a shared environment. It is what philosopher Immanuel Kant meant by the "categorical imperative" to treat others as valuable in and for themselves.

It is this feature that permits us to trust the morally responsible person. We know that such a person takes our point of view into account not merely as a useful precaution (as in "honesty is the best policy") but as important in its own right.

These components of moral responsibility are not too vague to be useful. Rationality and respect affect the manner in which a person approaches practical decision making: they affect the way in which the individual processes information and makes choices. A rational but not respectful Bill Jones will not lie to his friends *unless* he is reasonably sure he will not be found out. A rational but not respectful Mary Smith will defend an unjustly treated party *unless* she thinks it may be too costly to herself. A rational *and* respectful decision maker, however, notices – and cares – whether the consequences of his or her conduct lead to injuries or indignities to others.

Two individuals who take "the moral point of view" will not of course always agree on ethical matters, but they do at least have a basis for dialogue.

Projecting responsibility to corporations

Now that we have removed some of the vagueness from the notion of moral responsibility as it applies to persons, we can search for a frame of reference in which, by analogy with Bill Jones and Mary Smith, we can meaningfully and appropriately say that corporations are morally responsible. This is the issue reflected in the SSC case.

To deal with it, we must ask two questions: Is it meaningful to apply moral concepts to actors who are not persons but who are instead made up of persons? And even if meaningful, is it advisable to do so?

If a group can act like a person in some ways, then we can expect it to behave like a person in other ways. For one thing, we know that people organized into a group can act as a unit. As business people well know, legally a corporation is considered a unit. To approach unity, a group usually has some sort of internal decision structure, a system of rules that spell out authority relationships and specify the conditions under which certain individuals' actions become official actions of the group.[3]

If we can say that persons act responsibly only if they gather information about the impact of their actions on others and use it in making decisions, we can reasonably do the same for organizations. Our proposed frame of reference for thinking about and implementing corporate responsibility aims at spelling out the processes associated with the moral responsibility of individuals and projecting them to the level of organizations. This is similar to, though an inversion of, Plato's famous method in the *Republic*, in which justice in the community is used as a model for justice in the individual.

Hence, corporations that monitor their employment practices and the effects of their production processes and products on the environment and human health show the same kind of rationality and respect that morally responsible individuals do. Thus, attributing actions, strategies, decisions, and moral responsibilities to corporations as entities distinguishable from those who hold offices in them poses no problem.

And when we look about us, we can readily see differences in moral responsibility among corporations in much the same way that we see differences among persons. Some corporations have built features into their management incentive systems, board structures, internal control systems, and research agendas that in a person we would call self-control, integrity, and conscientiousness. Some have institutionalized awareness and concern for consumers, employees, and the rest of the public in ways that others clearly have not.

In an interview this week, Robert Kilpatrick, the chairman of the [Business Roundtable's] committee on the federal budget and president of the Connecticut General Insurance Corporation, said that his fellow executives had every intention of taking their "social responsibilities" seriously and working with other groups in the community to solve such national problems as unemployment, inflation, urban decay, stagnating productivity and low living standards.

"We know those problems will not go away," Mr. Kilpatrick said. "The ball is now in the private sector's court. Limited government is going to mean that the problems are going to have to be solved by the private sector alone or working closely with government. If we don't do the job now, we won't have another chance the next time around."

Leonard Silk

© 1981
The New York Times Company

2 See William K. Frankena, *Thinking About Morality* (Ann Arbor: University of Michigan Press, 1980), p. 26.

3 See Peter French, "The Corporation as a Moral Person," *American Philosophical Quarterly*, July 1979, p. 207.

If people are going to adopt the terminology of "responsibility" (with its allied concepts of corporate conscience) to suggest new, improved ways of dealing with corporations, then they ought to go back and examine in detail what "being responsible" entails — in the ordinary case of the responsible human being. Only after we have considered what being responsible calls for in general does it make sense to develop the notion of a corporation being responsible.

Christopher Stone

From *Where the Law Ends*
© 1975 by Christopher D. Stone
Reprinted with permission
of Harper & Row, Publishers, Inc.

As a matter of course, some corporations attend to the human impact of their operations and policies and reject operations and policies that are questionable. Whether the issue be the health effects of sugared cereal or cigarettes, the safety of tires or tampons, civil liberties in the corporation or the community, an organization reveals its character as surely as a person does.

Indeed, the parallel may be even more dramatic. For just as the moral responsibility displayed by an individual develops over time from infancy to adulthood,[4] so too we may expect to find stages of development in organizational character that show significant patterns.

Evaluating the idea of moral projection

Concepts like moral responsibility not only make sense when applied to organizations but also provide touchstones for designing more effective models than we now have for guiding corporate policy.

Now we can understand what it means to invite SSC as a corporation to be morally responsi-ble both in-house and in its community, but *should* we issue the invitation? Here we turn to the question of advisability. Should we require the organizational agents in our society to have the same moral attributes we require of ourselves?

Our proposal to spell out the processes associated with moral responsibility for individuals and then to project them to their organizational counterparts takes on added meaning when we examine alternative frames of reference for corporate responsibility.

Two frames of reference that compete for the allegiance of people who ponder the question of corporate responsibility are emphatically opposed to this principle of moral projection—what we might refer to as the "invisible hand" view and the "hand of government" view.

The invisible hand

The most eloquent spokesman of the first view is Milton Friedman (echoing many philosophers and economists since Adam Smith). According to this pattern of thought, the true and only social responsibilities of business organizations are to make profits and obey the laws. The workings of the free and competitive marketplace will "moralize" corporate behavior quite independently of any attempts to expand or transform decision making via moral projection.

A deliberate amorality in the executive suite is encouraged in the name of systemic morality: the common good is best served when each of us and our economic institutions pursue not the common good or moral purpose, advocates say, but competitive advantage. Morality, responsibility, and conscience reside in the invisible hand of the free market system, not in the hands of the organizations within the system, much less the managers within the organizations.

To be sure, people of this opinion admit, there is a sense in which social or ethical issues can and should enter the corporate mind, but the filtering of such issues is thorough: they go through the screens of custom, public opinion, public relations, and the law. And, in any case, self-interest maintains primacy as an objective and a guiding star.

The reaction from this frame of reference to the suggestion that moral judgment be inte-

---

4 A process that psychological researchers from Jean Piaget to Lawrence Kohlberg have examined carefully; see Jean Piaget, *The Moral Judgment of the Child* (New York: Free Press, 1965) and Lawrence Kohlberg, *The Philosophy of Moral Development* (New York: Harper & Row, 1981).

grated with corporate strategy is clearly negative. Such an integration is seen as inefficient and arrogant, and in the end both an illegitimate use of corporate power and an abuse of the manager's fiduciary role. With respect to our SSC case, advocates of the invisible hand model would vigorously resist efforts, beyond legal requirements, to make SSC right the wrongs of racial injustice. SSC's responsibility would be to make steel of high quality at least cost, to deliver it on time, and to satisfy its customers and stockholders. Justice would not be part of SSC's corporate mandate.

The hand of government

Advocates of the second dissenting frame of reference abound, but John Kenneth Galbraith's work has counterpointed Milton Friedman's with insight and style. Under this view of corporate responsibility, corporations are to pursue objectives that are rational and purely economic. The regulatory hands of the law and the political process rather than the invisible hand of the marketplace turns these objectives to the common good.

Again, in this view, it is a system that provides the moral direction for corporate decision making—a system, though, that is guided by political managers, the custodians of the public purpose. In the case of SSC, proponents of this view would look to the state for moral direction and responsible management, both within SSC and in the community. The corporation would have no moral responsibility beyond political and legal obedience.

What is striking is not so much the radical difference between the economic and social philosophies that underlie these two views of the source of corporate responsibility but the conceptual similarities. Both views locate morality, ethics, responsibility, and conscience in the systems of rules and incentives in which the modern corporation finds itself embedded. Both views reject the exercise of independent moral judgment by corporations as actors in society.

Neither view trusts corporate leaders with stewardship over what are often called noneconomic values. Both require corporate responsibility to march to the beat of drums outside. In the jargon of moral philosophy, both views press for a rule-centered or a system-centered ethics instead of an agent-centered ethics. In terms of the *Exhibit,* these frames of reference countenance corporate rule-following responsibility for corporations but not corporate decision-making responsibility.

Since we may have only weak confidence in our intuitions and judgments about the justice of the whole structure of society, we may attempt to aid our judgment by focusing on microsituations that we do have a firm grasp of. For many of us, an important part of the process of arriving at what [philosopher John] Rawls calls "reflective equilibrium" will consist of thought experiments in which we try out principles in hypothetical microsituations....Since Plato, at any rate, that has been our tradition; principles may be tried out in the large and in the small. Plato thought that writ large the principles are easier to discern; others may think the reverse.

Robert Nozick

From *Anarchy, State and Utopia*
© 1974 by Basic Books Inc.
Reprinted with permission of the publisher

The hand of management

To be sure, the two views under discussion differ in that one looks to an invisible moral force in the market while the other looks to a visible moral force in government. But both would advise against a principle of moral projection that permits or encourages corporations to exercise independent, noneconomic judgment over matters that face them in their short- and long-term plans and operations.

Accordingly, both would reject a third view of corporate responsibility that seeks to affect the thought processes of the organization itself—a sort of "hand of management" view—since neither seems willing or able to see the engines of profit regulate themselves to the degree that would be implied by taking the principle of moral projection seriously. Cries of inefficiency and moral imperialism from the right would be matched by cries of insensitivity and illegitimacy from the left, all in the name of preserving us from corporations and managers run morally amok.

Better, critics would say, that moral philosophy be left to philosophers, philanthropists, and politicians than to business leaders. Better that corporate morality be kept to glossy annual reports, where it is safely insulated from policy and performance.

Exhibit	Three uses of the term *responsible*	
	The causal sense	"He is responsible for this." Emphasis on holding to account for past actions, causality.
	The rule-following sense	"As a lawyer, he is responsible for defending that client." Emphasis on following social and legal norms.
	The decision-making sense	"He is a responsible person." Emphasis on an individual's independent judgment.

The two conventional frames of reference locate moral restraint in forces external to the person and the corporation. They deny moral reasoning and intent to the corporation in the name of either market competition or society's system of explicit legal constraints and presume that these have a better moral effect than that of rationality and respect.

Although the principle of moral projection, which underwrites the idea of a corporate conscience and patterns it on the thought and feeling processes of the person, is in our view compelling, we must acknowledge that it is neither part of the received wisdom, nor is its advisability beyond question or objection. Indeed, attributing the role of conscience to the corporation seems to carry with it new and disturbing implications for our usual ways of thinking about ethics and business.

Perhaps the best way to clarify and defend this frame of reference is to address the objections to the principle found in the ruled insert on pages 41-43. There we see a summary of the criticisms and counterarguments we have heard during hours of discussion with business executives and business school students. We believe that the replies to the objections about a corporation having a conscience are convincing.

Leaving the double standard behind

We have come some distance from our opening reflection on Southern Steel Company and its role in its community. Our proposal—clarified, we hope, through these objections and replies—suggests that it is not sufficient to draw a sharp line between individuals' private ideas and efforts and a corporation's institutional efforts but that the latter can and should be built upon the former.

Does this frame of reference give us an unequivocal prescription for the behavior of SSC in its circumstances? No, it does not. Persuasive arguments might be made now and might have been made then that SSC should not have used its considerable economic clout to threaten the community into desegregation. A careful analysis of the realities of the environment might have disclosed that such a course would have been counterproductive, leading to more injustice than it would have alleviated.

The point is that some of the arguments and some of the analyses are or would have been moral arguments, and thereby the ultimate decision that of an ethically responsible organization. The significance of this point can hardly be overstated, for it represents the adoption of a new perspective on corporate policy and a new way of thinking about business ethics. We agree with one authority, who writes that "the business firm, as an organic entity intricately affected by and affecting its environment, is as appropriately adaptive...to demands for responsible behavior as for economic service."[5]

The frame of reference here developed does not offer a decision procedure for corporate managers. That has not been our purpose. It does, however, shed light on the conceptual foundations of business ethics by training attention on the corporation as a moral agent in society. Legal systems of rules and incentives are insufficient, even though they may be necessary, as frameworks for corporate responsibility. Taking conceptual cues from the features of moral responsibility normally expected of the person in our opinion deserves practicing managers' serious consideration.

The lack of congruence that James Weston saw between individual and corporate moral responsibility can be, and we think should be, overcome. In the process, what a number of writers have characterized as a double standard—a discrepancy between our personal lives and our lives in organizational settings—might be dampened. The principle of moral projection not only helps us to conceptualize the kinds of demands that we might make of corporations and other organizations but also offers the prospect of harmonizing those demands with the demands that we make of ourselves.

5 See Kenneth R. Andrews,
The Concept of Corporate Strategy,
revised edition
(Homewood, Ill.:
Dow Jones-Irwin, 1980),
p. 99.

Is a corporation a morally responsible 'person'?

Objection 1
to the analogy:

Corporations are not persons. They are artificial legal constructions, machines for mobilizing economic investments toward the efficient production of goods and services. We cannot hold a corporation responsible. We can only hold individuals responsible.

Reply:

Our frame of reference does not imply that corporations are persons in a literal sense. It simply means that in certain respects concepts and functions normally attributed to persons can also be attributed to organizations made up of persons. Goals, economic values, strategies, and other such personal attributes are often usefully projected to the corporate level by managers and researchers. Why should we not project the functions of conscience in the same way? As for holding corporations responsible, recent criminal prosecutions such as the case of Ford Motor Company and its Pinto gas tanks suggest that society finds the idea both intelligible and useful.

Objection 2:

A corporation cannot be held responsible at the sacrifice of profit. Profitability and financial health have always been and should continue to be the "categorical imperatives" of a business operation.

Reply:

We must of course acknowledge the imperatives of survival, stability, and growth when we discuss corporations, as indeed we must acknowledge them when we discuss the life of an individual. Self-sacrifice has been identified with moral responsibility in only the most extreme cases. The pursuit of profit and self-interest need not be pitted against the demands of moral responsibility. Moral demands are best viewed as containments – not replacements – for self-interest.

This is not to say that profit maximization never conflicts with morality. But profit maximization conflicts with other managerial values as well. The point is to coordinate imperatives, not deny their validity.

Objection 3:

Corporate executives are not elected representatives of the people, nor are they anointed or appointed as social guardians. They therefore lack the social mandate that a democratic society rightly demands of those who would pursue ethically or socially motivated policies. By keeping corporate policies confined to economic motivations, we keep the power of corporate executives in its proper place.

Reply:

The objection betrays an oversimplified view of the relationship between the public and the private sector. Neither private individuals nor private corporations that guide their conduct by ethical or social values beyond the demands of law should be constrained merely because they are not elected to do so. The demands of moral responsibility are independent of the demands of political legitimacy and are in fact presupposed by them.

To be sure, the state and the political process will and must remain the primary mechanisms for protecting the public interest, but one might be forgiven the hope that the political process will not substitute for the moral judgment of the citizenry or other components of society such as corporations.

Objection 4:

Our system of law carefully defines the role of agent or fiduciary and makes corporate managers accountable to shareholders and investors for the use of their assets. Management cannot, in the name of corporate moral responsibility, arrogate to itself the right to manage those assets by partially noneconomic criteria.

Reply:

First, it is not so clear that investors insist on purely economic criteria in the management of their assets, especially if some of the shareholders' resolutions and board reforms of the last decade are any indication. For instance, companies doing business in South Africa have had stockholders question their activities, other companies have instituted audit committees for their boards before such auditing was mandated, and mutual funds for which "socially responsible behavior" is a major investment criterion now exist.

Second, the categories of "shareholder" and "investor" connote wider time spans than do immediate or short-term returns. As a practical matter, considerations of stability and long-term return on investment enlarge the class of principals to which managers bear a fiduciary relationship.

Third, the trust that managers hold does not and never has extended to "any means available" to advance the interests of the principals. Both legal and moral constraints must be understood to qualify that trust – even, perhaps, in the name of a larger trust and a more basic fiduciary relationship to the members of society at large.

Objection 5:

The power, size, and scale of the modern corporation – domestic as well as international – are awesome. To unleash, even partially, such power from the discipline of the marketplace and the narrow or possibly nonexistent moral purpose implicit in that discipline would be socially dangerous. Had SSC acted in the community to further racial justice, its purposes might have been admirable, but those purposes could have led to a kind of moral imperialism or worse. Suppose SSC had thrown its power behind the Ku Klux Klan.

Reply:

This is a very real and important objection. What seems not to be appreciated is the fact that power affects when it is used as well as when it is not used. A decision by SSC not to exercise its economic influence according to "non-economic" criteria is inevitably a moral decision and just as inevitably affects the community. The issue in the end is not whether corporations (and other organizations) should be "unleashed" to exert moral force in our society but rather how critically and self-consciously they should choose to do so.

The degree of influence enjoyed by an agent, whether a person or an organization, is not so much a factor recommending moral disengagement as a factor demanding a high level of moral awareness. Imperialism is more to be feared when moral reasoning is absent than when it is present. Nor do we suggest that the "discipline of the marketplace" be diluted; rather, we call for it to be supplemented with the discipline of moral reflection.

Objection 6:

The idea of moral projection is a useful device for structuring corporate responsibility only if our understanding of moral responsibility at the level of the person is in some sense richer than our understanding of moral responsibility on the level of the organization as a whole. If we are not clear about individual responsibility, the projection is fruitless.

Reply:

The objection is well taken. The challenge offered by the idea of moral projection lies in our capacity to articulate criteria or frameworks of reasoning for the morally responsible person. And though such a challenge is formidable, it is not clear that it cannot be met, at least with sufficient consensus to be useful.

For centuries, the study and criticism of frameworks have gone on, carried forward by many disciplines, including psychology, the social sciences, and philosophy. And though it would be a mistake to suggest that any single framework (much less a decision mechanism) has emerged as the right one, it is true that recurrent patterns are discernible and well enough defined to structure moral discussion.

In the body of the article, we spoke of rationality and respect as components of individual responsibility. Further analysis of these

components would translate them into social costs and benefits, justice in the distribution of goods and services, basic rights and duties, and fidelity to contracts. The view that pluralism in our society has undercut all possibility of moral agreement is anything but self-evident. Sincere moral disagreement is, of course, inevitable and not clearly lamentable. But a process and a vocabulary for articulating such values as we share is no small step forward when compared with the alternatives. Perhaps in our exploration of the moral projection we might make some surprising and even reassuring discoveries about ourselves.

Objection 7:

Why is it necessary to project moral responsibility to the level of the organization? Isn't the task of defining corporate responsibility and business ethics sufficiently discharged if we clarify the responsibilities of men and women in business as individuals? Doesn't ethics finally rest on the honesty and integrity of the individual in the business world?

Reply:

Yes and no. Yes, in the sense that the control of large organizations does finally rest in the hands of managers, of men and women. No, in the sense that what is being controlled is a cooperative system for a cooperative purpose. The

projection of responsibility to the organization is simply an acknowledgement of the fact that the whole is more than the sum of its parts. Many intelligent people do not an intelligent organization make. Intelligence needs to be structured, organized, divided, and recombined in complex processes for complex purposes.

Studies of management have long shown that the attributes, successes, and failures of organizations are phenomena that emerge from the coordination of persons' attributes and that explanations of such phenomena require categories of analysis and description beyond the level of the individual. Moral responsibility is an attribute that can manifest itself in organizations as surely as competence or efficiency.

Objection 8:

Is the frame of reference here proposed intended to replace or undercut the relevance of the "invisible hand" and the "government hand" views, which depend on external controls?

Reply:

No. Just as regulation and economic competition are not substitutes for corporate responsibility, so corporate responsibility is not a substitute for law and the market. The imperatives of ethics cannot be relied on – nor have they ever been relied on – without a context of external sanctions. And this is true as much for individuals as for organizations.

This frame of reference takes us beneath, but not beyond, the realm of external systems of rules and incentives and into the thought processes that interpret and respond to the corporation's environment. Morality is more than merely part of that environment. It aims at the projection of conscience, not the enthronement of it in either the state or the competitive process.

The rise of the modern large corporation and the concomitant rise of the professional manager demand a conceptual framework in which these phenomena can be accommodated to moral thought. The principle of moral projection furthers such accommodation by recognizing a new level of agency in society and thus a new level of responsibility.

Objection 9:

Corporations have always taken the interests of those outside the corporation into account in the sense that customer relations and public relations generally are an integral part of rational economic decision making. Market signals and social signals that filter through the market mechanism inevitably represent the interests of parties affected by the behavior of the company. What, then, is the point of adding respect to rationality?

Reply:

Representing the affected parties solely as economic variables in the environment of the company is treating them as means or resources and not as ends in themselves. It implies that the only voice which affected parties should have in organizational decision making is that of potential buyers, sellers, regulators, or boycotters. Besides, many affected parties may not occupy such roles, and those who do may not be able to signal the organization with messages that effectively represent their stakes in its actions.

To be sure, classical economic theory would have us believe that perfect competition in free markets (with modest adjustments from the state) will result in all relevant signals being "heard," but the abstractions from reality implicit in such theory make it insufficient as a frame of reference for moral responsibility. In a world in which strict self-interest was congruent with the common good, moral responsibility might be unnecessary. We do not, alas, live in such a world.

The element of respect in our analysis of responsibility plays an essential role in ensuring the recognition of unrepresented or underrepresented voices in the decision making of organizations as agents. Showing respect for persons as ends and not mere means to organizational purposes is central to the concept of corporate moral responsibility.

In the first part of the 17th century, Sir Edward Coke, one of Great Britain's most eminent jurists, concluded that a corporation was but an impersonal creation of the law—not a being, just a product of written rules and government fiat. But times have changed. Sir Edward could not have foreseen the results of the Industrial Revolution. He certainly did not foresee that 350 years after his pronouncements corporations would be the largest employers on earth, would generate the preponderance of the world's goods and services, and would be owned on a worldwide basis by millions of shareholders.

Although it may be true that Conoco remains an inanimate being for legalistic purposes, the company has a very personal existence for its shareholders, employees, officers, and directors. The success or failure of Conoco affects most of them during their working lives, and may affect them during their retirement. And to the employees, officers, and directors, Conoco's reputation concerns their reputation as well.

No one can deny that in the public's mind a corporation can break the law and be guilty of unethical and amoral conduct. Events of the early 1970s, such as corporate violations of federal law and failure of full disclosure, confirmed that both our government and our citizenry expect **corporations** *to act lawfully, ethically, and responsibly.*

Perhaps it is then appropriate in today's context to think of Conoco as a **living corporation;** *a sentient being whose conduct and personality are the collective effort and responsibility of its employees, officers, directors, and shareholders....*

The Conoco Conscience,
inhouse booklet on moral standards
© 1976
Continental Oil Company

The moral crisis in American capitalism

Robert Wuthnow

Headline-catching economic difficulties have emboldened the opponents of market capitalism to question its appropriateness to the American way of life. With its promise of abundance badly tarnished, they ask, does the market still have a useful role to play in shaping the values or legitimizing the institutions of American society? And if it does, just how is the market—that abstraction of classical economic thought—to exert its influence on the present-day world of fact and event?

These questions are, of course, not new, but they do have a new urgency. The author of this article seeks to answer them in an original way by showing both how the market creates opportunities for morally satisfying action for those who participate in it and how the assumptions on which the market system is based help support the exercise of individual freedom. New developments in technology, however, have put many of these old assumptions at risk, and the author gives an important place in his discussion of the market to the realities of technological change.

Robert Wuthnow is associate professor of sociology at Princeton University. He is the author of The Consciousness Reformation *(1976) and* Experimentation in American Religion *(1978), both at the University of California Press, and has been doing research on the logic of moral codes and belief systems in American culture.*

Illustration by Karen Watson.

Reprint 82212

*Do the assumptions
on which its market economy rests
still have meaning
for American society?*

Periods of economic uncertainty inevitably provoke questions about the vitality of America's economic system. Today, of course, inflation, unemployment, and lagging productivity inspire debate about the efficiency of the market system itself. But for Americans, at least, a market-based economy means something more than just the exchange of goods and services at prices determined by levels of supply and demand. True, the market system as Americans understand it differs from economies dependent on barter or central planning, but this is the market in just its narrow economic sense. In American culture, the market carries additional significance.

Whether we acknowledge it consciously or not, the market influences our basic values, helps shape our suppositions about reality, and figures centrally in our tacit assumptions about daily life. We invest the market with moral importance and associate it with many of our most deeply held beliefs.

In fact, the market system is so inextricably woven into our view of the world that any threat to the market endangers not only our standard of living but, more important, the very fabric of our society.

Some observers argue that such a period of danger is already upon us. In a speech delivered at Harvard University shortly after his arrival in the United States, Aleksandr Solzhenitsyn, widely known for his revealing criticisms of Soviet society, claimed that the American system indeed suffers from a pervasive sickness—a sickness that even extends to a fundamental uncertainty about the institutions of capitalism.[1] Noting the lack of public commitment, responsibility, and loyalty to the absolute values on which America was founded, Solzhenitsyn challenged us to renew our sense of moral obligation.

---

1 Aleksandr I. Solzhenitsyn,
A World Split Apart
(New York: Harper & Row, 1978).

Pollsters regularly identify rising skepticism about the ethics and values of public leaders and public institutions. Some cultural critics speak of a serious "disjuncture" between the economic realm and the values that once gave it legitimacy; others point to an alarming shift in what was once a civic-minded population toward a narcissistic concern for the self.[2]

But if in America the market system is intimately linked to personal values and commitments, what are the moral assumptions on which that system is based? What are its implications for industrial behavior and individual conscience?

The morality of the marketplace

Textbook economics holds that the marketplace is nothing more than a means for transacting business. This view is wrong. The marketplace provides one of the few arenas in modern society in which people have an opportunity to participate directly in public life. Indeed, with the possible exception of voting, market activities constitute the major form of such participation. Buying and selling, working and consuming link individuals to one another and to the collective goals of their society. In the market, therefore, one can discharge – or avoid – his or her moral responsibilities to society.

A historical view

The founders of modern economic theory clearly recognized the moral character of the marketplace. Adam Smith, the great eighteenth-century spokesman for laissez-faire economics, was as interested in moral philosophy as in economic theory. To Smith, the freely functioning market was an instrument of human betterment, for as buyers and sellers pursued their private interests, an "invisible hand" guaranteed that prosperity would accrue to them all.

What was good for the pin maker was, in Smith's view, good for England. After all, the pin maker contributed to the good of society by making pins. If he withdrew from the market, hoarded his pins, or took an extended vacation, he not only damaged his personal interests as a businessman but failed to keep the public trust as well. His moral obligation, therefore, was to participate in the market.

The eighteenth century also thought the marketplace a buttress to moral virtues in that it placed a check on the individual's most dangerous pas-

sions. By rationally pursuing one's own economic interest, one channeled unruly natural passions into socially desirable activities. Outside the market, these passions readily led to avarice, lust, fanaticism, and caprice; within it, they led to discipline and virtue. As Montesquieu once observed, "Commerce . . . polishes and softens barbarian ways."

Arguments like these also had political connotations. In the turbulent context of the eighteenth century, men of property and principle believed a strong market economy offered the best protection against the designs of the powerful, for by making social relations more predictable, it promoted both domestic and international peace. Yet the market was delicate, like a fine clock, and had to be treated with respect and devotion. By acting responsibly in the marketplace, a citizen discharged a moral duty.

How much these philosophical arguments actually swayed the merchants and industrialists of the time remains, of course, a matter for conjecture. At a minimum, historical evidence suggests that they were not the arguments of academicians alone. As Albert O. Hirschman has shown, eighteenth-century publications – and even eighteenth-century laws – were filled with debate about the moral quality of the market and about its responsibility for individual and social well-being.[3]

By the nineteenth century, the market system had come to be such a familiar feature of social organization that it scarcely required an explicit moral defense. It was simply a fact of life.

In the United States, for example, the market system was widely regarded as a source of individual freedom and dignity. The famous McGuffey readers, on which more than 150 million Americans were reared, extolled the virtues of the marketplace as a means of building moral character. Similarly, in the popular rags-to-riches stories of the period, only by struggling in the marketplace did the individual discover his talents and contribute to the good of his fellow man. To the readers of Horatio Alger, the market never appeared to be a strictly economic device; it was, first and foremost, an engine for shaping moral character.

The modern scene

These arguments may no longer carry the weight or conviction they once did, but neither have they altogether disappeared. Older notions of character and virtue may have given way to modern concepts of the self; yet people still need to think of themselves as moral individuals, and the market remains a primary arena in which to demonstrate moral responsibility.

Contemporary best-seller lists include moralistic defenses of the market system as the only way of protecting the free world and the affluent life. Public voices regularly call on consumers to conserve energy, buy American goods, regulate spending habits, and avoid hoarding and speculation. Even presidents and their advisers present economic policy in moral terms – often as the moral equivalent of a war against the enemies of the free market.

In all these ways and more, behavior in the marketplace takes on moral significance today. Because individuals' actions can affect the very well-being of society, they represent more than strict economic calculation; they are a way of discharging both civic and social responsibility.

Moral crusades

A society's moral sense also expresses itself in the kinds of "moral crusades" in which it engages. In the United States these crusades have ranged from the abolition and temperance movements to various nativistic campaigns against Jews and Catholics and to the more recent struggle for civil rights. At present, the profamily and antiabortion campaigns sponsored by such groups as the Moral Majority and the Conservative Caucus seek to impute a moral meaning to specific dimensions of public life.

Of late, however, a growing number of these crusades have had as their focus not the family or race or religion or personal conduct but the marketplace. The consumer protection, environmental, antismoking, and antinuclear movements, for example – no less than the drives for equal employment, fair housing, accurate advertising, and cleaned-up television – share the assumption that the marketplace is an important focus for moral behavior. Whether to smoke cigarettes, recycle beer cans, and install solar collectors have become decisions of moral as well as economic importance.

Individual commitment

How do these various moral claims help legitimize the market system? Let us assume for the moment that people prefer to think of themselves as decent, morally upright individuals and not as purely calculating utilitarians. If this is a reasonable assumption, as I believe it is, then responsible behavior in the marketplace can work to maintain a person's sense of self-worth. Not surprisingly, activities that promote a feeling of well-being tend to evoke strong individual commitment and thus to appear legitimate.[4]

In the past, the obligations of military service, kinship, religion, and philanthropy provided the most common ways of demonstrating one's moral stature. Today, however, the marketplace has surpassed them in making such opportunities available. Commitment to the market, therefore, stems only in part from strict economic necessity or from convictions about the market as a rational economic system. Its legitimacy and stability rest instead on the feeling of self-worth it affords to individuals who fulfill their moral responsibilities to society.

This argument assumes, of course, that the market actually does provide opportunities to fulfill moral obligations. This is the catch. If these occasions are not present even in symbolic form, it becomes difficult to maintain a sense of personal worth and thus to feel loyalty to the market. But whether the market is genuinely rich in such opportunities remains an important question.

Capitalism & freedom

The dynamics of self-esteem, therefore, provide one set of assumptions on which the legitimacy of American capitalism rests; the relation between capitalism and freedom constitutes a second. Linking an institution to the highest values of a society is an obvious way of legitimating that institution. No wonder, then, that some apologists for the free market have exploited the notion of freedom in order to oppose government intervention in the economy and to extol the virtues of private enterprise. Others go further. According to Milton Friedman, for example, the free market provides the only sure protection for freedom of speech, freedom of religion, and freedom of thought.[5]

But asserting a relation between capitalism and freedom is of little value unless that relation is thoroughly understood. Freedom assists in the day-to-day legitimation of the market system not so much by linking economic activity with abstract political phi-

2 See Daniel Bell,
  The Cultural Contradictions of Capitalism
  (New York: Basic Books, 1976) and
  Christopher Lasch,
  *The Culture of Narcissism:
  American Life in an Age of Diminishing Expectations*
  (New York: Norton, 1978).

3 Albert O. Hirschman,
  The Passions and the Interests
  (Princeton: Princeton University Press, 1977).

4 For a discussion of legitimacy,
  see Peter L. Berger's article
  "New Attack on the Legitimacy of Business,"
  HBR September-October 1981, p. 82.

5 Milton Friedman,
  Capitalism and Freedom
  (Chicago: University of Chicago Press, 1962).

losophy as by reinforcing the sense of moral worth that individuals derive from the marketplace. This understanding of freedom is a recent development.

The early idea of freedom

In societies lacking a fully developed market economy, freedom has generally been thought an attribute of groups. In traditional India, for example, the individual believed himself free insofar as he occupied a clearly defined rank within the hierarchical structure of the caste system. According to Louis Dumont, a French anthropologist who has devoted many years to the study of Indian culture, the Western concept of freedom as individual autonomy was virtually unknown in India until recent times. Even in societies where trade was well developed – among the Polynesian Islanders, for example, or in the Greek city-states – freedom was not associated with the individual merchant or trader but with the people collectively.

To the American colonists, freedom still lacked a focus on the individual. What they valued most was freedom from external political domination – in effect, the freedom to worship as they chose, to create fitting standards of government, and to build institutions appropriate to the New World. But these were all collective enterprises. The Puritan settlers of the seventeenth and eighteenth centuries were not the Protestant individualists of the nineteenth century. To the Puritans, freedom from external constraint meant not license but conformity to internal restraint.

Freedom in a market society

As the market economy grew to prominence during the nineteenth century, the idea of freedom became increasingly associated with individuals, not collective institutions. For Americans it was the rugged individualist on the frontier – the heroic woodsman, the pioneer, and the self-sufficient farmer – who then best symbolized freedom. And it was the market, not communal groups, that provided these newly autonomous individuals with an outlet for their produce and with the materials they needed for survival.

But self-sufficiency and autonomy, as definitions of freedom, were by themselves inadequate before the growing social complexity that accompanied the rise of large-scale industry. Contrary to what many observers have said, the growth of complex industrial bureaucracies did not erode the concept of freedom so much as give it a different meaning. No longer were free individuals able to think of themselves as purely separate creatures, like grains of sand on the seashore. Instead, freedom came to mean knowing one's place in the organization of society – that is, knowing what one's function was in relation to other individuals and groups.

The British anthropologist Mary Douglas likens this modern idea of freedom to a grid in which each cell is occupied by an individual who stands in specific, formal relation to the other occupants of the grid.[6] In his study of prisons, factories, and military units, the French historian Michel Foucault takes this concept one step further by arguing that the similarity between cells and the modern view of the individual is more than just analogy. According to Foucault, the market economy actually created cells – cubicles, offices, places on assembly lines – that in turn shaped a notion of the person based not on self-sufficiency but on functional responsibility to some large organization or system.[7]

True, in highly regimented settings like military units and assembly lines, the individual's functions are closely prescribed. As a market economy evolves, however, the opportunities for individual discretion increase, and it is in these acts of discretion that individual freedom is most vividly manifest. In setting priorities, in choosing among possible courses of action, in selecting jobs or career paths, and in making decisions as consumers, individuals dramatize their freedom.

The right to choose

In the contemporary marketplace, therefore, freedom means essentially the right to choose. But why is this type of freedom valued? To be sure, the freedom to explore personal talents and desires expresses fundamental beliefs about the value and dignity of the individual. But this is only part of the story – and perhaps not even the most important part, since many people readily sacrifice their individuality in favor of conformity to collective norms.

What the right to choose does, even if that right is often relinquished, is to make it possible for individuals to be held responsible for their actions. Responsibility for an action can, after all, be imputed to an individual only if he or she could have chosen to do otherwise. If a sergeant orders me to march, for

6 Mary Douglas,
Natural Symbols: Explorations in Cosmology
(New York: Vintage Books, 1973).

7 Michel Foucault,
Discipline and Punish: The Birth of the Prison
(New York: Vintage Books, 1979).

8 Karl Polanyi,
The Livelihood of Man,
Harry Pearson, ed.
(New York: Academic Press, 1977).

example, I can take little credit for my "decision" to march. But if I voluntarily purchase and maintain a home, the responsibility for that decision is mine alone.

Now, if the market works to sustain my loyalty by nurturing an image of myself as a good and decent person, it must not only provide me with opportunities to discharge moral obligations, it must also demonstrate to me that I am free to discharge them and can therefore be held responsible for them. The legitimacy of the market system depends heavily on its capacity to provide this sense of freedom.

Because the modern concept of freedom is largely subjective, it is difficult to determine in any absolute sense whether the market system actually reinforces freedom. No standard, easily measurable criteria like GNP or disposable income are available. The only relevant evidence is the feeling involved in making choices among the various products, services, and opportunities provided by the market.

But this kind of evidence is sufficient. As individuals make choices in their jobs and as consumers, they are likely to experience their freedom more vividly than in any Fourth of July celebration. This dramatically "experienced" freedom is real enough that it easily pushes into the background abstract questions about the freedom of those who cannot or who choose not to participate in the marketplace. Such questions are, of course, important, but their theoretical concern does not—and cannot—in practice disprove the mutual legitimation of marketplace and personal freedom.

Economic laws

A third set of assumptions also links capitalism with freedom and moral responsibility. We assume that economic forces exist over which we have no more control than over the laws of nature. Whenever our most conscientious choices lead to unexpected and undesired outcomes, these economic laws receive the blame. We believe these laws to be objectively real, to be beyond human control or manipulation, to operate according to principles of their own, and to function in ways only partly comprehensible to economic theorists. They provide us an excuse, so that we do not have to blame ourselves or question our moral responsibility—even when evil results from our well-intentioned activities.

All moral codes include assumptions that permit their adherents to excuse themselves from the consequences of some of their actions. Although moral codes are often thought a source of guilt, just the opposite is actually the case. Moral codes are generally constructed in such a way that guilt can be absolved and that individuals can be left with the sense that they are good and decent. In the world's great religions, for example, some notion of evil spirits, fate, original sin, or inherent contradiction has always been present to absolve individuals of full responsibility for their actions. Were these escape clauses not present, guilt and frustration would build up to such intolerable levels that the moral codes would probably fall apart.

So too with capitalism. It imputes moral meaning to the marketplace and holds individuals responsible for their economic choices, but it also absolves them of overwhelming guilt and frustration by providing a scapegoat for the failings of the system.

Just as fate and the demonic are objectified in other moral systems, so popular discourse objectifies the market economy as an ominous, willful, living creature. The economy gets "sick," suffers "blows," sustains "shocks," "recovers," "falls into a slump," "straightens itself out," "awakens," experiences "spurts," and "revives." Like earthly beings, interest rates "climb," inflation "soars," and productivity "staggers." Even the caretakers of the economy, much like wise physicians caring for an ailing patient, are said to seek "remedies" in their attempt to "heal" the economy and maintain its "health."

This talk livens up the newspapers, but it also plays an important role in sustaining commitment to the market system. Characterizing the economy as something "out there" for which individuals cannot be held morally accountable is, as all propagandists know, perhaps the most effective way of legitimating it. A mere idea can be questioned: Is it right? Could it have been otherwise? An objective fact, in contrast, simply exists. Standing outside the realm of choice, it appears natural and inevitable. Things could not be otherwise. When something goes wrong, therefore, no one need take the blame. Such problems, after all, result from the operation of the economy's natural laws.

Since the early part of the nineteenth century, Western culture has increasingly viewed the market system as a part of reality itself and has thus fallen prey to what Karl Polanyi, the late economist and historian, termed the "economist fallacy." This fallacy consists of the assumption that the market works according to economic laws that apply to all societies. It is true, of course, that all societies have had economies, but the market system is only one form of economic organization. It may seem a fact of nature, but the market system is as much a humanly constructed institution as are democracy, communism, and the mass media. There is nothing inevitable about it.[8]

Nevertheless, the temptation is to think of the market as an inevitable fact of nature because doing so limits the realm of moral responsibility. In a sense, people find it useful to have restrictions on their freedom so that they cannot be held accountable for everything that happens. Consumers can excuse themselves for not saving more of their income. Large corporations can excuse themselves for not making a profit. Even presidents of the United States can excuse their inability to perform economic miracles. Given our belief in economic laws to which we are all subject, we need think no less of ourselves for not doing better.

Is there a crisis?

The legitimacy of the American economic system rests, therefore, on more than its productive capacity. It derives support from three sets of largely unrecognized assumptions that, in combination, sustain the belief of those who participate in the market in their own goodness and decency. These assumptions do not require adherence to any formal creed, doctrine, or philosophical outlook. They are built into the fabric of American society itself.

The market system provides an arena in which some of the moral obligations incurred by members of society can be fulfilled. This is so because the capacity to make choices in the marketplace reveals a deep relation between capitalism and personal freedom. A belief in objective economic laws, then, limits this freedom and thereby defines realistically those areas to which moral responsibility applies. Together these assumptions provide individuals with a measure of security against doubt—doubt that what they are doing is right and doubt that the system as a whole is worthwhile.

Historians suggest that the market system gradually acquired these meanings during the eighteenth and nineteenth centuries. As the market economy incorporated ever more of the adult population into the production of goods and services for commercial exchange, it came to be an important determinant of how individuals felt about themselves. Indeed, some historians—Polanyi, for example—argue that by the end of the nineteenth century the market had become the single most important institution in the life of industrialized societies.

The implications of technology

Many observers now, however, believe that the market system is undergoing a crisis in legitimacy and commitment. To put the question bluntly:

Are the sets of assumptions we have discussed being eroded today by major events in the world?

I am convinced that the answer to this question is yes. The growing dependence of American society—and, in fact, of the world at large—on technology threatens to undermine each of the basic tenets of the market system's moral code. Although it is too soon to predict the final outcome of so fundamental a cultural transition, it is likely that, over the long haul, the market's legitimating assumptions will become reoriented around technology. If so, technology will take on an increasingly important role in determining how people think and act. Just as the market dominated the nineteenth century, so technology may well come to dominate not only the economic life but also the social and intellectual life of the modern world.

I do not mean that technology threatens to unravel the social fabric, as many have suggested, by provoking environmental catastrophe or accelerating the pace of social change. True, both of these may occur. But I think the more serious implications of current technology lie in the subtle and as yet largely imperceptible shifts it is causing in the assumptions undergirding the individual's sense of moral worth.

A moral code in flux

Signs of this process of change are already evident. The growing complexity of the marketplace makes it increasingly difficult to believe that participation contributes in any significant way to the public good or represents any genuine discharge of one's moral obligations to society. As a result, the activities that lead to moral gratification are more and more restricted to the "private" realms of family, leisure, and voluntary associations, where individual effort still makes a discernible difference.

To some extent, this tendency has been slowed by a professionalization of the work force that redefines work as a career from which personal fulfillment can and should be expected. But even here a serious decline in loyalty and commitment exists. A study of work values conducted a few years ago in the Detroit area, for example, found that over a 13-year period commitment to the work ethic among professionals had dropped precipitously.[9]

Though the meaning of these changes is not yet clear, the indications are that technology is

9 Larry Blackwood,
"Social Change and Commitment to
the Work Ethic,"
in Robert Wuthnow, ed.,
The Religious Dimension
(New York: Academic Press, 1979),
p. 241.

now taking on the kind of moral force once associated with the marketplace. Consider the accomplishments in which society takes pride: the moon landing, the space shuttle, sophisticated defense systems, improvements in transportation and communication, breakthroughs in laser technology, the latest generation of high-speed computers.

Or consider what it is that now leads to a sense of personal accomplishment: contributing to these technological feats; being knowledgeable enough to discuss them intelligently with co-workers, family, and neighbors; reaping the benefits of technology as consumers of home computers, microwave ovens, videodiscs, and the like.

Further, today's moral crusades still focus to some extent on the marketplace, but their emphasis is shifting toward technology. A small but growing number of individuals attribute the highest moral importance to opposing what they see as the worst dangers of technology—the threat of nuclear annihilation, the risk associated with nuclear energy, the invention of drugs that make euthanasia and abortion easy, and the use of communications technology for the dissemination of values potentially harmful to the moral fabric of society. It is no accident that the Moral Majority and similar groups have seized on these issues.

Then, too, the idea of freedom, so vital to the traditional legitimation of the market system, has been similarly affected by the rising prominence of technology. Contemporary discussions of freedom center on questions of technology, not the market, for no longer is it the market that provides the clearest dramatization of freedom.

Society has become sophisticated enough to realize that the production, consumption, and pricing of goods represents far more than the simple act of autonomous individuals freely expressing their personal preferences. It is the underlying technology to which society looks to expand its range of choices—and which society fears as the greatest potential threat to its right to choose.

As a result, technology now provides the key symbolism in discussions of freedom. On one issue after another ("the pill," abortion, genetic screening, sex selection, solar energy, fusion research, labor-saving consumer products, information processing), technology symbolizes what promises most to enhance, or threatens most to diminish, personal freedom.

Finally, the notion of objective economic laws, which have long been taken for granted as part of reality, is also undergoing a subtle process of revision. The growing use of fiscal planning by government agencies and the private sector alike undercuts the belief that economic realities are simply "there" in the nature of things. As planning agencies assume responsibility for the economy, society will increasingly hold them—and not some neutral law—morally accountable for the failings of the system.

This phenomenon has already played a significant role in recent elections, but it is really nothing new. It was, history tells us, not so much the stark hunger and economic destitution that led the peasantry to revolt in Old Regime France. That much they were used to. It was, rather, the growing belief that representatives of the regime could have forestalled the periodic misery that afflicted the masses.

Toward a new code

As the moral code underlying the market system falls open to challenge, a new technology-based code has begun to take its place as a guarantor—within limits—of personal freedom. Just as the idea of objective economic laws at one time justified the failure of morally respectable intentions, so the notion of finite "technical capacity" does so today. Because the technical capacity of society is still limited, oil and electricity cost as much as they do, nuclear power is necessary but risky, and space exploration is of uncertain benefit to life on earth. Or so runs the new rationale. What under other circumstances might appear the failure of managers, breadwinners, and consumers can now be attributed to the limited "state of the art."

Society may have lost its former confidence in the market as a reflection of immutable laws of nature, but it has no doubt that technology rests on proven evidence about the world itself. Individuals can thus be held responsible for what current technology allows; what falls outside its limitations, however, is beyond human responsibility as well. Technology, then, promises society not only economic value but also a new legitimating moral code. Technology, in turn, acquires legitimacy because it promotes economic progress and—more important—because it supports the self-worth of individuals.

A look to the future

What do these developments portend? The market economy is, after all, already heavily reliant on scientific technology. R&D figures centrally in projections for corporate profits and productivity. Government plays an increasing role in organizing and funding large-scale technical projects. Much of the labor force is associated, directly or indirectly, with the production and distribution of technical knowledge.

To say that technology will become increasingly important, therefore, is to suggest only a continuation of society's dependence on technology.

Strengthening the linkages between the individual's concept of self and technology, however, represents a qualitative deepening and broadening of that dependence. When, for example, personal gratification comes less from making choices in the marketplace than from making contributions to technological projects, society may have to restructure the organization of work itself.

Major technological projects require vast sums of capital, the application of expert knowledge, and the cooperation of corporations, universities, national labs, and government agencies. These "technical systems," to give them a name, represent as dramatically new a form of social organization as the modern corporation did in the late eighteenth century. They already exist in knowledge-intensive areas such as nuclear waste disposal, solar photovoltaic applications, millimeter wave technology, and the gene-splicing industry, and they are likely to become even more prominent.

The new moral code linking self-worth with participation in the production of technology should, of course, contribute to the legitimacy of these technical systems and their capacity to elicit personal commitment. To the extent that the marketplace continues to be an arena for the discharge of moral obligations, however, some conflict will inevitably arise between the market and emerging technical systems. The two do overlap in that the market distributes the tangible products of technology, but at heart they are quite different in both organization and legitimating assumptions.

Technical systems require communication networks, collective planning, and a degree of centralized administration that is out of place in the traditional view of the market. They also put a value on innovation and scientific calculation that was only implicit, if present at all, in the legitimating assumptions of the market.

For the present, then, these two systems for conferring legitimacy on American society and the American economy will exist in uneasy balance. We have weathered periods of uncertainty in the past, perhaps most notably during the Great Depression, but we have never felt so direct a challenge to our deepest legitimating assumptions. As a new moral code slowly takes shape, a delicate balance must again be struck between the moral demands we as Americans perceive in our work and our ability to fulfill them – that is, between the freedom undergirding moral responsibility and our perception of unchangeable forces in the external world. Getting this balance right is as vital to the functioning of the economy as the economy is to the society itself. ▽

2

The executive on the spot

What makes an executive successful — the size of the profit, his
sense of personal fulfillment, the
approval of other people?

Moral Hazards of an Executive

By Louis William Norris

No business, educational, or political executive today would be so foolhardy as to reiterate
Cornelius Vanderbilt in saying, "Let the public
be damned." He knows he would not be able to
market his product or gain public support on
such a platform. Nor would he be caught mut-
tering even under his breath, "Let the employees
be damned." His success depends too much on
their contentment for any such invective, even
when he is positively sure their wage demands
are preposterous. His shiny office intercom may,
on the other hand, bring in a detectable, "Let
the president be damned." For the executive is
knowingly involved in the private lives of more
people than ever before in history. They let
him know what they think of *his* policies.

For an executive, the chief crises are moral.
Since his job is so rarely impersonal, his principal problems are what he does about people.
He may have started out as a master craftsman,
teacher, or production expert, but as an executive he is daily putting into action plans for
people to carry out, which will in turn affect
other people. The criteria that guide his actions — his morals, in short — are therefore
the most important features of his term of service as an executive. He is continuously on the
radarscope of public judgment.

¹ Garden City, New York, Doubleday & Company, Inc.,
1956.

Reprint 60512

It is my thesis in this article that one of the
key tests of an executive is his capacity to face
the hazards and problems of:

1. Living with the necessity of compromise —
   but never compromising too much.
2. Being free to disclose only parts of the truth
   on many occasions, yet needing to see the
   whole truth.
3. Having to make final decisions but on the
   basis of incomplete facts.
4. Accepting responsibility for the mistakes of
   subordinates while not allowing them to
   make *too many* mistakes.
5. Living up to the image that the public and
   his associates demand of a man in high office, but not becoming the victim of it.
6. Succeeding as a man of thought as well as
   a man of action.

No Recipes

Many have taken pity on the harried executive and tried to show him how to succeed. For
example:

◀ In *The Executive Life*,¹ the editors of *Fortune*
get down to fundamentals of how to become an
executive, how to avoid getting fired, how to manage raises, control the threat of overwork, and similar questions, but they do not identify or provide
guidance through the crucial tests of the executive.
These tests are moral, for they concern not only
what the executive *does*, but what he *should* do.

❧ Others have looked to the education of the executive. The Fund for Adult Education compiled some essays under the title, *Toward the Liberally Educated Executive*.[2] These have been reprinted by popular demand. We are told here that the executive must have a cultivated mind, but not that he must have a cultivated set of morals.

❧ David Lilienthal's *Big Business: A New Era*,[3] shows that America's destiny will be best realized through big organizations and, therefore, through the aid of big executives. Their social, political, and economic influence is enormous, to be sure. He does not, however, show the moral import of such a condition.

❧ The big executives belong to *The Power Elite*,[4] as C. Wright Mills notes. But while the moral standards of the power elite constitute the crux of their social function, that fact remains to be elaborated.

❧ William H. Whyte, Jr., in *The Organization Man*[5] and Alan Harrington in *Life in the Crystal Palace*[6] warn of the hazards in bureaucracy. But what of the moral hazards?

Moral Maze

Success is demanded of an executive, whether of a distillery or a college. He must stay in office to exercise his functions. He does not become prime minister to preside over the dissolution of his majesty's empire. Even if he and his family own the company, he must succeed in the competitive whirl, or there will be no company over which he may reign as an executive. Hence, a standard of success, which must derive ultimately from moral issues, becomes inevitable. The thoughtful businessman may wonder what test measures his success. Is it

— Growth of his organization?
— Development of efficiency in production?
— Gain in good will toward the corporation?
— Extension of service to the public?

If any or all these criteria figure in the executive's mind, should they? Does his business *need* to grow? Is there any point to improving production? Suppose the public comes to think better of his organization? Is this change worth the executive's ulcers? Does the public deserve to have the services an executive makes available to them? Or is a supposed service really a luxury that has become a necessity, or even a threat to health and emotional well-being?

Let it not be affirmed with fine disdain that such moral questions are impertinent, impractical, or ephemeral. Some standard of values is assumed or expressed in all thought and action. The executive thinks and acts in the interest of a "better" alternative. He is all wrapped up in moral hazards before he gets into his clothes in the morning. He puts them aside only with the skillful aid of Morpheus again that night — though if Freud is right, they even cling to him in his dreams.

What are the hazards which no executive can bypass, jump over, or wave out of his way?

I. Living With Compromise

First of all, the executive in any organization, even of modest complexity, must live on a diet of compromise. Democracy has come to be expected in business, education, and nearly every form of administration, as well as in politics. Leadership rests on an amalgamation of opinion, a fusion of standards. A healthy administrative organization encourages differences and originality of judgment. All this is to the good, but it makes for everyday aches and pains. To illustrate:

❧ The junior executive must be a "comer" — an idea man. Not always will he see eye to eye with senior, more experienced men. Whose counsel shall the chief executive take?

❧ The judgment of the public served is a potent force to be considered in product styling, community relations, and other areas. Shall the policy of the company agree with, educate, or ignore the public? Usually a combination of these factors is chosen.

❧ Every school and college seeks to educate its students to avoid the errors of their elders. To secure the support of these elders, while their youth are being set 25 years ahead of them, takes some doing. Typically it requires compromise of ideals. At least they must be indirectly sought or delayed. The school administrator in large areas of the country, including some districts north of the Mason-Dixon Line, must let integration remain an ideal, while the real feelings of his community play themselves out in some form of intolerance.

❧ Woodrow Wilson found it impossible to compromise on the location of the graduate school at Princeton, or on America's entry into the League

[2] Robert A. Goldwin, editor (White Plains, New York, Fund for Adult Education, 1957).
[3] New York, Harper & Brothers, 1953.
[4] New York, Oxford University Press, Inc., 1956.
[5] New York, Simon and Schuster, Inc., 1956.
[6] New York, Alfred A. Knopf, Inc., 1959.

of Nations. In the one case, it was expedient for him to resign from Princeton; and, in the other, he brought on the break in his health which was to shorten his life. Was he merely a poor diplomat, or was he illustrating that some issues do not lend themselves to compromise? He had to act, as every executive must, whether his constituents were ready to move with him or not.

Conflicts of Interest

Let the executive be alert to the kinds of compromise he inevitably makes.

For one thing, he must choose between present and long-term values. Shall the dividends be higher or the capital improvements greater? Is a curriculum change to meet the needs of the time as important as one that fulfills the needs that are timeless? Secondly, a conflict between individual and institutional values must often be resolved. Loyalty to an institution is fundamental to the institution's success. Yet an individual can hinder its success in spite of his loyalty. It might be better for the company for the vice president to be dismissed, though this could ruin his health and reputation. A student might be better off to be permitted continuance in college, though forgiveness of his offense would smirch the honor of old Siwash.

Again, shall decisions be made in the interests of few or many? Democratic morality commonly holds its nose when legislative or executive action is taken or threatened that favors the few. Witness Teapot Dome, or the Dixon-Yates contract. Yet who can say with certainty that F.D.R. should not have run for a third or fourth term? Would anyone else have brought the war to a close sooner? As pressure mounts for admission to college, should a college plan to concentrate its efforts on the intellectual elite, or serve a cross section of the masses?

Unquestionably the most significant compromises are those that balance material and nonmaterial values. Although advertising that plays on the vanity, fear, craving for status, and pride of purchasers may sell the product, the advertising executive may do well to resist trying to win his promotion by performance on these keys alone. And a trade union executive may emphasize the economic needs of his union to such an extent that other and more spiritual advantages already possessed dim out of sight in the eyes of members.

[7] See *Experiment in Education* (Chicago, Henry Regnery Company, 1954).

There are benefits in compromise. Often it is the only way to secure group action. The price of diverse wisdom among differing people may be mutual adjustment before action is possible. Further, such compromise educates differing individuals, who try out hypotheses urged by their opponents. In the end, compromise may be the way ideals actualize themselves. Executives of the church found it necessary to compromise with the Roman Empire, property owners, and social leaders to prevent its ideals from remaining a kingdom of heaven, found only in heaven.

Perhaps the chief evil in compromise lies in its apparent disregard of universal principle. An executive undermines his own influence if he becomes motivated largely by expediency. The great executives have been considered "men of principle," no matter how much they may have trimmed their sales on minor points. Virtue remains largely a habit of the will to follow principle, as Aristotle and Kant emphasized. Members of any institution want the security supplied by the knowledge that their executive is "unpurchasable," to use a term made prominent by William Ernest Hocking.[7] Deviation from principle may become habit forming. Fear of mediocrity, shortsightedness, or unpredictability sets in when principle falls out.

Implications for Action

Every executive must calculate the strength in the tension between the values of compromise and adherence to principle. He will safeguard himself if he seeks to become clearly conscious of the compromises made in nearly every important decision. Choices between black and white are easy. But they never come to a top executive! He is also well advised to keep a chronic idealist in his organization. His conscience should be pricked by this trusted aid every time matters of principle are brought down into the dusty flats of earthy action.

II. Control of Truth

Another moral hazard besetting the executive resides in his control of truth on many occasions. It is rare that an executive has the privilege of telling the truth, the whole truth, and nothing but the truth. To take a common illustration, truth, bluntly told, may hurt a subordinate who is incompetent or misguided. When improvement by this subordinate is possible, tactful treatment of the fault to be corrected will involve adroit selection of truths that can be told. So far, so good. But if the executive withholds truth on this occasion, he will on others. Can he be trusted to withhold the *right* truths?

And let us not delude ourselves about the frequency with which these occasions occur in and out of the office. No manager can escape all of them:

◖ A college executive who pointed out to a prospective benefactor, even though truly, that his wealth was accumulated through exploitational labor practices or questionable marketing policies, would soon be looking for another job. He would, in this case, hold to the theory of transubstantiation as far as wealth given to his institution is concerned. The truth about his benefactor would have to wait!

◖ Would a successful sales executive counsel his staff not to sell to those who could not afford to buy? Certainly not very often, and probably never at all.

◖ If an executive consoles himself by saying that even marital bliss requires him not to tell all to his wife when he returns from a business trip, he must realize that he gambles regularly one truth against another, and there is danger in such gambling.

◖ Timing the release of information to the public may involve manipulation of the truth. For instance, though it has been known for some time, figures about the stockpiling of surpluses may be released just before a labor contract runs out; a rise in college fees may be announced at Christmastime when good cheer neutralizes the chilling news that more dollars are needed for education; and a political executive may advise against additional taxes in an election year, knowing they will be necessary the next year.

Obviously, no executive tells all he knows as soon as he knows it!

Emphasis on the value of one's own product or service may suggest the idea (sometimes false, sometimes not) that other products or services are inferior or even nonexistent. An executive of nearly any organization serves as a promoter of it. The ever-present possibility exists that his special pleading will be too successful. In *The Hidden Persuaders*,[8] Vance Packard has shown vividly (even if exaggeratedly) how controllable the public is. The moral issue for

[8] New York, David McKay Company, Inc., 1957.

the executive consists in whether his organization deserves to control the public in such measure as it seeks to do. For control usually results from withholding some truths while emphasizing others. One need only recall that this has been the avowed means of propaganda used by dictators, if he wants to recognize the gravity of such an issue.

The Test of Integrity

Of course, to possess partial truth about a subject, or to give out partial truth to others, does not invalidate necessarily the truth as far as it goes. Indeed, it is rarely possible to set forth the whole truth about anything in a single sentence. For truth is a whole system of propositions, values, and relations, and only part of a system can be handled at a time.

The crux of the matter lies in how much importance is attached to that part of the whole which is mentioned, and in how much implied significance is assigned to the remainder that is unmentioned. And how plain is it made that there is a larger whole of truth within which a given proposition or plan of action rests? This must be taken as crucial also. The executive has to look to the orientation of the truth he chooses to emphasize. An advertising statement like "More people are buying one" *could* mean that only three have bought one, as long as just two did last year!

It may be asked whether an executive must be responsible if the publics with which he deals lack powers of critical thought. The answer lies in the fact that every man is responsible in some measure for his actions *and for their effects*.

Surely if a man were idolized as a public hero, he would scarcely think of his position as an accident, but as a consequence of his actions. So, too, must he recognize responsibility for those of his actions that are not considered noble, or might not be so considered if all the facts were recognized.

Integrity becomes the chief requirement for the executive. He can be trusted with the direction of his organization only if he is able to interrelate in one whole all of its affairs. He must see the whole truth about the operations of his institution, and handle the partial truths called for on each occasion by reference to this whole. A man of integrity is a fully integrated man. He can become so and remain so only by constant regard for the whole system of facts he knows — those he does not disclose as well as those he does.

III. Finality of Decisions

A third moral dilemma for the executive arises from the many occasions when his judgment alone must be taken as final. Broad matters of policy are usually set by a board of directors, but these are often recommended by the chief executive and, when approved, they are interpreted and applied by him. Often responsibility for a decision can be lodged nowhere else. Some subordinates relish freedom from basic decisions and delight in passing them up the line of command. The president is indeed "the recipient of the ultimate buck." Democracy is more fun for subordinates than it is for top executives!

Time often requires decisions before all the facts are in, or can be obtained. General Eisenhower rightly chose to invade Normandy during bad weather. He counted on the Nazis' belief that the Allied Powers would not risk such weather. He did not *know* they would leave some positions thinly guarded for this reason, but he judged correctly. This is essentially the definition of genius given by the late Justice Holmes. "Genius," he said, "is the capacity to reach the proper conclusion before all the facts are in." The executive is often called on to be a genius. He dare not be wrong, though it may be his own judgment alone he can trust. If he is wrong, the disaster may be overwhelming.

A responsible executive seeks counsel where possible. But some problems cannot be discussed with others. For instance, financial and personnel questions are sometimes so confidential as to require complete secrecy. Besides, no one else has the point of view or responsibility of the chief executive, and rarely the relevant experience. Friendships with associates must remain temperate, for the executive cannot avoid sitting in judgment on the work of his colleagues. He must avoid bias, both seeming and real. A measure of aloofness becomes the price of objectivity.

Perspective Through Values

A certain unavoidable loneliness is attached, consequently, to administrative leadership. The executive may vacillate between overconfidence

[9] Alfred North Whitehead (New York, The Macmillan Company, 1925).

and underconfidence in his own judgment. Persistent success may breed overconfidence, while too many failures crack morale. If this loneliness becomes apparent to colleagues, the boss finds himself an object of pity and a cause of hushed conversations on his approach. He must like his job, however severe the discipline of issues he must handle alone.

Presumably the executive is one of the best informed men about his organization, else he would not be put in office. He must demand of every subordinate information, in relevant form, about his business, and he must call on "idea men" for help in making changes. But his *chief* need is for help on problems no one else knows much about. He will find himself searching for principles to guide him where his judgment alone is required. And the fulcrum of his judgment comes at last to be a scheme of values.

What are the aims of my organization? What values does it contribute to my generation, and to those yet to come? What satisfactions should my employees derive from their work? And when I die, what do I hope to be my life's chief accomplishment?

These are questions whose answers serve as a base line for proceeding to handle problems where the boss's judgment alone prevails. Aristotle's *Ethics*, "The Sermon on the Mount," and Whitehead's *Science and the Modern World* [9] should provide perspective. A diet of these discerning analyses of value helps to remove an executive from worry about "his" problems, keep him fresh and humble, and set him on the road to the discovery that there are solutions. All of his problems have been faced before.

An organization of complexity usually succeeds in providing the executive with enough failures to make him quit, if he does nothing to counteract them. Let him use the best judgment he can muster; but when his judgment fails, he needs to do something in which he wins or finds pleasure. This may be a game in which he excels, a hobby he has mastered, or a family outing in which he counts as a necessary feature. Thromboses, ulcers, suicides, and neurasthenia should not invade the executive's office if he has the support of values in the office and of achievements outside.

IV. Responsibility for Errors

Some hazards come in the form of responsibility for the mistakes of a subordinate. For instance, Sherman Adams' involvement with Bernard Goldfine became a serious moral problem for President Eisenhower. He remained loyal to Adams though the latter's acceptance of gifts for apparent political favors suggested that the President approved of this practice. Had Eisenhower repudiated Adams, he would have withdrawn the support which a subordinate must be allowed to presuppose if he is to do his best work.

Originality and initiative are essential in the subordinates of a healthy organization. Experimentation brings fresh values. A dean who has no new ideas about how a college can improve its instruction is a liability to his president. Conversely, a dean who is not allowed to experiment should resign. Delegated authority implies that a subordinate has the right to make mistakes — and the duty to accept responsibility for his mistakes.

Responsibility given to subordinates obviously matures their judgment. They may learn from their failures. The moral issue enlarges when those failures mount to such proportions that they become expensive or harmful to the prestige of the institution and to the welfare of colleagues. It may be profitable to allow subordinates to annoy each other with their mistakes. Friction, up to a point, defines issues and tests the resourcefulness of colleagues. If a finance vice president will not recommend approval of requests by a production vice president, both are likely to have taken a careful measure of each other.

Extent of Involvement

How far should the executive go in assuming responsibility for the serious errors of his subordinates? Certainly there are limits. The manager of a baseball team usually gets fired when his team consistently fails to win; there was a shake-up of top executives in the Edsel Division of the Ford Motor Company when the Edsels failed to sell in expected numbers; and the president of a midwestern university was recently dismissed because a strong alumni group felt, among other things, that he was not interested in a winning football team. A board of directors is bound to hold an executive accountable for what goes wrong in his organization. If he tolerates failure too often on the part of subordi-

[10] See *Human Nature and Conduct: An Introduction to Social Psychology* (New York, Henry Holt and Company, Inc., 1922), Part I, Section 1.

nates, he becomes a failure himself. His duty lies in cultivating conditions that prevent his subordinates' failure. If they win, he wins.

No executive can administer his organization on an atomistic theory of morals. While he cannot be his brother's keeper, especially if the brother makes too many serious errors, he can be his brother's brother. John Dewey would doubtless say, "If my neighbor steals, I, too, am a thief." [10] That overstates the case, though it emphasizes the mutual involvement of all men in moral questions. It is both right and expedient, therefore, that the executive assume some responsibility for the errors of his subordinates. If they cannot be corrected, his obligations cease, and a new man must be put on the payroll.

Democratic administration depends for its success on common aims individually shared. The democratic administrator stands in a position of mutual influence with his subordinates. He profits from their joint wisdom. He may judge and discipline them when they err, if he has developed for himself sufficiently reliable standards of private judgment. Note, however, that his judgment will consist largely in continuously setting before them high standards of excellence with which they cannot fail to compare themselves. Their ability or inability to reach these standards will generally become so apparent to themselves and their colleagues that they will respond with better effort, or resign.

This means that the executive is a leader, not a boss. Rigid discipline, which once meant enforced obedience, only results in fear, suspicion, hatred, resistance, and similar negative reactions. The executive must be a morale builder who engenders willingness to work, to cooperate, and to improve.

V. Images & Mirages

Some interesting issues arise from the nature of a top executive's office. Let us examine just a few of them.

Picture of Success

For one thing, the chief executive — or possibly the man aspiring to succeed to that position — is called on to live up to, or fit into, an image of the head of his organization that is pre-established in most cases. For example:

The "success" impression must be maintained. A bank, college, retail store, or political office rests on public confidence. The chief office holders must manifest present success and confidence in the future. Credit ratings and sales are related to the "success" atmosphere they generate. Philanthropists and investors are most often interested only in a going concern. Hence the dress, home and furnishings, car, vacations, and general approach of the executive to life all assume basic importance.

Whether or not the executive lives up to the public image expected of him may become a critical question. He may support the image sincerely (else he should not support it at all), but sincerity does not solve his problem. "The good of the company" often comes ahead of his personal pleasures or convenience. He must be the life of the party, whether he feels like it or not. If his fatigue, indigestion, boredom, or even disagreement on moral questions become too evident to his friends, there is something wrong with the company, or he must be a bad choice for the office. The test is a hard one. Any Dr. Jekyll, when he is honest, will want to be a Mr. Hyde at least once a month, and particularly after the annual board meeting!

Illusions of Praise

Another problem, strange as it may seem, is that the office of the executive often receives a great deal of recognition and praise. The danger is that the executive may be deceived into receiving this recognition for himself rather than for his office. The president presides at all meetings, actually or by implication, and leads all processions, receptions, and delegations. He sometimes forgets that his office requires this prominence, not his personal eminence apart from the office. As awards, citations, and publicity come to the executive for his organization, as if he had done the work himself, it is a subtle temptation to forget that he is the mouthpiece only of his institution, not of the whole body.

Politeness and official protocol may so obscure the true nature of an executive's work as to prevent him from ever securing a true appraisal of what he does. The most reliable judges of his work are not likely to be his subordinates. If they believe themselves unappreciated, they may seek recognition either by excessive praise or by too severe condemnation. As for members of the board of directors, they are likely to represent other interests and to occupy positions far removed from the executive's daily task. Acquaintances outside the firm may not be helpful, either.

There are always some well-meaning friends who praise a well-known figure if he merely stays out of jail. The executive needs to remember the caution Charles Reynolds Brown, formerly dean of the Yale Divinity School, was wont to give young theologues before they received their diplomas: "You will always have about you some kind old ladies, both male and female, who will tell you you are the greatest prophet since Amos. But that won't make it so!"

The executive is, therefore, in a quandary. If he accepts too facilely the public image of his office, he becomes insincere. If he departs too radically from it, he may disturb his constituents. If he accepts the recognition and achievements of his office as his own, he may remove himself from discriminating critics, and ride unjustly on the shoulders of his colleagues' achievements. He must, therefore, come back once more to his own scheme of professional and moral values. His recourse lies in developing for his own use a public image for his office and a private image for himself. This will deliver him from the strait jacket of public opinion. It will also deliver him from the cynicism that he might develop if he tried to stay completely detached from the role of his company and public demand.

VI. Cultural Development

Another dilemma lies in the relation of personal development to official activity. An executive continually carries out plans of action, and he must do so intelligently. At the same time, however, he wants to give time and attention to self-cultivation. He wants to be fresh and original. How far should he defer appointments at the office while he studies his problems, or defer decisions while he attends professional conferences, or takes a vacation?

As the cold war drags on, it becomes more and more evident that the battle of the century is for men's minds. An executive who ignores this fact may find himself administering an operation of vanishing importance. The involvement of his institution in the changing social, political, and economic conditions of the time requires him to know much about other managers' jobs as well as his own. He serves his own company as he studies conditions not directly related, but nonetheless surely related, to his own post. He must know what his organization is heading for.

In Europe, *the* American philosophy has often been considered pragmatism. The go-getting, successful American, particularly the businessman, is supposed to live by the doctrine that what is true is that which works. But this is a case where we do not want to see ourselves as others see us — or, at least, only as others see us. For in reality the thoughtful American executive has in his mind many a plan that has not worked, but that he knows must be true. He finds himself seeking more satisfactions than mere success. He discovers, too, that many of his employees have other goals than mere financial success.

The Institute for Executives at Aspen, Colorado, like the seminars at the University of Pennsylvania sponsored by the Bell Telephone Company, are interesting efforts to fill the void of cultural ideas and ideals that many an executive has begun to feel.[11] Doubtless the late Justice Holmes was right in saying, "It is required of a man that he share the action and passion of his time at peril of being judged not to have lived." [12] But all action and passion make Jack a dangerous, even if not a dull, boy. I find it significant, for example, that early American life was led by men who were able to unite thought and action in an admirable way. The John Cottons were ministers as well as cultural and political leaders. Thomas Jefferson was a scholar of prodigious practical accomplishment too. Woodrow Wilson was too academic for some, but his ideas are still demanding world acceptance.

The Ultimate Question

The executive must manage his life so that he can fill up his mind with interesting ideas that supply a context and guide for his actions. He is entitled, even obligated, to read books, to travel, and to confer with leaders outside his line of work so that life can be richer for him.

The thoughtful leader comes at last to face the ultimate question of whether he is big enough for the office. If he is, it will be in a large measure because he is adequate to deal with the moral issues put before him.

[11] See Charles A. Nelson, "The Liberal Arts in Management," HBR May–June 1958, p. 91.

[12] Memorial Day Address, Keene, New Hampshire, May 30, 1884; published in *The Mind and Faith of Justice Holmes*, edited by Max Lerner (Boston, Little, Brown and Company, 1946), p. 10.

WITHOUT indulging in too great refinements, let us remind ourselves that communication also has at bottom a moral aspect. It does, when all is said, anticipate a change in the conduct of the recipient. If the change has any large significance it means an interposing or interference with the autonomy of the other person or persons. And the tampering with personal drives and desires is a moral act even if its upshot is not a far-reaching one, or is a beneficial result. To seek to persuade behavior into a new direction may be wholly justifiable and the result in terms of behavior consequences may be salutary. But the judgment of benefit or detriment is not for the communicator safely to reach by himself. He is assuming a moral responsibility. And he had better be aware of the area with which he concerns himself and the responsibility he assumes. He should be willing to assert as to any given new policy, "I stand behind this as having good personal consequences for the individuals whom it will affect." That judgment speaks a moral concern and desired moral outcome.

Ordway Tead, *Administration: Its Purpose and Performance*
New York, Harper & Brothers, 1959, p. 46.

Saul W. Gellerman

Why 'good' managers make bad ethical choices

How could top-level executives at the Manville Corporation have suppressed evidence for decades that proved that asbestos inhalation was killing their own employees?

What could have driven the managers of Continental Illinois Bank to pursue a course of action that threatened to bankrupt the institution, ruined its reputation, and cost thousands of innocent employees and investors their jobs and their savings?

Why did managers at E.F. Hutton find themselves pleading guilty to 2,000 counts of mail and wire fraud, accepting a fine of $2 million, and putting up an $8 million fund for restitution to the 400 banks that the company had systematically bilked?

How can we explain the misbehavior that took place in these organizations – or in any of the others, public and private, that litter our newspapers' front pages: workers at a defense contractor who accused their superiors of falsifying time cards; alleged bribes and kickbacks that honeycombed New York City government; a company that knowingly marketed an unsafe birth control device; the decision-making process that led to the space shuttle Challenger tragedy.

"When in doubt, don't."

The stories are always slightly different; but they have a lot in common since they're full of the oldest questions in the world, questions of human behavior and human judgment applied in ordinary day-to-day situations. Reading them we have to ask how usually honest, intelligent, compassionate human beings could act in ways that are callous, dishonest, and wrongheaded.

In my view, the explanations go back to four rationalizations that people have relied on through

Mr. Gellerman is dean of the University of Dallas Graduate School of Management. He is the author of eight books on management and of the HBR article "Supervision: Substance and Style" (March-April 1976).

Reprint 86402

the ages to justify questionable conduct: believing that the activity is not "really" illegal or immoral; that it is in the individual's or the corporation's best interest; that it will never be found out; or that because it helps the company the company will condone it. By looking at these rationalizations in light of these cases, we can develop some practical rules to more effectively control managers' actions that lead to trouble – control, but not eliminate. For the hard truth is that corporate misconduct, like the lowly cockroach, is a plague that we can suppress but never exterminate.

Three cases

Amitai Etzioni, professor of sociology at George Washington University, recently concluded that in the last ten years, roughly two-thirds of America's 500 largest corporations have been involved, in varying degrees, in some form of illegal behavior. By taking a look at three corporate cases, we may be able to identify the roots of the kind of misconduct that not only ruins some people's lives, destroys institutions, and gives business as a whole a bad name but that also inflicts real and lasting harm on a large number of innocent people. The three cases that follow should be familiar. I present them here as examples of the types of problems that confront managers in all kinds of businesses daily.

Manville Corporation

A few years ago, Manville (then Johns Manville) was solid enough to be included among the giants of American business. Today Manville is in the process of turning over 80% of its equity to a trust representing people who have sued or plan to sue it for liability in connection with one of its principal former products, asbestos. For all practical purposes, the entire company was brought down by questions of corporate ethics.

More than 40 years ago, information began to reach Johns Manville's medical department – and through it, the company's top executives – implicating asbestos inhalation as a cause of asbestosis, a debilitating lung disease, as well as lung cancer and mesothelioma, an invariably fatal lung disease. Manville's managers suppressed the research. Moreover, as a matter of policy, they apparently decided to conceal the information from affected employees. The company's medical staff collaborated in the cover-up, for reasons we can only guess at.

Money may have been one motive. In one particularly chilling piece of testimony, a lawyer recalled how 40 years earlier he had confronted Manville's corporate counsel about the company's policy of concealing chest X-ray results from employees. The lawyer had asked, "Do you mean to tell me you would let them work until they dropped dead?" The reply was, "Yes, we save a lot of money that way."

Based on such testimony, a California court found that Manville had hidden the asbestos danger from its employees rather than looking for safer ways to handle it. It was less expensive to pay workers' compensation claims than to develop safer working conditions. A New Jersey court was even blunter: it found that Manville had made a conscious, cold-blooded business decision to take no protective or remedial action, in flagrant disregard of the rights of others.

How can we explain this behavior? Were more than 40 years' worth of Manville executives all immoral?

Such an answer defies common sense. The truth, I think, is less glamorous – and also less satisfying to those who like to explain evil as the actions of a few misbegotten souls. The people involved were probably ordinary men and women for the most part, not very different from you and me. They found themselves in a dilemma, and they solved it in a way that seemed to be the least troublesome, deciding not to disclose information that could hurt their product. The consequences of what they chose to do – both to thousands of innocent people and, ultimately, to the corporation – probably never occurred to them.

The Manville case illustrates the fine line between acceptable and unacceptable managerial behavior. Executives are expected to strike a difficult balance – to pursue their companies' best interests but not overstep the bounds of what outsiders will tolerate.

Even the best managers can find themselves in a bind, not knowing how far is too far. In retrospect, they can usually easily tell where they should have drawn the line, but no one manages in retrospect. We can only live and act today and hope that whoever looks back on what we did will judge that we struck the proper balance. In a few years, many of us may be found delinquent for decisions we are making now about tobacco, clean air, the use of chemicals, or some other seemingly benign substance. The managers at Manville may have believed that they were acting in the company's best interests, or that what they were doing would never be found out, or even that it wasn't really wrong. In the end, these were only rationalizations for conduct that brought the company down.

Continental Illinois Bank

Until recently the ninth largest bank in the United States, Continental Illinois had to be saved from insolvency because of bad judgment by management. The government bailed it out, but at a price. In effect it has been socialized: about 80% of its equity now belongs to the Federal Deposit Insurance Corporation. Continental seems to have been brought down by managers who misunderstood its real interests. To their own peril, executives focused on a single-minded pursuit of corporate ends and forgot about the means to the ends.

In 1976, Continental's chairman declared that within five years the magnitude of its lending would match that of any other bank. The goal was attainable; in fact, for a time, Continental reached it. But it dictated a shift in strategy away from conservative corporate financing and toward aggressive pursuit of borrowers. So Continental, with lots of lendable funds, sent its loan officers into the field to buy loans that had originally been made by smaller banks that had less money.

The practice in itself was not necessarily unsound. But some of the smaller banks had done more than just lend money – they had swallowed hook, line, and sinker the extravagant, implausible dreams of poorly capitalized oil producers in Oklahoma, and they had begun to bet enormous sums on those dreams. Eventually, a cool billion dollars' worth of those dreams found their way into Continental's portfolio, and a cool billion dollars of depositors' money flowed out to pay for them. When the price of oil fell, a lot of dry holes and idle drilling equipment were all that was left to show for most of the money.

Continental's officers had become so entranced by their lending efforts' spectacular results that they hadn't looked deeply into how they had been achieved. Huge sums of money were lent at fat rates of interest. If the borrowers had been able to repay the loans, Continental might have become the eighth or even the seventh largest bank in the country. But that was a very big "if." Somehow there was a failure of control and judgment at Continental – probably because the officers who were buying those shaky loans

"...So that's how the destabilization is going down here. How's the deregulation going up there?"

were getting support and praise from their superiors. Or at least they were not hearing enough tough questions about them.

At one point, for example, Continental's internal auditors stumbled across the fact that an officer who had purchased $800 million in oil and gas loans from the Penn Square Bank in Oklahoma City had also borrowed $565,000 for himself from Penn Square. Continental's top management investigated and eventually issued a reprimand. The mild rebuke reflected the officer's hard work and the fact that the portfolio he had obtained would have yielded an average return of nearly 20% had it ever performed as planned. In fact, virtually all of the $800 million had to be written off. Management chose to interpret the incident charitably; federal prosecutors later alleged a kickback.

On at least two other occasions, Continental's own control mechanisms flashed signals that something was seriously wrong with the oil and gas

portfolio. A vice president warned in a memo that the documentation needed to verify the soundness of many of the purchased loans had simply never arrived. Later, a junior loan officer, putting his job on the line, went over the heads of three superiors to tell a top executive about the missing documentation. Management chose not to investigate. After all, Continental was doing exactly what its chairman had said it would do: it was on its way to becoming the leading commercial lender in the United States. Oil and gas loans were an important factor in that achievement. Stopping to wait for paperwork to catch up would only slow down reaching the goal.

Eventually, however, the word got out about the instability of the bank's portfolio, which led to a massive run on its deposits. No other bank was willing to come to the rescue, for fear of being swamped by Continental's huge liabilities. To avoid going under, Continental in effect became a ward of the federal government. The losers were the bank's shareholders, some officers who lost their jobs, at least one who was indicted, and some 2,000 employees (about 15% of the total) who were let go, as the bank scaled down to fit its diminished assets.

Once again, it is easy for us to sit in judgment after the fact and say that Continental's loan officers and their superiors were doing exactly what bankers shouldn't do: they were gambling with their depositors' money. But on another level, this story is more difficult to analyze – and more generally a part of everyday business. Certainly part of Continental's problem was neglect of standard controls. But another dimension involved ambitious corporate goals. Pushed by lofty goals, managers could not see clearly their real interests. They focused on ends, overlooked the ethical questions associated with their choice of means – and ultimately hurt themselves.

E.F. Hutton

The nation's second largest independent broker, E.F. Hutton & Company, recently pleaded guilty to 2,000 counts of mail and wire fraud. It had systematically bilked 400 of its banks by drawing against uncollected funds or in some cases against nonexistent sums, which it then covered after having enjoyed interest-free use of the money. So far, Hutton has agreed to pay a fine of $2 million as well as the government's investigation costs of $750,000. It has set up an $8 million reserve for restitution to the banks – which may not be enough. Several officers have lost their jobs, and some indictments may yet follow.

But worst of all, Hutton has tarnished its reputation, never a wise thing to do – certainly not when your business is offering to handle other people's money. Months after Hutton agreed to appoint new directors – as a way to give outsiders a solid majority on the board – the company couldn't find people to accept the seats, in part because of the bad publicity.

Apparently Hutton's branch managers had been encouraged to pay close attention to cash management. At some point, it dawned on someone that using other people's money was even more profitable than using your own. In each case, Hutton's overdrafts involved no large sums. But cumulatively, the savings on interest that would otherwise have been owed to the banks was very large. Because Hutton always made covering deposits, and because most banks did not object, Hutton assured its managers that what they were doing was sharp – and not shady. They presumably thought they were pushing legality to its limit without going over the line. The branch managers were simply taking full advantage of what the law and the bankers' tolerance permitted. On several occasions, the managers who played this game most astutely were even congratulated for their skill.

Hutton probably will not suffer a fate as drastic as Manville's or Continental Illinois's. Indeed, with astute damage control, it can probably emerge from this particular embarrassment with only a few bad memories. But this case has real value because it is typical of much corporate misconduct. Most improprieties don't cut a corporation off at the knees the way Manville's and Continental Illinois's did. In fact, most such actions are never revealed at all – or at least that's how people figure things will work out. And in many cases, a willingness to gamble thus is probably enhanced by the rationalization – true or not – that everyone else is doing something just as bad or would if they could; that those who wouldn't go for their share are idealistic fools.

Four rationalizations

Why do managers do things that ultimately inflict great harm on their companies, themselves, and people on whose patronage or tolerance their organizations depend? These three cases, as well as the current crop of examples in each day's paper, supply ample evidence of the motivations and instincts that underlie corporate misconduct. Although the particulars may vary – from the gruesome dishonesty surrounding asbestos handling to the mundanity of illegal money management – the motivating beliefs are pretty much the same. We may examine them in the context of the corporation, but we know that these feelings are basic throughout society; we find them wherever we go because we take them with us.

When we look more closely at these cases, we can delineate four commonly held rationalizations that can lead to misconduct:

A belief that the activity is within reasonable ethical and legal limits – that is, that it is not "really" illegal or immoral.

A belief that the activity is in the individual's or the corporation's best interests – that the individual would somehow be expected to undertake the activity.

A belief that the activity is "safe" because it will never be found out or publicized; the classic crime-and-punishment issue of discovery.

A belief that because the activity helps the company the company will condone it and even protect the person who engages in it.

☐   The idea that an action is not really wrong is an old issue. How far is too far? Exactly where is the line between smart and too smart? Between sharp and shady? Between profit maximization and illegal conduct? The issue is complex: it involves an interplay between top management's goals and middle managers' efforts to interpret those aims.

Put enough people in an ambiguous, ill-defined situation, and some will conclude that whatever hasn't been labeled specifically wrong must be OK – especially if they are rewarded for certain acts. Deliberate overdrafts, for example, were not proscribed at Hutton. Since the company had not spelled out their illegality, it could later plead guilty for itself while shielding its employees from prosecution.

Top executives seldom ask their subordinates to do things that both of them know are against the law or imprudent. But company leaders sometimes leave things unsaid or give the impression that there are things they don't want to know about. In other words, they can seem, whether deliberately or otherwise, to be distancing themselves from their subordinates' tactical decisions in order to keep their own hands clean if things go awry. Often they lure ambitious lower level managers by implying that rich rewards await those who can produce certain results – and that the methods for achieving them will not be examined too closely. Continental's simple wrist-slapping of the officer who was caught in a flagrant conflict of interest sent a clear message to other managers about what top management really thought was important.

How can managers avoid crossing a line that is seldom precise? Unfortunately, most know that they have overstepped it only when they have gone too far. They have no reliable guidelines about what will be overlooked or tolerated or what will be condemned or attacked. When managers must operate in murky borderlands, their most reliable guideline is an old principle: when in doubt, don't.

That may seem like a timid way to run a business. One could argue that if it actually took hold among the middle managers who run most companies, it might take the enterprise out of free enterprise. But there is a difference between taking a worthwhile economic risk and risking an illegal act to make more money.

The difference between becoming a success and becoming a statistic lies in knowledge – including self-knowledge – not daring. Contrary to popular mythology, managers are not paid to take risks; they are paid to know which risks are worth taking. Also, maximizing profits is a company's second priority, not its first. The first is ensuring its survival.

All managers risk giving too much because of what their companies demand from them. But the same superiors who keep pressing you to do more, or to do it better, or faster, or less expensively, will turn on you should you cross that fuzzy line between right and wrong. They will blame you for exceeding instructions or for ignoring their warnings. The smartest managers already know that the best answer to the question, "How far is too far?" is don't try to find out.

☐   Turning to the second reason why people take risks that get their companies into trouble, believing that unethical conduct is in a person's or corporation's best interests nearly always results from a parochial view of what those interests are. For example, Alpha Industries, a Massachusetts manufacturer of microwave equipment, paid $57,000 to a Raytheon manager, ostensibly for a marketing report. Air force investigators charged that the report was a ruse to cover a bribe: Alpha wanted subcontracts that the Raytheon manager supervised. But those contracts ultimately cost Alpha a lot more than they paid for the report. After the company was indicted for bribery, its contracts were suspended and its profits promptly vanished. Alpha wasn't unique in this transgression: in 1984, the Pentagon suspended 453 other companies for violating procurement regulations.

Ambitious managers look for ways to attract favorable attention, something to distinguish them from other people. So they try to outperform their peers. Some may see that it is not difficult to look remarkably good in the short run by avoiding things that pay off only in the long run. For example, you can skimp on maintenance or training or customer service, and you can get away with it – for a while.

The sad truth is that many managers have been promoted on the basis of "great" results obtained in just those ways, leaving unfortunate successors to inherit the inevitable whirlwind. Since this is not necessarily a just world, the problems that such people create are not always traced back to them. Companies cannot afford to be hoodwinked in this way. They must be concerned with more than just results. They have to look very hard at how results are obtained.

Evidently, in Hutton's case there were such reviews, but management chose to interpret favorably what government investigators later interpreted unfavorably. This brings up another dilemma: management quite naturally hopes that any of its borderline actions will be overlooked or at least interpreted charitably if noticed. Companies must accept human nature for what it is and protect themselves with watchdogs to sniff out possible misdeeds.

An independent auditing agency that reports to outside directors can play such a role. It can provide a less comfortable, but more convincing, review of how management's successes are achieved. The discomfort can be considered inexpensive insurance and serve to remind all employees that the real interests of the company are served by honest conduct in the first place.

☐   The third reason why a risk is taken, believing that one can probably get away with it, is perhaps the most difficult to deal with because it's often true. A great deal of proscribed behavior escapes detection.

We know that conscience alone does not deter everyone. For example, First National Bank of Boston pleaded guilty to laundering satchels of $20 bills worth $1.3 billion. Thousands of satchels must have passed through the bank's doors without incident before the scheme was detected. That kind of heavy, unnoticed traffic breeds complacency.

How can we deter wrongdoing that is unlikely to be detected? Make it more likely to be detected. Had today's "discovery" process – in which plaintiff's attorneys can comb through a company's records to look for incriminating evidence – been in use when Manville concealed the evidence on asbestosis, there probably would have been no cover-up. Mindful of the likelihood of detection, Manville would have chosen a different course and could very well be thriving today without the protection of the bankruptcy courts.

The most effective deterrent is not to increase the severity of punishment for those caught but to heighten the perceived probability of being caught in the first place. For example, police have found that parking an empty patrol car at locations where motorists often exceed the speed limit reduces the frequency of speeding. Neighborhood "crime watch" signs that people display decrease burglaries.

Simply increasing the frequency of audits and spot checks is a deterrent, especially when combined with three other simple techniques: scheduling audits irregularly, making at least half of them unannounced, and setting up some checkups soon after others. But frequent spot checks cost more than big sticks, a fact that raises the question of which approach is more cost-effective.

A common managerial error is to assume that because frequent audits uncover little behavior that is out of line, less frequent, and therefore less costly, auditing is sufficient. But this condition overlooks the important deterrent effect of frequent checking. The point is to prevent misconduct, not just to catch it.

A trespass detected should not be dealt with discreetly. Managers should announce the misconduct and how the individuals involved were punished. Since the main deterrent to illegal or unethical behavior is the perceived probability of detection, managers should make an example of people who are detected.

□   Let's look at the fourth reason why corporate misconduct tends to occur, a belief that the company will condone actions that are taken in its interest and will even protect the managers responsible. The question we have to deal with here is, How do we keep company loyalty from going berserk?

That seems to be what happened at Manville. A small group of executives and a succession of corporate medical directors kept the facts about the lethal qualities of asbestos from becoming public knowledge for decades, and they managed to live with that knowledge. And at Manville, the company – or really, the company's senior management – did condone their decision and protect those employees.

Something similar seems to have happened at General Electric. When one of its missile projects ran up costs greater than the air force had agreed to pay, middle managers surreptitiously shifted those costs to projects that were still operating under budget. In this case, the loyalty that ran amok was primarily to the division: managers want their units' results to look good. But GE, with one of the finest reputations in U.S. industry, was splattered with scandal and paid a fine of $1.04 million.

One of the most troubling aspects of the GE case is the company's admission that those involved were thoroughly familiar with the company's ethical standards before the incident took place. This suggests that the practice of declaring codes of ethics and teaching them to managers is not enough to deter unethical conduct. Something stronger is needed.

Top management has a responsibility to exert a moral force within the company. Senior executives are responsible for drawing the line between loyalty to the company and action against the laws and values of the society in which the company must operate. Further, because that line can be obscured in the heat of the moment, the line has to be drawn well short of where reasonable men and women could begin to suspect that their rights had been violated. The company has to react long before a prosecutor, for instance, would have a strong enough case to seek an indictment.

Executives have a right to expect loyalty from employees against competitors and detractors, but not loyalty against the law, or against common morality, or against society itself. Managers must warn employees that a disservice to customers, and especially to innocent bystanders, cannot be a service to the company. Finally, and most important of all, managers must stress that excuses of company loyalty will not be accepted for acts that place its good name in jeopardy. To put it bluntly, superiors must make it clear that employees who harm other people allegedly for the company's benefit will be fired.

The most extreme examples of corporate misconduct were due, in hindsight, to managerial failures. A good way to avoid management oversights is to subject the control mechanisms themselves to periodic surprise audits, perhaps as a function of the board of directors. The point is to make sure that internal audits and controls are functioning as planned. It's a case of inspecting the inspectors and taking the necessary steps to keep the controls working efficiently. Harold Geneen, former head of ITT, has suggested that the board should have an independent staff, something analogous to the Government Accounting Office, which reports to the legislative rather than the executive branch. In the end, it is up to top management to send a clear and pragmatic message to all employees that good ethics is still the foundation of good business. ▽

The parable of the sadhu

After encountering a dying pilgrim on a climbing trip in the Himalayas, a businessman ponders the differences between individual and corporate ethics

Bowen H. McCoy

Mr. McCoy is a managing director of Morgan Stanley & Co., Inc., and president of Morgan Stanley Realty, Inc. He is also an ordained ruling elder of the United Presbyterian Church.

Illustration by Geoffrey Moss.

Reprint 83512

It was early in the morning before the sun rose, which gave them time to climb the treacherous slope to the pass at 18,000 feet before the ice steps melted. They were also concerned about their stamina and altitude sickness, and felt the need to press on. Into this chance collection of climbers on that Himalayan slope an ethical dilemma arose in the guise of an unconscious, almost naked sadhu, an Indian holy man. Each climber gave the sadhu help but none made sure he would be safe. Should somebody have stopped to help the sadhu to safety? Would it have done any good? Was the group responsible? Since leaving the sadhu on the mountain slope, the author, who was one of the climbers, has pondered these issues. He sees many parallels for business people as they face ethical decisions at work.

Last year, as the first participant in the new six-month sabbatical program that Morgan Stanley has adopted, I enjoyed a rare opportunity to collect my thoughts as well as do some traveling. I spent the first three months in Nepal, walking 600 miles through 200 villages in the Himalayas and climbing some 120,000 vertical feet. On the trip my sole Western companion was an anthropologist who shed light on the cultural patterns of the villages we passed through.

During the Nepal hike, something occurred that has had a powerful impact on my thinking about corporate ethics. Although some might argue that the experience has no relevance to business, it was a situation in which a basic ethical dilemma suddenly intruded into the lives of a group of individuals. How the group responded I think holds a lesson for all organizations no matter how defined.

The sadhu

The Nepal experience was more rugged and adventuresome than I had anticipated. Most commercial treks last two or three weeks and cover a quarter of the distance we traveled.

My friend Stephen, the anthropologist, and I were halfway through the 60-day Himalayan part of the trip when we reached the high point, an 18,000-foot pass over a crest that we'd have to traverse to reach to the village of Muklinath, an ancient holy place for pilgrims.

Six years earlier I had suffered pulmonary edema, an acute form of altitude sickness, at 16,500 feet in the vicinity of Everest base camp, so we were understandably concerned about what would happen at 18,000 feet. Moreover, the Himalayas were having their wettest spring in 20 years; hip-deep powder and ice had already driven us off one ridge. If we failed to cross the pass, I feared that the last half of our "once in a lifetime" trip would be ruined.

The night before we would try the pass, we camped at a hut at 14,500 feet. In the photos taken at that camp, my face appears wan. The last village we'd passed through was a sturdy two-day walk below us, and I was tired.

During the late afternoon, four backpackers from New Zealand joined us, and we spent most of the night awake, anticipating the climb. Below we could see the fires of two other parties, which turned out to be two Swiss couples and a Japanese hiking club.

To get over the steep part of the climb before the sun melted the steps cut in the ice, we departed at 3:30 A.M. The New Zealanders left first, followed by Stephen and myself, our porters and Sherpas, and then the Swiss. The Japanese lingered in their camp. The sky was clear, and we were confident that no spring storm would erupt that day to close the pass.

At 15,500 feet, it looked to me as if Stephen were shuffling and staggering a bit, which are symptoms of altitude sickness. (The initial stage of altitude sickness brings a headache and nausea. As the condition worsens, a climber may encounter difficult breathing, disorientation, aphasia, and paralysis.) I felt strong, my adrenaline was flowing, but I was very concerned about my ultimate ability to get across. A couple of our porters were also suffering from the height, and Pasang, our Sherpa sirdar (leader), was worried.

Just after daybreak, while we rested at 15,500 feet, one of the New Zealanders, who had gone ahead, came staggering down toward us with a body slung across his shoulders. He dumped the almost naked, barefoot body of an Indian holy man—a sadhu—at my feet. He had found the pilgrim lying on the ice, shivering and suffering from hypothermia. I cradled the sadhu's head and laid him out on the rocks. The New Zealander was angry. He wanted to get across the pass before the bright sun melted the snow. He said, "Look, I've done what I can. You have porters and Sherpa guides. You care for him. We're going on!" He turned and went back up the mountain to join his friends.

I took a carotid pulse and found that the sadhu was still alive. We figured he had probably visited the holy shrines at Muklinath and was on his way home. It was fruitless to question why he had chosen this desperately high route instead of the safe, heavily traveled caravan route through the Kali Gandaki gorge. Or why he was almost naked and with no shoes, or how long he had been lying in the pass. The answers weren't going to solve our problem.

Stephen and the four Swiss began stripping off outer clothing and opening their packs. The sadhu was soon clothed from head to foot. He was not able to walk, but he was very much alive. I looked down the mountain and spotted below the Japanese climbers marching up with a horse.

Without a great deal of thought, I told Stephen and Pasang that I was concerned about withstanding the heights to come and wanted to get over the pass. I took off after several of our porters who had gone ahead.

On the steep part of the ascent where, if the ice steps had given way, I would have slid down about 3,000 feet, I felt vertigo. I stopped for a breather, allowing the Swiss to catch up with me. I inquired about the sadhu and Stephen. They said that the sadhu was fine and that Stephen was just behind. I set off again for the summit.

Stephen arrived at the summit an hour after I did. Still exhilarated by victory, I ran down the snow slope to congratulate him. He was suffering from altitude sickness, walking 15 steps, then stopping, walking 15 steps, then stopping. Pasang accompanied him all the way up. When I reached them, Stephen glared at me and said: "How do you feel about contributing to the death of a fellow man?"

I did not fully comprehend what he meant.

"Is the sadhu dead?" I inquired.

"No," replied Stephen, "but he surely will be!"

After I had gone, and the Swiss had departed not long after, Stephen had remained with the sadhu. When the Japanese had arrived, Stephen had asked to use their horse to transport the sadhu down to the hut. They had refused. He had then asked Pasang to have a group of our porters carry the sadhu. Pasang had resisted the idea, saying that the porters would have to exert all their energy to get themselves over the pass. He had thought they could not carry a man down 1,000 feet to the hut, reclimb the slope, and get across safely before the snow melted. Pasang had pressed Stephen not to delay any longer.

The Sherpas had carried the sadhu down to a rock in the sun at about 15,000 feet and had pointed out the hut another 500 feet below. The Japanese had given him food and drink. When they had last seen him he was listlessly throwing rocks at the Japanese party's dog, which had frightened him.

We do not know if the sadhu lived or died.

For many of the following days and evenings Stephen and I discussed and debated our behavior toward the sadhu. Stephen is a committed Quaker with deep moral vision. He said, "I feel that what happened with the sadhu is a good example of the breakdown between the individual ethic and the corporate ethic. No one person was willing to assume ultimate responsibility for the sadhu. Each was willing to do his

bit just so long as it was not too inconvenient. When it got to be a bother, everyone just passed the buck to someone else and took off. Jesus was relevant to a more individualistic stage of society, but how do we interpret his teaching today in a world filled with large, impersonal organizations and groups?"

I defended the larger group, saying, "Look, we all cared. We all stopped and gave aid and comfort. Everyone did his bit. The New Zealander carried him down below the snow line. I took his pulse and suggested we treat him for hypothermia. You and the Swiss gave him clothing and got him warmed up. The Japanese gave him food and water. The Sherpas carried him down to the sun and pointed out the easy trail toward the hut. He was well enough to throw rocks at a dog. What more could we do?"

"You have just described the typical affluent Westerner's response to a problem. Throwing money—in this case food and sweaters—at it, but not solving the fundamentals!" Stephen retorted.

"What would satisfy you?" I said. "Here we are, a group of New Zealanders, Swiss, Americans, and Japanese who have never met before and who are at the apex of one of the most powerful experiences of our lives. Some years the pass is so bad no one gets over it. What right does an almost naked pilgrim who chooses the wrong trail have to disrupt our lives? Even the Sherpas had no interest in risking the trip to help him beyond a certain point."

Stephen calmly rebutted, "I wonder what the Sherpas would have done if the sadhu had been a well-dressed Nepali, or what the Japanese would have done if the sadhu had been a well-dressed Asian, or what you would have done, Buzz, if the sadhu had been a well-dressed Western woman?"

"Where, in your opinion," I asked instead, "is the limit of our responsibility in a situation like this? We had our own well-being to worry about. Our Sherpa guides were unwilling to jeopardize us or the porters for the sadhu. No one else on the mountain was willing to commit himself beyond certain self-imposed limits."

Stephen said, "As individual Christians or people with a Western ethical tradition, we can fulfill our obligations in such a situation only if (1) the sadhu dies in our care, (2) the sadhu demonstrates to us that he could undertake the two-day walk down to the village, or (3) we carry the sadhu for two days down to the village and convince someone there to care for him."

"Leaving the sadhu in the sun with food and clothing, while he demonstrated hand-eye coordination by throwing a rock at a dog, comes close to fulfilling items one and two," I answered. "And it wouldn't have made sense to take him to the village where the people appeared to be far less caring than the Sherpas, so the third condition is impractical. Are you really saying that, no matter what the implications, we should, at the drop of a hat, have changed our entire plan?"

The individual vs. the group ethic

Despite my arguments, I felt and continue to feel guilt about the sadhu. I had literally walked through a classic moral dilemma without fully thinking through the consequences. My excuses for my actions include a high adrenaline flow, a superordinate goal, and a once-in-a-lifetime opportunity—factors in the usual corporate situation, especially when one is under stress.

Real moral dilemmas are ambiguous, and many of us hike right through them, unaware that they exist. When, usually after the fact, someone makes an issue of them, we tend to resent his or her bringing it up. Often, when the full import of what we have done (or not done) falls on us, we dig into a defensive position from which it is very difficult to emerge. In rare circumstances we may contemplate what we have done from inside a prison.

Had we mountaineers been free of physical and mental stress caused by the effort and the high altitude, we might have treated the sadhu differently. Yet isn't stress the real test of personal and corporate values? The instant decisions executives make under pressure reveal the most about personal and corporate character.

Among the many questions that occur to me when pondering my experience are: What are the practical limits of moral imagination and vision? Is there a collective or institutional ethic beyond the ethics of the individual? At what level of effort or commitment can one discharge one's ethical responsibilities?

Not every ethical dilemma has a right solution. Reasonable people often disagree; otherwise there would be no dilemma. In a business context, however, it is essential that managers agree on a process for dealing with dilemmas.

The sadhu experience offers an interesting parallel to business situations. An immediate response was mandatory. Failure to act was a decision in itself. Up on the mountain we could not resign and submit our résumés to a headhunter. In contrast to philosophy, business involves action and implementation—getting things done. Managers must come up with answers to problems based on what they see and what they allow to influence their decision-making processes. On the mountain, none of us but

Stephen realized the true dimensions of the situation we were facing.

One of our problems was that as a group we had no process for developing a consensus. We had no sense of purpose or plan. The difficulties of dealing with the sadhu were so complex that no one person could handle it. Because it did not have a set of preconditions that could guide its action to an acceptable resolution, the group reacted instinctively as individuals. The cross-cultural nature of the group added a further layer of complexity. We had no leader with whom we could all identify and in whose purpose we believed. Only Stephen was willing to take charge, but he could not gain adequate support to care for the sadhu.

Some organizations do have a value system that transcends the personal values of the managers. Such values, which go beyond profitability, are usually revealed when the organization is under stress. People throughout the organization generally accept its values, which, because they are not presented as a rigid list of commandments, may be somewhat ambiguous. The stories people tell, rather than printed materials, transmit these conceptions of what is proper behavior.

For 20 years I have been exposed at senior levels to a variety of corporations and organizations. It is amazing how quickly an outsider can sense the tone and style of an organization and the degree of tolerated openness and freedom to challenge management.

Organizations that do not have a heritage of mutually accepted, shared values tend to become unhinged during stress, with each individual bailing out for himself. In the great takeover battles we have witnessed during past years, companies that had strong cultures drew the wagons around them and fought it out, while other companies saw executives supported by their golden parachutes, bail out of the struggles.

Because corporations and their members are interdependent, for the corporation to be strong the members need to share a preconceived notion of what is correct behavior, a "business ethic," and think of it as a positive force, not a constraint.

As an investment banker I am continually warned by well-meaning lawyers, clients, and associates to be wary of conflicts of interest. Yet if I were to run away from every difficult situation, I wouldn't be an effective investment banker. I have to feel my way through conflicts. An effective manager can't run from risk either; he or she has to confront and deal with risk. To feel "safe" in doing this, managers need the guidelines of an agreed-on process and set of values within the organization.

After my three months in Nepal, I spent three months as an executive-in-residence at both Stanford Business School and the Center for Ethics and Social Policy at the Graduate Theological Union at Berkeley. These six months away from my job gave me time to assimilate 20 years of business experience. My thoughts turned often to the meaning of the leadership role in any large organization. Students at the seminary thought of themselves as antibusiness. But when I questioned them they agreed that they distrusted all large organizations, including the church. They perceived all large organizations as impersonal and opposed to individual values and needs. Yet we all know of organizations where peoples' values and beliefs are respected and their expressions encouraged. What makes the difference? Can we identify the difference and, as a result, manage more effectively?

The word "ethics" turns off many and confuses more. Yet the notions of shared values and an agreed-on process for dealing with adversity and change – what many people mean when they talk about corporate culture – seem to be at the heart of the ethical issue. People who are in touch with their own core beliefs and the beliefs of others and are sustained by them can be more comfortable living on the cutting edge. At times, taking a tough line or a decisive stand in a muddle of ambiguity is the only ethical thing to do. If a manager is indecisive and spends time trying to figure out the "good" thing to do, the enterprise may be lost.

Business ethics, then, has to do with the authenticity and integrity of the enterprise. To be ethical is to follow the business as well as the cultural goals of the corporation, its owners, its employees, and its customers. Those who cannot serve the corporate vision are not authentic business people and, therefore, are not ethical in the business sense.

At this stage of my own business experience I have a strong interest in organizational behavior. Sociologists are keenly studying what they call corporate stories, legends, and heroes as a way organizations have of transmitting the value system. Corporations such as Arco have even hired consultants to perform an audit of their corporate culture. In a company, the leader is the person who understands, interprets, and manages the corporate value system. Effective managers are then action-oriented people who resolve conflict, are tolerant of ambiguity, stress, and change, and have a strong sense of purpose for themselves and their organizations.

If all this is true, I wonder about the role of the professional manager who moves from company to company. How can he or she quickly absorb the values and culture of different organizations? Or is there, indeed, an art of management that is totally transportable? Assuming such fungible managers do exist, is it proper for them to manipulate the values of others?

What would have happened had Stephen and I carried the sadhu for two days back to the village and become involved with the villagers in his care? In four trips to Nepal my most interesting experiences occurred in 1975 when I lived in a Sherpa home in the Khumbu for five days recovering from altitude sickness. The high point of Stephen's trip was an invitation to participate in a family funeral ceremony in Manang. Neither experience had to do with climbing the high passes of the Himalayas. Why were we so reluctant to try the lower path, the ambiguous trail? Perhaps because we did not have a leader who could reveal the greater purpose of the trip to us.

Why didn't Stephen with his moral vision opt to take the sadhu under his personal care? The answer is because, in part, Stephen was hard-stressed physically himself, and because, in part, without some support system that involved our involuntary and episodic community on the mountain, it was beyond his individual capacity to do so.

I see the current interest in corporate culture and corporate value systems as a positive response to Stephen's pessimism about the decline of the role of the individual in large organizations. Individuals who operate from a thoughtful set of personal values provide the foundation for a corporate culture. A corporate tradition that encourages freedom of inquiry, supports personal values, and reinforces a focused sense of direction can fulfill the need for individuality along with the prosperity and success of the group. Without such corporate support, the individual is lost.

That is the lesson of the sadhu. In a complex corporate situation, the individual requires and deserves the support of the group. If people cannot find such support from their organization, they don't know how to act. If such support is forthcoming, a person has a stake in the success of the group, and can add much to the process of establishing and maintaining a corporate culture. It is management's challenge to be sensitive to individual needs, to shape them, and to direct and focus them for the benefit of the group as a whole.

For each of us the sadhu lives. Should we stop what we are doing and comfort him; or should we keep trudging up toward the high pass? Should I pause to help the derelict I pass on the street each night as I walk by the Yale Club en route to Grand Central Station? Am I his brother? What is the nature of our responsibility if we consider ourselves to be ethical persons? Perhaps it is to change the values of the group so that it can, with all its resources, take the other road. ▽

Harvard Business Review

To resolve the confusion and controversy about "corporate morality" and "business ethics," here is a statesmanlike proposal addressed to the problems of individual business managers.

Code of Conduct for Executives

By Robert W. Austin

In the past year we have heard much discussion of price fixing and conflicts of interest in business and government. The ethics of many top-level executives have been questioned; the reputations of various organizations have suffered. Much of the argument, it seems to me, is confused. The controversy does not seem to be getting us anywhere. Accordingly, in this article I shall propose a different way of thinking about the whole problem. I believe that:

❡ "Business ethics," "corporate morality," "corporate ethics," and similar phrases mean nothing. The public's opinion of the ethics of business and of the corporation is based entirely on the actions of *individual* business managers.

❡ Codes of conduct imposed by statutes or by corporate statements of policy are external in character and are prohibitive in kind. They largely consist of "Thou shalt not"s — psychologically unsound and, by their very phrasing, creating an attitude of suspicion on the part of the public.

❡ If business management is to be a profession, it must meet the basic requirements of the professions. One of these requirements is an internally developed code of conduct that can be and is professed as the code by which the members of the profession will live.

❡ The code should call on the executive to assume the duty of: (a) placing the interests of his company before his private interests; (b) placing the interests of society before his own and his company's interests; and (c) revealing the truth in all cases of involvement. (The same code would apply to governmental executives with the substitution of the appropriate state or federal organization for "company.")

After describing the proposed code I shall show how its provisions would have applied to

EDITORS' NOTE: This article was conceived as a part of a general discussion of "incentives for executives" (New York: McGraw-Hill, 1962).

Reprint 61502

executives in the price-fixing, five-percenter, and other cases, and helped to avoid much needless trouble and embarrassment. To begin, however, we must backtrack from the main argument and examine some of the incentives and ideas about ethics that often enter into the controversy.

Starting Points

An incentive, according to the dictionary, is "that which incites or tends to incite to determination or action." There are two kinds of incentives — external and internal. Also, there are external and internal "disincentives." I define a disincentive as "that which impedes or tends to impede determination or action."

Types of Incentive

An *external* incentive is a neutral or amoral thing. The incentive, whatever it is, can incite toward action or decisions which may be defined as either good or bad, but the incentive itself is neutral. Incentives designed to induce executives to take more effective action, or to make better decisions to accomplish some purpose, are external incentives. Examples are stock options, profit sharing, bonuses, early retirement, and threat of punishment. The purpose of using such devices is to create a more profitable operation of the enterprises run by executives thus incited.

But profit is also a neutral or amoral concept. There either is or is not a difference between income and outgo. If income exceeds outgo, the venture is profitable; if outgo exceeds income, the venture is not. But the fact of either profit or loss is not "good" or "bad," using these words in a moral sense. It is how the difference, or the profit, is produced which may be moral, immoral, or amoral. Thus it is the action the external incentive produces that may be judged by an ethical standard, not the external incentive itself, nor the resulting profit or loss.

Another, and very different, kind of incentive is *internal*. It is the kind which is created by the executive himself, which wells up from within. It does not act like the carrot or the stick, but is something very different. A personal ethic or philosophy, an overweening ambition for power or material gain, greed, fear — all these could be internal incentives. They may themselves be thought of as good or evil, moral or immoral, depending on the standards by which they are judged; and they may be good or evil in result

as the action caused by the internal incentive is judged.

There must also be external and internal *dis*incentives. Examples of external disincentives are poor pay, a bad boss, unhappiness at home, the mores of the society in which one lives, and statutory prohibitions with threats of punishment; examples of internal disincentives are lack of education, laziness, being naturally an introvert in an extrovert's job, and a neurosis of some sort.

It is obvious, of course, that one man's incentive — external or internal — may be another man's disincentive. A disagreeable boss may make one type of man work his head off to advance past the boss or move away from him; such a boss is an external incentive. But the same disagreeable manager could make another man fold up, do less work, and fail to produce what is expected of him, and so be an external disincentive. Similarly, my personal ambition may make me work hard, study nights to improve myself, and thus be an internal incentive to act; but that same ambition may make me fail to act where my duty is to do so, because I am afraid my action will offend superiors who control my advancement, and thus it may be an internal *dis*incentive to act. In short, it all depends on circumstances and people.[1]

Mirages of Ethics

What about the phrase "business ethics"? Now that we have categorized incentives and disincentives, we must know what we mean by business ethics, to see whether they can be categorized as incentives or disincentives, external or internal.

Unfortunately, "business ethics" is one of those phrases used by all with a different meaning for each user — and, indeed, a different meaning at different times when used by the same person. This is true of similar phrases like "corporate morality" or "corporate ethics," also. This lack of definition causes confusion on the part of business managers and greater confusion among observers of the acts of managers. "Business" means so many things to so many people that when used as an adjective to modify the noun "ethics," which itself is a term meaning many things to many people, the resultant phrase becomes meaningless. Similarly, "corporate" has little meaning when used to modify terms such

[1] See Raymond C. Baumhart, "Problems in Review: How Ethical Are Businessmen?" HBR July–August 1961, p. 6.

as "ethics" or "morality," for a corporation is not a person or individual and the concept of ethics or morals is one relating to right and wrong actions of individuals, not of artificial entities created by law.

Yet, in general discussions of recent problems of right and wrong in the business world, spokesmen for all classes and segments of our society have used such terms as if they had a clear and definable meaning. To illustrate:

◖ A leading industrialist, speaking before the Minneapolis Junior Chamber of Commerce, said that "if corporations are corrupt, then it will be assumed that the society itself is corrupt." But a corporation cannot be corrupt; it may employ men who are corrupt and who act for the corporation contrary to society's rules, but the corporation itself can neither be corrupt nor ethical, for it is not the kind of being that can be so judged.

◖ The president of one of our largest oil companies in a letter to supervisors in March said that if his letters had titles, "perhaps the heading of this one should be 'Business Ethics' or 'Corporate Morality.' " He then went on to talk about a corporate *policy* with respect to standards of conduct for executives in the company. This latter idea makes sense: while a corporation may itself have neither morals nor ethics, its board of directors may adopt a policy setting forth standards of conduct which will be required of its executives. When this is done, that policy and those standards of conduct become meaningful, for they represent standards of right and wrong for individual conduct.

◖ A Kiplinger *Washington Letter* in April 1961 started off by saying, "Business ethics are about to be questioned in an even bigger way," and referred to "outright frauds" in government contracts. Here again it is unclear to talk about business ethics. Fraud, a crime, is perpetrated by *individuals*, and not by "business," which is a vague and amorphous word.

◖ President Kennedy in his special message to Congress on conflict-of-interest statutes was more precise than most. He did use the phrase "ethics in government," which might have been thought to indicate that a government could have ethics, but he soon made clear that what he meant to do was to create standards of conduct for individuals engaged in government.

"Business ethics" is a poor phrase to use, but properly interpreted it can only mean the standards of conduct of individual businessmen, *not* the standards of business as a whole. It is in this sense that I approach the subject in this article. The questions before us are these: Are individual codes of conduct incentives or disincentives? Is it possible to have a common code of conduct for business managers which can be categorized as an incentive for good?

Price-Fixing Cases

The electrical manufacturers' price-fixing suit makes an interesting case study showing how codes of conduct act as incentives or as disincentives. What were the codes of conduct of the executives involved — both externally and internally imposed?

Antitrust Laws

The antitrust laws, externally imposed, are a code of conduct stating that (a) competing businessmen should not agree as to the prices at which their products are to be sold, (b) competing businessmen should not agree to allocate shares of the market between themselves, and (c) businessmen must not monopolize a market. These statutory codes of conduct are stated as "Thou shalt not"s and carry sanctions for failure to conform — fine or imprisonment.

For the executives in the electrical firms the codes were either external incentives to compete vigorously *or* external disincentives to conspire, insofar as agreements in restraint of trade were concerned. However, where monopolization was concerned, in the case of the large companies they were either external incentives to hold the umbrella over smaller companies in the industry *or* external disincentives to compete.

As the widely publicized experience with the so-called "white sales" showed, if General Electric and Westinghouse really set prices at competitive levels, their percentage share of the market rose, and thus they ran an increasing danger of being charged with monopolization. Here, then, was a situation where external codes of conduct imposed by the same statute were, or certainly seemed to be, contradictory. Whether the codes were incentives or disincentives, they created conflicts and problems of judgment in the minds of the individuals involved.

Company Directive

General Electric's Directive 20.5 created a standard of conduct for individual employees insofar as the antitrust laws were concerned. It was distributed to all decision-making executives once a year; each was expected to sign it to indicate his understanding and agreement to comply. Aside from general provisions directing executives to comply with the antitrust laws and a general suggestion that counsel be consulted where doubt existed, the only specific statements forbade discussions of price or agreements as to market share with competitors, and clearly implied sanctions if this code of conduct were violated.

This directive was an external incentive to compete, if it meant what it said, or an external disincentive to conspire. It did not *explicitly* state a code of conduct with respect to monopolization, however, and this omission left it up to individual executives to decide where vigorous competition ended and monopolization began. Thus, depending on how sophisticated the men were about the antitrust laws, the directive might have been either an external incentive to compete vigorously *or* an external disincentive to compete all out — *or*, perhaps, an external incentive to stabilize prices to the greatest extent possible without getting caught. This corporate policy as to conduct was clearly worded as a "Thou shalt not."

Decentralization Policy

General Electric's policy of decentralization was not stated as a code of conduct but as a philosophy of management. That philosophy was to create separate profit centers within the organization, giving to top executives both responsibility and authority to run that segment of the whole as if it were a separate business. One of the responsibilities imposed was to earn a fixed percentage of return on the investment involved.

This was an externally imposed dual incentive. It was, first, an incentive to reach the level in the business where one could gain the prestige, power, and material rewards going with the position held, and, second, an incentive to make the profit required. It was also an external disincentive to act in any way that might lower return on investment, and so lessen the individual's prestige, power, and material reward.

If a rigorous competitive policy carried out by the individual executive in accordance with the antitrust laws and Directive 20.5's code of conduct resulted in lower profit, or none, or a failure to earn the necessary return on investment, then these externally imposed incentives or disincentives conflicted with the codes imposed by law and corporate policy and necessi-

tated a judgment, a decision, as to personal action by the executive involved.

Personal Beliefs

In the price-fixing case each man had his own code of conduct: honesty and integrity; duty to family; ambition for prestige, power, material rewards; sense of obligation to his company or to superiors within the company; respect in both the community he lived in and the community he worked in; his innate desire, true of all men, to feel that in his daily activity he was making a significant contribution to a significant goal.

We cannot, of course, unravel how all of these incentives and disincentives worked in the individuals. Surely a personal code of honesty would have acted as an internal incentive to comply with Directive 20.5 even though it might not have acted as an internal incentive to make him comply with the antitrust laws. A man could convince himself in all honesty that it was illegal, but not dishonest, to disobey what to him was a bad and contradictory law; but it would have been much more difficult to disobey after signing a statement yearly that he agreed with a company directive to obey that bad law.

This situation raises a question as to whether or not the executive thought that the externally imposed corporate code of conduct was *really* believed by his superiors who drafted it. If he could convince himself that it was not so believed, then all the pressures driving him toward success — some coming from his superiors and some from his internal desires or incentives — could well push him in the unfortunate direction of disobeying both the law and the company directive unless he had some basic code of conduct, necessarily *internal*, upon which he could rely to steer him through this labyrinth of conflicting incentives and disincentives.

Actual Motives

If all this seems highly theoretical, let us look at the testimony of two executives before the Senate Antitrust and Monopoly Subcommittee "explaining" their "motives" for attending the illegal meetings to fix prices. Each man listed:

1. A desire to keep workers employed during a time of poor business.

2. A desire to make sure their company had enough money to engage in research that would help public and private utilities.

3. A desire to protect their company from sharp competitive practices.

These are laudable motives based on an internal incentive to make — in one's daily work — a significant contribution to a significant goal.

If an executive's internal incentive can convince him that by his actions he is benefiting workers for whose employment he is responsible, serving the society in which he lives, and protecting his company from unscrupulous and fraudulent competition, and if the internal incentive competes with the externally imposed and confusing incentives and disincentives of a "bad" law, can we blame him for deciding to follow his own code of good conduct? I should think not — unless, once again, there is some affirmative, internal "Thou shalt," rather than an external "Thou shalt not," which will carry him unscathed to the best decision.

In this case there were external and internal codes of conduct acting both as incentives and disincentives. The requirements were confused, contradictory, and primarily of the "Thou shalt not" character rather than the "Thou shalt" — negative rather than affirmative, requiring fallible individual judgments as to proper conduct.

Conflicts of Interest

Another interesting series of case studies lies in the area of so-called "conflicts of interest." In recent years, for instance, we have had cases concerning an executive assistant to the President of the United States, a Secretary of the Air Force, and the president of a large corporation.

Governing Codes

I shall return to the specifics of these situations presently. First, however, let us consider the more general question: What codes of conduct apply to men involved in cases of this sort? There are at least four variations:

(1) There are externally imposed codes for government officers in the various federal and state statutes relating to conflicts of interest, mostly stated as "Thou shalt not"s. Thus:

• Thou shalt not accept gifts from people with whom you transact government business.

• Thou shalt not as an ex-government employee work on a matter on which you worked while in government.

• Thou shalt not use official information for private gain.

• Thou shalt not have outside employment that conflicts with government work.

• Thou shalt not seek favors from those affected by your government job.

• Thou shalt not own property which may induce you to act in your own interest rather than that of the government.

(2) For businessmen acting in a fiduciary capacity there are externally imposed codes of conduct growing out of the development of the English Common Law relating to fiduciaries:

• *For trustees* — Thou shalt not act so as to place your personal benefit ahead of that of the beneficiary of the trust, nor shall you act so as to profit at the expense of the trust.

• *For agents* — Thou shalt not serve as agent for two principals in the same transaction unless both know and approve of your so acting.

• *For corporate officers and directors* — Thou shalt not act on matters which involve your private interests.

(3) There are codes of conduct externally imposed on businessmen by statutes such as the Securities Act of 1933, the Securities Exchange Act of 1934, the Federal Trade Commission Act, and the Food, Drug, and Cosmetic Act. They make such stipulations as:

• Thou shalt not mislead the public in a statement of facts describing a company prior to an offer of securities to the public.

• Thou shalt not fail to reveal the stock ownership of directors and large stockholders in a proxy statement sent to stockholders.

• Thou shalt not fail to reveal when a nominee for the office of director does business with the corporation for whose board he is a candidate.

• Thou shalt not profit from inside knowledge by purchase and sale of stock of a company of which you are a director.

• Thou shalt not be guilty of false or misleading advertising.

• Thou shalt not be guilty of adulteration or misbranding.

Most significant is the emergence in the last 30 years in statutes such as the Securities Acts and the Federal Trade Commission Act of a duty to reveal *all* the facts. Of additional significance is the fact that the conflicts of interest considered are not only between the person involved and the organization by which he is employed, but also between the individual involved and society as a whole.

(4) There are externally imposed codes of conduct for businessmen embodied in corporate statements of policy on conflicts of interest. Almost all I have seen have been couched in "Thou shalt not" terms. Here, for example, are statements from a document recently adopted by a company with which I am familiar:

❡ "No employee shall take outside employment with a competitor, supplier, or customer of ——— Company without prior clearance by an officer of the company who is a member of the president's executive committee."

❡ "No employee of ——— Company shall purchase, trade, or deal in commodities in which the company trades, deals, or purchases without prior clearance by an officer of the company who is a member of the president's executive committee."

❡ "No director or employee shall have a financial interest in a company or enterprise which is competing with ——— Company, or with which ——— Company does business exceeding $5,000 per annum unless such ownership is less than 10% of the equity in such company or enterprise. Ownership of any interest in a customer, supplier, or competitor by an individual's wife or minor children shall be attributed to him in determining such equity percentages. A list of all such interests totaling more than 2% shall be filed with the secretary of this company and supplements filed within 30 days after any changes. Deviations from this policy shall only be authorized by the board of directors on consideration of specific circumstances."

You will note that the language is "No employee shall" — equivalent to "Thou shalt not." On the other hand, this code has the saving grace of creating the *affirmative duty to reveal facts* to a superior, thus relieving the individual of the decision as to whether or not the code stated applies to his situation.

Purposes & Limitations

Almost all of these externally imposed codes have sanctions of some kind attached to them: discharge for government employees; responsibility for financial loss, or even fine or imprisonment, for trustees or agents; fine or imprisonment for false advertisers; and discharge for employees violating corporate statements of policy.

What kinds of incentives or disincentives are these codes? Externally imposed, they are designed to reduce or avoid conflicts of interest which, if not properly avoided or resolved, result in damage to individuals or business entities. The codes may be characterized as incentives for honest dealing or disincentives for dishonest actions.

There is not too much chance here of having internally imposed codes of conduct conflict with externally imposed codes of conduct, for most men would agree that honesty is the best policy. But there is the very difficult problem of *interpretation* of the rules.

Problems of Judgment

Now let us return to our case histories. What went wrong? How useful were the codes?

The Case of the Presidential Assistant. Here a man in a position of great power in government accepted gifts from a businessman who had constant dealings with various branches of government where the Presidential Assistant had great influence. The fact of the gifts and their value were unknown to his superiors.

There was no conflict here as to whether the relevant code of conduct was right or wrong. Both the giver and the recipient affirmed that a gift for the purpose of inducing special treatment was wrong. Therefore, the code as an incentive to honest dealing was a good one. But both giver and recipient felt that a gift between friends where no special services were sought was all right and did not violate the code. Whether or not the code acted as an incentive or disincentive depended on the individual's judgment as to whether a given act fell within the purview of the provisions. If — as in this case — in his opinion, it did not, then the code, although accepted, was neither an incentive nor a disincentive.

The Case of the Secretary of the Air Force. Here the Secretary revealed to a Congressional Committee that he had retained an interest as a special partner in an industrial engineering company. He wrote letters on his official stationery to executives of large companies doing business with his branch of the service, recommending highly the services of his partner and the industrial engineering firm of which he was a special partner.

Again, there was no question about the incentive toward honest dealing intended by the code of conduct expressed in the statute. But the Secretary quite honestly could not see that his letters could be interpreted as using his official position to his personal benefit; that is, that recipients of the letters would be induced to engage the services of his partner in the hope that they would receive favored treatment in their dealings with his branch of the government. Once more the external code was not effective as an incentive or disincentive, since, in the Secretary's judgment, it was not applicable to the situation.

The Case of the President of a Large Corporation. The president had substantial equity interests in suppliers of his company. In his fiduciary capacity he would and did agree that he should not profit at the expense of his employer, but he failed either to see or agree that his ownership might result in that supplier being favored over other suppliers to the possible detriment of his employer. Thus he failed to reveal his interest to his board of directors. So, again, the application of the code was a matter of his individual judgment, and since in the president's judgment it did not apply to the case at hand, it was neither an incentive nor a disincentive for him to act.

Incentives at Dead Center

While there are differences of degree — and differences of interpretation — some clear conclusions grow out of this discussion:

(1) Codes of conduct, whether internal or external, may be either incentives or disincentives.

(2) Codes of conduct may result in conflict between their incentive or disincentive value, and may thus require fallible individual judgment as to what is right and what is wrong.

(3) Externally imposed codes of conduct are more often stated as "Thou shalt not"s rather than "Thou shalt"s. Being essentially negative in character, they create problems of individual judgment as to what is prohibited, and fail to create a positive sense of duty or responsibility.

(4) Some commonly accepted codes, phrased as "Thou shalt not"s, are neither incentives nor disincentives, because they are so phrased and so negative in character that the manager may honestly say, "The code is good and I agree with its prohibitions, but it does not apply to me." Thus, a code acceptable to all in theory may not be effective either as an incentive or disincentive in a given situation, and so will be valueless and meaningless.

Threat to Public Confidence

There is no question but that the five percenters in Washington, the deep freeze and mink coats and Oriental rugs for government employees, the payola in television programs, the collusion of businessmen and union leaders with organized crime, the price-fixing cases in the electrical industry, and the conflict-of-interest revelations about business leaders have all raised public questions about the standards of conduct of businessmen. More and more people are wondering whether business leaders have a code of conduct other than that of making a profit, which business leaders have asserted for many years is the primary purpose for their being in business.

Clearly this is a problem for businessmen. Henry Ford II in Minneapolis said this was so, and that top corporate executives must accept full responsibility for setting up high ethical standards and strict policies and for policing them. He said:

"I suggest we look not only at the obvious areas of danger, where we may run afoul of the law, but also at those borderline areas of corporate action which might have unfortunate social consequences for our fellow man. Around the world, we are often described as a corporate society. If . . . it is judged that corporations are corrupt, then it will be assumed that the society itself is corrupt."

These are wise words, but I am not sure that this general approach is the answer. I am not sure that this is the way to create a code of conduct which will act as a positive incentive for good among corporate employees. I doubt that this incentive will carry the fallible individual through the conflicts of incentive and disincentive created by various codes of conduct (external and internal) and by other external and internal incentives and disincentives such as fear and greed — or past the danger point of deciding that a given code of conduct does not apply to his situation.

When one speaks of "policing" standards, I am afraid it means standards expressed in terms of "Thou shalt not"s. I am convinced that in this or any other area of conduct "Thou shalt not"s imposed from above do not enlist support.

Proposed Solution

But business leaders must face and solve the problem, else they will no doubt find "Thou shalt not"s imposed by society.

What can we do? Over the years we have read more and more about business management as a profession. More often than not we hear executives characterized as "professional managers." Is there a clue here?

I think that there is. Unfortunately that word "professional" has two meanings when used as an adjective. And executives and educators are guilty of using it both ways. The first meaning is "professional" in the sense of the professional golf pro or professional baseball player; that is, a "professional manager" is one who is paid to manage, and this usage unfortunately carries the connotation that he performs only for pay and for no other reason. We all know that top executives in industry do not devote their time and effort to performing their function as managers for pay alone.

The other meaning of "professional" is for one who is engaged in a profession. This is the important meaning, since one who is a member of a profession assumes affirmative obligations and duties beyond that of simply practicing his profession. Another way to put this is to say that one who is a member of a profession actually professes — that for the privilege of becoming a member of that profession he assumes an affirmative obligation to society.

Principles of a Sound Code

All of the recognized professions have three basic characteristics in common:

1. The requirement that a member of the profession demonstrate an acceptable standard of excellence within a recognized body of knowledge. (An ancillary requirement is the affirmative duty to attempt to expand that body of knowledge and pass it on to others succeeding him.)

2. A code of conduct, produced by the profession and *not* imposed on it by others, which each member affirms or professes that he will follow. (The standard should be affirmative — "Thou shalt" in character rather than "Thou shalt not.")

3. Recognition and assertion of the fact that each member of that profession will place the interests of society before his own personal interest.

If the profession of business management is to develop and truly meet the standards of other recognized professions, it is essential that its members meet these three requirements.

Insofar as the first is concerned, business management is and has been developing rapidly. Colleges and universities have contributed to the development of an ever-expanding body of knowledge necessary for good management. Contributions have also been made by business executives in organizations such as the Committee for Economic Development and by individuals writing about management and business administration.

It is in the other two areas that the profession has not advanced. There is as yet no simple affirmative code of conduct which has been generated by and within the profession and which the public knows business managers affirm and profess. Nor has there been an affirmative statement of the business manager's recognition that as an individual his obligation to society overrides any other obligation he may have.

Can we devise such a code — one which will be simple, easy to understand, and convincing? I suggest the following:

1. The professional business manager affirms that he will place the interest of the business for which he works before his own private interests.

2. The professional business manager affirms that he will place his duty to society above his duty to his company and above his private interest.

3. The professional business manager affirms that he has a duty to reveal the facts in any situation where (a) his private interests are involved with those of his company or (b) where the interests of his company are involved with those of the society in which it operates.

4. The professional business manager affirms that when business managers follow this code of conduct, the profit motive is the best incentive for the development of a sound, expanding, and dynamic economy.

Resolving Conspiracy

What might have happened in the electrical manufacturers' conspiracy cases if this standard of conduct had been operable in that situation? The externally imposed codes of conduct — that is, the prohibitions contained in the antitrust laws and in General Electric's Directive 20.5 — may have led the individual executive (as I have already pointed out) into trying to resolve conflicts between external and internal incentives, between his judgment as to what his company policy was and how he best could carry it out in the light of his own personal incentives and the profit purpose of his company. These codes placed on fallible individuals the pressures of conflicting incentives and disincentives and resulted in unhappy consequences for both the individuals and their company — and, indeed, for the society in which the company operated.

On the other hand, the code of conduct I have suggested would have led the individual executive to go up the ladder to reveal the facts to the president of the company. Then more than one fallible man would have been involved in looking at the external codes and at the company's and individual's positions with respect thereto. When the facts were revealed to the president and he recognized the conflict between (a) the antitrust law's prohibitions against restraints of trade and (b) the same law's prohibitions against monopolization, it would have been his duty under the proposed code to reveal, in turn, the facts to his board of directors. I am sure that at this point the decision would have been made to compete vigorously in spite of any dangers apparently inherent in so doing, i.e., the threat of being charged with monopolization.

Thus, the problem of the individuals involved would have been solved and their affirmative code of conduct would have carried them all through a difficult time. On the other hand, having made the correct decision to comply with the law, the board of directors of General Electric Company, with the facts in their possession and complying with this suggested code, would have had a responsibility, and a clear one, to reveal the truth and the facts about the problem faced by companies of this kind to the society in which they operated.

How would that have been done? There were several alternative courses of action open. One would have been to develop a presentation of the facts about the dilemma in which companies of this character were (and still are) placed by the prohibitions of Sections 1 and 2 of the Sherman Act, and then to reveal these facts to the Department of Justice. Another possible course of action would have been to prepare a presentation to place on the record of a Congressional Committee investigating monopoly. The third possibility would have been to bring to the attention of the public through institutional advertising the fact that the problem existed not only for the giants in the electrical industry, but for those in many other industries as well.

I have often wondered about the wisdom of the policy adopted by so many leaders of large business enterprises, of affirming time and time again that they agree with and support the antitrust laws when, in fact, those statutes create problems for them which are well-nigh insuperable in terms of corporate policy. Let me also add that I sometimes wonder about well-publicized members of the United States Congress demanding strict enforcement of the antitrust laws when it is clear that the knowledge they have acquired over years of public hearings must have convinced them that the industrial society in which we now live no longer fits the theoretical society for which the original concepts of pure competition and pure monopoly were developed.

Clarifying Interests

What of the many different kinds of conflict-of-interest cases about which we hear so much? What would this code of conduct have meant in such situations? To go back to our three examples:

❧ The Secretary of the Air Force, since his personal interests were clearly involved, would have revealed the facts to his superior, and have been told whether or not the external code of conduct applied to him.

❧ The Presidential Assistant would have gone to the President of the United States, or to the Attorney General, and revealed the facts.

❧ The president who had an equity interest in his corporation's suppliers would have revealed his interest to the board of directors of his company and asked whether or not that interest conflicted with the interests of his company.

In each case the individual would not have relied on his own judgment in a difficult situation, would have avoided future trouble, and would have enhanced his standing in his job.

In essence, then, the simple code of conduct I propose affirms that business managers have overriding obligations to others, and that they have a duty to reveal the facts where their personal interests are involved. In contrast to statutes and corporate policies, this code would be an *internal* incentive to sound decision making.

"Of course,
honesty is one of the better policies."

Ethics without the sermon

*Plain speaking
about
an often obscure subject in
the form of 12 questions
to ask
when making
a business decision*

Laura L. Nash

"Like some Triassic reptile, the theoretical view of ethics lumbers along in the far past of Sunday School and Philosophy 1, while the reality of practical business concerns is constantly measuring a wide range of competing claims on time and resources against the unrelenting and objective marketplace." So writes the author of this article as she introduces a procedure to test pragmatically the ethical content and human fallout of everyday decisions in business and other organizational settings. First you have to define the problem as you see it, then (insofar as possible) examine it as outsiders might see it. You explore where your loyalties lie and consider both your intentions in making the decision and whom your action might affect. You proceed to the consequences of disclosing your action to those you report to or respect, and then analyze the symbolic meaning to all affected. In her conclusion the author attacks the sticky question of the proper moral standpoint of the organization as a whole.

Laura Nash is assistant professor of business administration at the Harvard Business School, where she teaches business policy. Formerly a teacher of classics at Brown, Brandeis, and Harvard universities, she recently spent a year and a half at the Harvard Business School doing research on business and ethics.

Illustrations by Saxon;
drawing on facing page © *1981,*
The New Yorker Magazine, Inc.

Reprint 81609

As if via a network TV program on the telecommunications satellite, declarations such as these are being broadcast throughout the land:

Scene 1. Annual meeting, Anyproducts Inc.; John Q. Moneypockets, chairman and CEO, speaking: "Our responsibility to the public has always come first at our company, and we continue to strive toward serving our public in the best way possible in the belief that good ethics is good business. . . . Despite our forecast of a continued recession in the industry through 1982, we are pleased to announce that 1981's earnings per share were up for the twenty-sixth year in a row."

Scene 2. Corporate headquarters, Anyproducts Inc.; Linda Diesinker, group vice president, speaking: "Of course we're concerned about minority development and the plight of the inner cities. But the best place for our new plant would be Horsepasture, Minnesota. We need a lot of space for our operations and a skilled labor force, and the demographics and tax incentives in Horsepasture are perfect."

Scene 3. Interview with a financial writer; Rafe Shortstop, president, Anyproducts Inc., speaking: "We're very concerned about the state of American business and our ability to compete with foreign companies. . . . No, I don't think we have any real ethical problems. We don't bribe people or anything like that."

Scene 4. Jud McFisticuff, taxi driver, speaking: "Anyproducts? You've got to be kidding! I wouldn't buy their stuff for anything. The last thing of theirs I bought fell apart in six months. And did you see how they were dumping wastes in the Roxburg water system?"

Scene 5. Leslie Matriculant, MBA '82, speaking: "Join Anyproducts? I don't want to risk my reputation working for a company like that. They recently acquired a business that turned out to have ten class-action discrimination suits against it. And when Anyproducts tried to settle the whole thing out of court, the president had his picture in *Business Week* with the caption, 'His secretary still serves him coffee'."

Whether you regard it as an unchecked epidemic or as the first blast of Gabriel's horn, the trend toward focusing on the social impact of the corporation is an inescapable reality that must be factored into today's managerial decision making. But for the executive who asks, "How do we as a corporation examine our ethical concerns?" the theoretical insights currently available may be more frustrating than helpful.

As the first scene in this article implies, many executives firmly believe that corporate operations and corporate values are dynamically intertwined. For the purposes of analysis, however, the executive needs to uncoil the business-ethics helix and examine both strands closely.

Unfortunately, the ethics strand has remained largely inaccessible, for business has not yet developed a workable process by which corporate values can be articulated. If ethics and business are part of the same double helix, perhaps we can develop a microscope capable of enlarging our perception of both aspects of business administration—what we do and who we are.

Sidestepping Triassic reptiles

Philosophy has been sorting out issues of fairness, injury, empathy, self-sacrifice, and so on for more than 2,000 years. In seeking to examine the ethics of business, therefore, business logically assumes it will be best served by a "consultant" in philosophy who is already familiar with the formal discipline of ethics.

As the philosopher begins to speak, however, a difficulty immediately arises; corporate executives and philosophers approach problems in radically different ways. The academician ponders the intangible, savors the paradoxical, and embraces the peculiar; he or she speaks in a special language of categorical imperatives and deontological viewpoints that must be taken into consideration before a statement about honesty is agreed to have any meaning.

Like some Triassic reptile, the theoretical view of ethics lumbers along in the far past of Sunday School and Philosophy 1, while the reality of practical business concerns is constantly measuring a wide range of competing claims on time and resources against the unrelenting and objective marketplace.

Not surprisingly, the two groups are somewhat hostile. The jokes of the liberal intelligentsia are rampant and weary: "*Ethics and Business*—the shortest book in the world." "Business and ethics—a subject confined to the preface of business books." Accusations from the corporate cadre are delivered with an assurance that rests more on an intuition of social climate than on a certainty of fact: "You do-gooders are ruining America's ability to compete in the world." "Of course, the cancer reports on ———— [choose from a long list] were terribly exaggerated."

What is needed is a process of ethical inquiry that is immediately comprehensible to a group of executives and not predisposed to the utopian, and sometimes anticapitalistic, bias marking much of the work in applied business philosophy today. So I suggest, as a preliminary solution, a set of 12 questions that draw on traditional philosophical frameworks but that avoid the level of abstraction normally associated with formal moral reasoning.

I offer the questions as a first step in a very new discipline. As such, they form a tentative model that will certainly undergo modifications after its parts are given some exercise. The *Exhibit* on page 87 poses the 12 questions.

To illustrate the application of the questions, I will draw especially on a program at Lex Service Group, Ltd., whose top management prepared a statement of financial objectives and moral values as a part of its strategic planning process.[1] Lex is a British company with operations in the United Kingdom and the United States. Its sales total about $1.2 billion. In 1978 its structure was

---

1. The process is modeled after ideas in Kenneth R. Andrews's book *The Concept of Corporate Strategy* (Homewood, Ill.: Richard D. Irwin, 1980, revised edition) and in Richard F. Vancil's article "Strategy Formulation in Complex Organizations," *Sloan Management Review*, Winter 1976, p. 4.

partially decentralized, and in 1979 the chairman's policy group began a strategic planning process. The intent, according to its statement of values and objectives, was "to make explicit the sort of company Lex was, or wished to be."

Neither a paralegal code nor a generalized philosophy, the statement consisted of a series of general policies regarding financial strategy as well as such aspects of the company's character as customer service, employee-shareholder responsibility, and quality of management. Its content largely reflected the personal values of Lex's chairman and CEO, Trevor Chinn, whose private philanthropy is well known and whose concern for social welfare has long been echoed in the company's personnel policies.

In the past, pressure on senior managers for high profit performance had obscured some of these ideals in practice, and the statement of strategy was a way of radically realigning various competing moral claims with the financial objectives of the company. As one senior manager remarked to me, "The values seem obvious, and if we hadn't been so gross in the past we wouldn't have needed the statement." Despite a predictable variance among Lex's top executives as to the desirability of the values outlined in the statement, it was adopted with general agreement to comply and was scheduled for reassessment at a senior managers' meeting one year after implementation.

The 12 questions

1   Have you defined the problem accurately?

How one assembles the facts weights an issue before the moral examination ever begins, and a definition is rarely accurate if it articulates one's loyalties rather than the facts. The importance of factual neutrality is readily seen, for example, in assessing the moral implications of producing a chemical agent for use in warfare. Depending on one's loyalties, the decision to make the substance can be described as serving one's country, developing products, or killing babies. All of the above may be factual statements, but none is neutral or accurate if viewed in isolation.

Similarly, the recent controversy over marketing U.S.-made cigarettes in Third World countries rarely noted that the incidence of lung cancer in underdeveloped nations is quite low (from one-tenth to one-twentieth the rate for U.S. males) due primarily to the lower life expectancies and

Exhibit	Twelve questions for examining the ethics of a business decision
1	Have you defined the problem accurately?
2	How would you define the problem if you stood on the other side of the fence?
3	How did this situation occur in the first place?
4	To whom and to what do you give your loyalty as a person and as a member of the corporation?
5	What is your intention in making this decision?
6	How does this intention compare with the probable results?
7	Whom could your decision or action injure?
8	Can you discuss the problem with the affected parties before you make your decision?
9	Are you confident that your position will be as valid over a long period of time as it seems now?
10	Could you disclose without qualm your decision or action to your boss, your CEO, the board of directors, your family, society as a whole?
11	What is the symbolic potential of your action if understood? if misunderstood?
12	Under what conditions would you allow exceptions to your stand?

earlier predominance of other diseases in these nations. Such a fact does not decide the ethical complexities of this marketing problem, but it does add a crucial perspective in the assignment of moral priorities by defining precisely the injury that tobacco exports may cause.

Extensive fact gathering may also help defuse the emotionalism of an issue. For instance, local statistics on lung cancer incidence reveal that the U.S. tobacco industry is not now "exporting death," as has been charged. Moreover, the substantial and immediate economic benefits attached to tobacco may be providing food and health care in these countries. Nevertheless, as life expectancy and the standards of living rise, a higher incidence of cigarette-related diseases appears likely to develop in these nations. Therefore, cultivation of the nicotine habit may be deemed detrimental to the long-term welfare of these nations.

According to one supposedly infallible truth of modernism, technology is so complex that its results will never be fully comprehensible or predictable. Part of the executive's frustration in responding to question 1 is the real possibility that the "experts" will find no grounds for agreement about the facts.

As a first step, however, defining fully the factual implications of a decision determines to a large degree the quality of one's subsequent moral position. Pericles' definition of true courage rejected the Spartans' blind obedience in war in preference to the courage of the Athenian citizen who, he said, was able to make a decision to proceed in full knowledge of the probable danger. A truly moral decision is an informed decision. A decision that is based on blind or convenient ignorance is hardly defensible.

One simple test of the initial definition is the question:

2 How would you define the problem if you stood on the other side of the fence?

The contemplated construction of a plant for Division X is touted at the finance committee meeting as an absolute necessity for expansion at a cost saving of at least 25%. With plans drawn up for an energy-efficient building and an option already secured on a 99-year lease in a new industrial park in Chippewa County, the committee is likely to feel comfortable in approving the request for funds in a matter of minutes.

The facts of the matter are that the company will expand in an appropriate market, allocate its resources sensibly, create new jobs, increase Chippewa County's tax base, and most likely increase its returns to the shareholders. To the residents of Chippewa County, however, the plant may mean the destruction of a customary recreation spot, the onset of severe traffic jams, and the erection of an architectural eyesore. These are also facts of the situation, and certainly more immediate to the county than utilitarian justifications of profit performance and rights of ownership from an impersonal corporation whose headquarters are 1,000 miles from Chippewa County and whose executives have plenty of acreage for their own recreation.

The purpose of articulating the other side, whose needs are understandably less proximate than operational considerations, is to allow some mechanism whereby calculations of self-interest (or even of a project's ultimate general beneficence) can be interrupted by a compelling empathy for those who might suffer immediate injury or mere annoyance as a result of a corporation's decisions. Such empathy is a necessary prerequisite for shouldering voluntarily some responsibility for the social consequences of corporate operations, and it may be the only solution to today's overly litigious and anarchic world.

There is a power in self-examination: with an exploration of the likely consequences of a proposal, taken from the viewpoint of those who do not immediately benefit, comes a discomfort or an embarrassment that rises in proportion to the degree of the likely injury and its articulation. Like Socrates as gadfly, who stung his fellow citizens into a critical examination of their conduct when they became complacent, the discomfort of the alternative definition is meant to prompt a disinclination to choose the expedient over the most responsible course of action.

Abstract generalities about the benefits of the profit motive and the free market system are, for some, legitimate and ultimate justifications, but when unadorned with alternative viewpoints, such arguments also tend to promote the complacency, carelessness, and impersonality that have characterized some of the more injurious actions of corporations. The advocates of these arguments are like the reformers in Nathaniel Hawthorne's short story "Hall of Fantasy" who "had got possession of some crystal fragment of truth, the brightness of which so dazzled them that they could see nothing else in the whole universe."

In the example of Division X's new plant, it was a simple matter to define the alternate facts; the process rested largely on an assumption that certain values were commonly shared (no one likes a traffic jam, landscaping pleases more than an unadorned building, and so forth). But the alternative definition often underscores an inherent disparity in values or language. To some, the employment of illegal aliens is a criminal act (fact #1); to others, it is a solution to the 60% unemployment rate of a neighboring country (fact #2). One country's bribe is another country's redistribution of sales commissions.

When there are cultural or linguistic disparities, it is easy to get the facts wrong or to invoke a pluralistic tolerance as an excuse to act in one's own self-interest: "That's the way they do things over there. Who are we to question their beliefs?" This kind of reasoning can be both factually inaccurate (many generalizations about bribery rest on hearsay and do not represent the complexities of a culture) and philosophically inconsistent (there are plenty of beliefs, such as those of the environmentalist, which the same generalizers do not hesitate to question).

3 How did this situation occur in the first place?

Lex Motor Company, a subsidiary of Lex Service Group Ltd., had been losing share at a 20% rate in a declining market; and Depot B's performance was the worst of all. Two nearby Lex depots could easily absorb B's business, and closing it down seemed the only sound financial decision. Lex's chairman, Trevor Chinn, hesitated to approve the closure, however, on the grounds that putting 100 people out of work was not right when the corporation itself was not really jeopardized by B's existence. Moreover, seven department managers, who were all within five years of retirement and had had 25 or more years of service at Lex, were scheduled to be made redundant.

The values statement provided no automatic solution, for it placed value on both employees' security and shareholders' interest. Should they close Depot B? At first Chinn thought not: Why should the little guys suffer disproportionately when the company was not performing well? Why not close a more recently acquired business where employee service was not so large a factor? Or why not wait out the short term and reduce head count through natural attrition?

As important as deciding the ethics of the situation was the inquiry into its history. Indeed, the history gave a clue to solving the dilemma: Lex's traditional emphasis on employee security *and* high financial performance had led to a precipitate series of acquisitions and subsequent divestitures when the company had failed to meet its overall objectives. After each rationalization, the people serving the longest had been retained and placed at Depot B, so that by 1980 the facility had more managers than it needed and a very high proportion of long-service employees.

So the very factors that had created the performance problems were making the closure decision difficult, and the very solution that Lex was inclined to favor again would exacerbate the situation further!

In deciding the ethics of a situation it is important to distinguish the symptoms from the disease. Great profit pressures with no sensitivity to the cycles in a particular industry, for example, may force division managers to be ruthless with employees, to short-weight customers, or even to fiddle with cash flow reports in order to meet headquarters' performance criteria.

Dealing with the immediate case of lying, quality discrepancy, or strained labor relations—when the problem is finally discovered—is only a temporary solution. A full examination of how the situation occurred and what the traditional solutions have been may reveal a more serious discrepancy of values and pressures, and this will illuminate the real significance and ethics of the problem. It will also reveal recurring patterns of events that in isolation appear trivial but that as a whole point up a serious situation.

Such a mechanism is particularly important because very few executives are outright scoundrels. Rather, violations of corporate and social values usually occur inadvertently because no one recognizes that a problem exists until it becomes a crisis. This tendency toward initial trivialization seems to be the biggest ethical problem in business today. Articulating answers to my first three questions is a way of reversing that process.

Aristotle   *Contemplation is the best activity.*
It is also the most continuous
since we can contemplate truth
more continuously
than we can perform any action.

4 To whom and what do you give your loyalties as a person and as a member of the corporation?

Every executive faces conflicts of loyalty. The most familiar occasions pit private conscience and sense of duty against corporate policy, but equally frequent are the situations in which one's close colleagues demand participation (tacit or explicit) in an operation or a decision that runs counter to company policy. To whom or what is the greater loyalty—to one's corporation? superior? family? society? self? race? sex?

The good news about conflicts of loyalty is that their identification is a workable way of smoking out the ethics of a situation and of discovering the absolute values inherent in it. As one executive in a discussion of a Harvard case study put it, "My corporate brain says this action is O.K., but my noncorporate brain keeps flashing these warning lights."

The bad news about conflicts of loyalty is that there are few automatic answers for placing priorities on them. "To thine own self be true" is a murky quagmire when the self takes on a variety of roles, as it does so often in this complex modern world.

Supposedly, today's young managers are giving more weight to individual than to corporate identity, and some older executives see this tendency as being ultimately subversive. At the same time, most of them believe individual integrity is essential to a company's reputation.

The U.S. securities industry, for example, is one of the most rigorous industries in America in its requirements of honesty and disclosure. Yet in the end, all its systematic precautions prove inadequate unless the people involved also have a strong sense of integrity that puts loyalty to these principles above personal gain.

A system, however, must permit the time and foster the motivation to allow personal integrity to surface in a particular situation. An examination of loyalties is one way to bring this about. Such an examination may strengthen reputations but also may result in blowing the whistle (freedom of thought carries with it the risk of revolution). But a sorting out of loyalties can also bridge the gulf between policy and implementation or among various interest groups whose affiliations may mask a common devotion to an aspect of a problem—a devotion on which consensus can be built.

How does one probe into one's own loyalties and their implications? A useful method is simply to play various roles out loud, to call on one's loyalty to family and community (for example) by asking, "What will I say when my child asks me why I did that?" If the answer is "That's the way the world works," then your loyalties are clear and moral passivity inevitable. But if the question presents real problems, you have begun a demodulation of signals from your conscience that can only enhance corporate responsibility.

5 What is your intention in making this decision?

6 How does this intention compare with the likely results?

These two questions are asked together because their content often bears close resemblance and, by most calculations, both color the ethics of a situation.

Corporation Buglebloom decides to build a new plant in an underdeveloped minority-populated district where the city has been trying with little success to encourage industrial development. The media approve and Buglebloom adds another star to its good reputation. Is Buglebloom a civic leader and a supporter of minorities or a canny investor about to take advantage of the disadvantaged? The possibilities of Buglebloom's intentions are endless and probably unfathomable to the public; Buglebloom may be both canny investor and friend of minority groups.

I argue that despite their complexity and elusiveness, a company's intentions *do* matter. The "purity" of Buglebloom's motives (purely profit-seeking or purely altruistic) will have wide-reaching effects inside and outside the corporation—on attitudes toward minority employees in other parts of the company, on the wages paid at the new plant, and on the number of other investors in the same area—that will legitimize a certain ethos in the corporation and the community.

Sociologist Max Weber called this an "ethics of attitude" and contrasted it with an "ethics of absolute ends." An ethics of attitude sets a standard to ensure a certain action. A firm policy at headquarters of not cheating customers, for example, may also deter salespeople from succumbing to a tendency to lie by omission or purchasers from continuing to patronize a high-priced supplier when the costs are automatically passed on in the selling price.

What about the ethics of result? Two years later, Buglebloom wishes it had never begun Project Minority Plant. Every good intention has been lost in the realities of doing business in an unfamiliar area, and Buglebloom now has dirty hands: some of those payoffs were absolutely unavoidable if the plant was to open, operations have been plagued with vandalism and language problems, and local resentment at the industrialization of the neighborhood has risen as charges of discrimination have surfaced. No one seems to be benefiting from the project.

The goodness of intent pales somewhat before results that perpetrate great injury or simply do little good. Common sense demands that the "responsible" corporation try to align the two more closely, to identify the probable consequences and also the limitations of knowledge that might lead to more harm than good. Two things to remember in comparing intention and results are that knowledge of the future is always inadequate and that overconfidence often precedes a disastrous mistake.

These two precepts, cribbed from ancient Greece, may help the corporation keep the disparities between intent and result a fearsome reality to consider continuously. The next two questions explore two ways of reducing the moral risks of being wrong.

7 Whom could your decision or action injure?

The question presses whether injury is intentional or not. Given the limits of knowledge about a new product or policy, who and how many will come into contact with it? Could its inadequate disposal affect an entire community? two employees? yourself? How might your product be used if it happened to be acquired by a terrorist radical group or a terrorist military police force? Has your distribution system or disposal plan ensured against such injury? Could it ever?

If not, there may be a compelling moral justification for stopping production. In an integrated society where business and government share certain values, possible injury is an even more important consideration than potential benefit. In policymaking, a much likelier ground for agreement than benefit is avoidance of injury through those "universal nos"—such as no mass death, no totalitarianism, no hunger or malnutrition, no harm to children.

To exclude *at the outset* any policy or decision that might have such results is to reshape the way modern business examines its own morality. So often business formulates questions of injury only after the fact in the form of liability suits.

8 Can you engage the affected parties in a discussion of the problem before you make your decision?

If the calculus of injury is one way of responding to limitations of knowledge about the probable results of a particular business decision, the participation of affected parties is one of the best ways of informing that consideration. Civil rights groups often complain that corporations fail to invite participation from local leaders during the planning stages of community development projects and charitable programs. The corporate foundation that builds a tennis complex for disadvantaged youth is throwing away precious resources if most children in the neighborhood suffer from chronic malnutrition.

In the Lex depot closure case I have mentioned, senior executives agonized over whether the employees would choose redundancy over job transfer and which course would ultimately be more beneficial to them. The managers, however, did not consult the employees. There were more than 200 projected job transfers to another town. But all the affected employees, held by local ties and uneasy about possibly lower housing subsidies, refused relocation offers. Had the employees been allowed to participate in the redundancy discussions, the company might have wasted less time on relocation plans or might have uncovered and resolved the fears about relocating.

The issue of participation affects everyone. (How many executives feel that someone else should decide what is in *their* best interest?) And yet it is a principle often forgotten because of the pressure of time or the inconvenience of calling people together and facing predictably hostile questions.

9 Are you confident that your position will be as valid over a long period of time as it seems now?

As anyone knows who has had to consider long-range plans and short-term budgets simultaneously, a difference in time frame can change the meaning of a problem as much as spring and autumn change the colors of a tree. The ethical coloring of a business decision is no exception to this generational aspect of decision making. Time alters circumstances, and few corporate value systems are immune to shifts in financial status, external political pressure, and personnel. (One survey now places the average U.S. CEO's tenure in office at five years.)

At Lex, for example, the humanitarianism of the statement of objectives and values depended on financial prosperity. The values did not fully anticipate the extent to which the U.K. economy would undergo a recession, and the resulting changes had to be examined, reconciled, and fought if the company's values were to have any meaning. At the Lex annual review, the managers asked themselves repeatedly whether hard times were the ultimate test of the statement or a clear indication that a corporation had to be able to "afford" ethical positions.

Ideally, a company's articulation of its values should anticipate changes of fortune. As the hearings for the passage of the Foreign Corrupt Practices Act of 1977 demonstrated, doing what you can get away with today may not be a secure moral standard, but short-term discomfort for long-term sainthood may require irrational courage or a rational reasoning system or, more likely, both. These 12 questions attempt to elicit a rational system. Courage, of course, depends on personal integrity.

Another aspect of the ethical time frame stretches beyond the boundaries of question 9 but deserves special attention, and that is the timing of the ethical inquiry. When and where will it be made?

We do not normally invoke moral principles in our everyday conduct. Some time ago the participants in a national business ethics conference had worked late into the night preparing the final case for the meeting, and they were very anxious the next morning to get the class under way. Just before the session began, however, someone suggested that they all donate a dollar apiece as a gratuity for the dining hall help at the institute.

Then just as everyone automatically reached into his or her pocket, another person questioned the direction of the gift. Why tip the person behind the counter but not the cook in the kitchen? Should the money be given to each person in proportion to salary or divided equally among all? The participants laughed uneasily—or groaned—as they thought of the diversion of precious time from the case. A decision had to be made.

With the sure instincts of efficient managers, the group chose to forgo further discussion of distributive justice and, yes, appoint a committee. The committee doled out the money without further group consideration, and no formal feedback on the donation was asked for or given.

The questions offered here do not solve the problem of making time for the inquiry. For suggestions about creating favorable conditions for examining corporate values, drawn from my field research, see the ruled insert on page 95.

10   Could you disclose without qualm your decision or action to your boss, your CEO, the board of directors, your family, or society as a whole?

The old question, "Would you want your decision to appear on the front page of the *New York Times*?" still holds. A corporation may maintain that there's really no problem, but a survey of how many "trivial" actions it is reluctant to disclose might be interesting. Disclosure is a way of sounding those submarine depths of conscience and of searching out loyalties.

Kant

Nothing can possibly be conceived in the world, or even out of it, which can be called good without qualification, except a Good Will.

It is also a way of keeping a corporate character cohesive. The Lex group, for example, was once faced with a very sticky problem concerning a small but profitable site with unpleasant (though in no way illegal) working conditions, where two men with 30 years' service worked. I wrote up the case for a Lex senior managers' meeting on the promise to disguise it heavily because the executive who supervised the plant was convinced that, if the chairman and the personnel director knew the plant's true location, they would close it down immediately.

At the meeting, however, as everyone became involved in the discussion and the chairman himself showed sensitivity to the dilemma, the executive disclosed the location and spoke of his own feelings about the situation. The level of mutual confidence was apparent to all, and by other reports it was the most open discussion the group had ever had.

The meeting also fostered understanding of the company's values and their implementation. When the discussion finally flagged, the chairman spoke up. Basing his views on a full knowledge of the group's understanding of the problem, he set the company's priorities. "Jobs over fancy conditions, health over jobs," Chinn said, "but we always *must disclose*." The group decided to keep the plant open, at least for the time being.

Disclosure does not, however, automatically bring universal sympathy. In the early 1970s, a large food store chain that repeatedly found itself embroiled in the United Farm Workers (UFW) disputes with the Teamsters over California grape and lettuce contracts took very seriously the moral implications of a decision whether to stop selling these products. The company endlessly researched the issues, talked to all sides, and made itself available to public representatives of various interest groups to explain its position and to hear out everyone else.

When the controversy started, the company decided to support the UFW boycott, but three years later top management reversed its position. Most of the people who wrote to the company or asked it to send representatives to their local UFW support meetings, however, continued to condemn the chain even after hearing its views, and the general public apparently never became aware of the company's side of the story.

11 What is the symbolic potential of your action if understood? if misunderstood?

Jones Inc., a diversified multinational corporation with assets of $5 billion, has a paper manufacturing operation that happens to be the only major industry in Stirville, and the factory has been polluting the river on which it is located. Local and national conservation groups have filed suit against Jones Inc. for past damages, and the company is defending itself. Meanwhile, the corporation has adopted plans for a new waste-efficient plant. The legal battle is extended and local resentment against Jones Inc. gets bitter.

As a settlement is being reached, Jones Inc. announces that, as a civic-minded gesture, it will make 400 acres of Stirville woodland it owns available to the residents for conservation and recreation purposes. Jones's intention is to offer a peace pipe to the people of Stirville, and the company sees the gift as a symbol of its own belief in conservation and a way of signaling that value to Stirville residents and national conservation groups. Should Jones Inc. give the land away? Is the symbolism significant?

If the symbolic value of the land is understood as Jones Inc. intends, the gift may patch up the company's relations with Stirville and stave off further disaffection with potential employees as the new plant is being built. It may also signal to employees throughout the corporation that Jones Inc. places a premium on conservation efforts and community relations.

If the symbolic value is misunderstood, however, or if completion of the plant is delayed and the old one has to be put back in use—or if another Jones operation is discovered to be polluting another community and becomes a target of the press—the gift could be interpreted as nothing more than a cheap effort to pay off the people of Stirville and hasten settlement of the lawsuit.

The Greek root of our word *symbol* means both signal and contract. A business decision —whether it is the use of an expense account or a corporate donation—has a symbolic value in signaling what is acceptable behavior within the corporate culture and in making a tacit contract with employees and the community about the rules of the game. How the symbol is actually perceived (or misperceived) is as important as how you intend it to be perceived.

12 Under what conditions would you allow exceptions to your stand?

If we accept the idea that every business decision has an important symbolic value and a contractual nature, then the need for consistency is obvious. At the same time, it is also important to ask under what conditions the rules of the game may be changed. What conflicting principles, circumstances, or time constraints would provide a morally acceptable basis for making an exception to one's normal institutional ethos? For instance, how does the cost of the strategy to develop managers from minority groups over the long term fit in with short-term hurdle rates? Also to be considered is what would mitigate a clear case of employee dishonesty.

Questions of consistency—if you would do X, would you also do Y?—are yet another way of eliciting the ethics of the company and of oneself, and can be a final test of the strength, idealism, or practicality of those values. A last example from the experience of Lex illustrates this point and gives temporary credence to the platitude that good ethics is good business. An article in the Sunday paper about a company that had run a series of racy ads, with pictures of half-dressed women and promises of free merchandise to promote the sale of a very mundane product, sparked an extended examination at Lex of its policies on corporate inducements.

One area of concern was holiday giving. What was the acceptable limit for a gift—a bottle of whiskey? a case? Did it matter only that the company did not *intend* the gift to be an inducement, or did the mere possibility of inducement taint the gift? Was the cut-off point absolute? The group could agree on no halfway point for allowing some gifts and not others, so a new value was added to the formal statement that prohibited the offering or receiving of inducements.

The next holiday season Chinn sent a letter to friends and colleagues who had received gifts of appreciation in the past. In it he explained that, as a result of Lex's concern with "the very complex area of business ethics," management had decided that the company would no longer send any gifts, nor would it be appropriate for its employees to receive any. Although the letter did not explain Lex's reasoning behind the decision, apparently there was a large untapped consensus about such gift giving: by return mail Chinn received at least 20 letters from directors, general managers, and chairmen of companies with which Lex had done business congratulating him for his decision, agreeing with the new policy, and thanking him for his holiday wishes.

The 'good puppy' theory

The 12 questions are a way to articulate an idea of the responsibilities involved and to lay them open for examination. Whether a decisive policy is also generated or not, there are compelling reasons for holding such discussions:

☐   The process facilitates talk as a group about a subject that has traditionally been reserved for the privacy of one's conscience. Moreover, for those whose consciences twitch but don't speak in full sentences, the questions help sort out their own perceptions of the problem and various ways of thinking about it.

☐   The process builds a cohesiveness of managerial character as points of consensus emerge and people from vastly different operations discover that they share common problems. It is one way of determining the values and goals of the company, and that is a key element in determining corporate strategy.

☐   It acts as an information resource. Senior managers learn about other parts of the company with which they may have little contact.

☐   It helps uncover ethical inconsistencies in the articulated values of the corporation or between these values and the financial strategy.

☐   It helps uncover sometimes dramatic differences between the values and the practicality of their implementation.

☐   It helps the CEO understand how the senior managers think, how they handle a problem, and how willing and able they are to deal with complexity. It reveals how they may be drawing on the private self to the enhancement of corporate activity.

☐   In drawing out the private self in connection with business and in exploring the significance of the corporation's activities, the process derives meaning from an environment that is often characterized as meaningless.

☐   It helps improve the nature and range of alternatives.

☐   It is cathartic.

The process is also reductive in that it limits the level of inquiry. For example, the 12 questions ask what injury might result from a decision and what good is intended, but they do not ask the meaning of *good* or whether the result is "just."

Socrates asked how a person could talk of pursuing the good before knowing what the good is; and the analysis he visualized entailed a lifelong process of learning and examination. Do the 12 short questions, with their explicit goal of simplifying the ethical examination, bastardize the Socratic ideal? To answer this, we must distinguish between personal philosophy and participation as a corporate member in the examination of a *corporate* ethos, for the 12 questions assume some difference between private and corporate "goodness."

This distinction is crucial to any evaluation of my suggested process for conducting

Shared conditions of some successful ethical inquiries

Fixed time frame	Understanding and identifying moral issues takes time and causes ferment, and the executive needs an uninterrupted block of time to ponder the problems.	**Credo**	Articulating the corporation's values and objectives provides a reference point for group inquiry and implementation. Ethical codes, however, when drawn up by the legal department, do not always offer a realistic and full representation of management's beliefs. The most important ethical inquiry for management may be the very formulation of such a statement, for the *process* of articulation is as useful as the values agreed on.
Unconventional location	Religious groups, boards of directors, and professional associations have long recognized the value of the retreat as a way of stimulating fresh approaches to regular activities. If the group is going to transcend normal corporate hierarchies, it should hold the discussion on neutral territory so that all may participate with the same degree of freedom.	**Homegrown topics**	In isolating an ethical issue, drawing on your own experience is important. Philosophical business ethics has tended to reflect national social controversies, which though relevant to the corporation may not always be as relevant – not to mention as easily resolved – as some internal issues that are shaping the character of the company to a much greater degree. Executives are also more likely to be informed on these issues.
Resource person	The advantage of bringing in an outsider is not that he or she will impose some preconceived notion of right and wrong on management but that he will serve as a midwife for bringing the values already present in the institution out into the open. He can generate closer examination of the discrepancies between values and practice and draw on a wider knowledge of instances and intellectual frameworks than the group can. The resource person may also take the important role of arbitrator – to ensure that one person does not dominate the session with his or her own values and that the dialogue does not become impossibly emotional.	**Resolution**	In all the programs I observed except one, there was a point at which the inquiry was slated to have some resolution: either a vote on the issue, the adoption of a new policy, a timetable for implementation, or the formulation of a specific statement of values. The one program observed that had no such decision-making structure was organized simply to gather information about the company's activities through extrahierarchical channels. Because the program had no tangible goals or clearly articulated results, its benefits were impossible to measure.
Participation of CEO	In most corporations the chief executive still commands an extra degree of authority for the intangible we call corporate culture, and the discussion needs the perspective of and legitimization by that authority if it is to have any seriousness of purpose and consequence. One of the most interesting experiments in examining corporate policy I have observed lacked the CEO's support, and within a year it died on the vine.		

an ethical inquiry and needs to be explained. What exactly do we expect of the "ethical," or "good," corporation? Three examples of goodness represent prevailing social opinions, from that of the moral philosopher to the strict Friedmaniac.

1   The most rigorous moral analogy to the good corporation would be the "good man." An abstract, philosophical ideal having highly moral connotations, the good man encompasses an intricate relation of abstractions such as Plato's four virtues (courage, godliness or philosophical wisdom, righteousness, and prudence). The activities of this kind of good corporation imply a heavy responsibility to collectively know the good and to resolve to achieve it.

2   Next, there is the purely amoral definition of good, as in a "good martini"—an amoral fulfillment of a largely inanimate and functional purpose. Under this definition, corporate goodness would be best achieved by the unadorned accrual of profits with no regard for the social implications of the means whereby profits are made.

3   Halfway between these two views lies the good as in "good puppy"—here goodness consists

primarily of the fulfillment of a social contract that centers on avoiding social injury. Moral capacity is perceived as present, but its potential is limited. A moral evaluation of the good puppy is possible but exists largely in concrete terms; we do not need to identify the puppy's intentions as utilitarian to understand and agree that its "ethical" fulfillment of the social contract consists of not soiling the carpet or biting the baby.

It seems to me that business ethics operates most appropriately for corporate man when it seeks to define and explore corporate morality at the level of the good puppy. The good corporation is expected to avoid perpetrating irretrievable social injury (and to assume the costs when it unintentionally does injury) while focusing on its purpose as a profit-making organization. Its moral capacity does not extend, however, to determining by itself what will improve the general social welfare.

The good puppy inquiry operates largely in concrete experience; just as the 12 questions impose a limit on our moral expectations, so too they impose a limit (welcome, to some) on our use of abstraction to get at the problem.

The situations for testing business morality remain complex. But by avoiding theoretical inquiry and limiting the expectations of corporate goodness to a few rules for social behavior that are based on common sense, we can develop an ethic that is appropriate to the language, ideology, and institutional dynamics of business decision making and consensus. This ethic can also offer managers a practical way of exploring those occasions when their corporate brains are getting warning flashes from their noncorporate brains. ▽

The rabbit and the goat

A Goat once approached a peanut stand that was kept by a Rabbit, purchased five cents worth of peanuts, laid down a dime, and received a punched nickel in change. In a few days the Goat came back, called for another pint of peanuts, and offered the same nickel in payment; but in the meantime had stopped the hole in it with a peg.

"I can't take that nickel," said the Rabbit.

"This is the very nickel you gave me in change a few days ago," replied the Goat.

"I know it is," continued the Rabbit, "but I made no attempt to deceive you about it. When you took the coin the hole was wide open, and you could see it for yourself. In working that mutilated coin off on you I sim-ply showed my business sagacity; but now you bring it back with the hole stopped up and try to pass it, with a clear intent to deceive. That is fraud. My dear Goat, I'm afraid the grand jury will get after you if you are not more careful about little things of this sort."

Moral:
This Fable teaches that the moral quality of a business transaction often depends upon the view you take of it.

From
"The Rabbit and the Goat,"
in *Life,*
October 8, 1885, p. 208.
Reprinted with the permission of the copyright owners.

Personal Values and Business Decisions

* *Does right make might?*
* *Does honesty always pay the honest man?*
* *Does good ethics mean good business in the long run?*

*By Edmund P. Learned,
Arch R. Dooley,
and Robert L. Katz*

Among thoughtful businessmen there is growing concern with the spiritual implications of their everyday activities. Some of these men are seeking greater meaning in their business lives than the accumulation of profits for the enterprise or of wealth, power, and prestige for themselves. Others are struggling with the problem of squaring their corporate responsibilities with their personal religious beliefs. Still others are attempting to define their personal values in the context of their business experience.

Symptoms of this concern are to be found everywhere. A tremendous number of speeches and articles on "religion and business" are receiving eager and enthusiastic response. In the pages of this magazine over the last two years, as just one example, every issue has contained at least one article dealing with ethical or moral problems. And, even more significant, the demand for reprints of these articles has held its own with groups of articles on such timely topics as statistical decision making, human relations, marketing, and executive development.

Why This Concern?

What has caused this current upsurge of businessmen's interest in questions of ultimate values? By tracing the roots of the trend, it will perhaps be more nearly possible to determine its nature and probable hardiness. A variety of partial answers have been advanced. Thus:

❡ Some suggest that the development merely reflects the concessions that have been wrung from businessmen by the pressure of circumstances. The strength of organized labor, the fear of communism, the memories of the recent past in which business emerged as a political whipping boy — all have been cited to explain the growing introspection evidenced by businessmen.

❡ Some push this analysis further and suggest that business has become conscious of its opportunities and responsibilities in other than purely economic affairs because of a guilty conscience. There is, for example, a persistent hard core of opinion that suggests that all manifestations of interest in ultimate values (particularly those which have been associated with outstandingly successful business careers) are an attempt to "buy respectability" — that is, to atone for the accumulation of great wealth and economic power through practices which cannot measure up to the highest ethical standards.

❡ A variation on this basic theme is the suggestion that actually there has been no genuine change in the ethical standards of business or of businessmen. Any evidence to the contrary, it is suggested, is merely carefully mounted public relations campaigns — window dressing to conceal the fact that business motives and tactics remain what they always have been.

❡ On the other hand, some commentators offer a far less cynical interpretation. Some, for exam-

Reprint 59205

ple, suggest that the period of uncertainty through which the world has recently passed and the period of equal uncertainty in which it now lives have forced each thoughtful individual, in business or in any other form of human endeavor, to give increasing thought to ultimate values and to seek certain unyielding premises on which he can fix his convictions.

❮ Other opinion centers upon a quite different characteristic of the contemporary era. It has been, these men suggest, a time that has lent itself to the "luxuries of conscience." Satisfying the basic needs for food, shelter, and so on has been increasingly easy for a broad section of the population. For the man of genuine ability in business, the challenge has often been not that of finding an adequate job but that of choosing among a variety of promising alternatives. In increasing numbers, men are able to ask themselves what they would like to do with their lives, with reasonable expectation of being able to move tangibly toward fulfillment of their goals.

Unavoidable Conflict

It is probable that each of these various explanations contains some element of truth. To the writers of this article, however, neither singly nor in combination do any of these reasons provide as meaningful an explanation as is to be found in the very fact that the businessman is, first of all, a *man*. As a man, he shares the universal trait of wanting to be certain that his life has meaning and purpose. But the nature of his role as a businessman places him continuously in a position of conflict. It forces him constantly to choose between alternative courses of action reflecting differing priorities of values.

In his analysis of these alternatives, and in his consideration of the values they represent, the businessman inevitably finds himself in a state of inner conflict. He wants to do the right thing, but he does not always find it easy to know what that right thing is. Efforts to deny the existence of such conflict, however persistently pursued, offer only temporary and superficial relief. Like all men, the businessman inevitably returns to the questions of ultimate values and to the question of whether his total life is serving those values in the way he would wish.

Evidence of Concern

A particularly cogent example of the nature and the strength of business's growing concern

with spiritual values was evident in the Harvard Business School Association's Fiftieth Anniversary Conference in September 1958, which had as its theme, "Management's Mission in a New Society." It is significant that every major speaker stressed the importance of more attention to spiritual values, and that no fewer than one fourth of the panel discussions, set up to consider topics of major importance to the participants, were directly concerned with these issues.[1]

Erwin D. Canham, editor of *The Christian Science Monitor*, had this to say:

"The only valid social goal is improvement of the lot of man and the better relationship of men to one another and to God, to fundamental truth. . . . This thesis is incontrovertible, and once we tended to live by it. . . .

"There is nothing inherently wrong with the satisfaction of man's material wants. . . . In fact, the attainment of a better standard of living is itself a spiritual victory, insofar as it exemplifies man's mastery of his physical environment. Behind all our technological, industrial, or mercantile attainments lies this kind of true victory. But we do not often recognize it as such, nor have we made any progress in explaining to the rest of the world that the real American achievement is spiritual instead of material."

Charles S. Malik, formerly Minister of Foreign Affairs of Lebanon and President of the General Assembly of the United Nations, discussed "The Businessman and the Challenge of Communism." After raising the question of the meaning men attach to their work, he went on to say:

"The businessman is judged by more than his product and his performance: his humanity is at stake. Rising above his individual interests to the proper consideration of the common good and soaring even beyond the common good to the spiritual significance of his wondrous material civilization, the businessman can clothe his humanity with a shining new splendor. He will put to shame every culture that ends in boredom, self-sufficiency, and human pride. His spiritualized materialism will have something profound to say and give to all men. He will identify himself with their human state. He will be proud of his business and its achievements, but he will be even prouder of that which is beyond business in his culture. He will say, 'Let others compete with me in material things and let them even excel, but there is one thing in

[1] See *Management's Mission in a New Society*, edited by Dan H. Fenn, Jr. (New York, McGraw-Hill Book Company, Inc., scheduled for Spring 1959 publication).

which they cannot excel because they do not know it and are not even seeking it. That is the power and depth and freedom of the spirit in which man is fully himself.' In this way Communism's challenge to the businessman will turn into the businessman's challenge to Communism."

Later in the same program, Stanley F. Teele, dean of the Harvard Business School, described the requirements for "The Businessman of the Future" as being "more rational, more responsible, more religious." He said:

"Personally, I am troubled by our apparent continued emphasis on material progress alone as the measure of success or failure in this kind of competition [with the Soviet Union]. . . . We are falling into a trap of our own making; we have become so impressed by the world's reaction to our tremendous material progress that there is risk that we shall consider this the true measure of our greatness and the most important contribution which we have made and can make to the world. In our hearts we know better; we know that the demonstration of how 170 million people can live together in peace, with basic goals of human dignity, morality, and justice, is our real contribution."

Mission vs. Material Progress

These and many other distinguished men who participated in the program were all pointing at the same thing: the need to place stronger emphasis on spiritual goals, not only so that each man may find greater meaning in his work and in his life, but, even more dramatically, so that our nation and our way of life may survive in the international battle for men's hearts and minds.

As Arnold J. Toynbee, the distinguished historian, pointed out at the conference, no society has ever flourished without a spiritual mission; the quest for material progress alone is insufficient to spur men on to the achievements which are required to create an enduring, dynamic, progressive nation. In fact, his conclusion is that all through history material progress as a national goal has led to stagnation, boredom, and moral decay.

It is significant that the great concern for more spirituality in business comes at a time when our material progress has achieved extraordinary heights. The high level of satisfaction of material wants, taken as a goal, threatens stagnation and destruction of our society; but, at the same time, it provides an unparalleled opportunity for freeing men's minds and ambitions for loftier goals.

What Is Spirituality?

When we talk about seeking loftier goals and about finding "spirituality" in our business lives, what do we really mean? There is nothing mysterious in the word spirituality. Spirituality in business, as we see it, is the process of seeking to discover, however imperfectly, God's law in each everyday work situation, and of trying to behave in each situation as nearly in accord with that law as we are able to. Perhaps this broad generalization will be clearer and more meaningful if we define our terms:

We conceive of God as that force in the universe which has created and maintained all that is real and true. We believe that God's creation has an order and symmetry which relates all things to one another. We consider the ultimate fulfillment of man, *as man*, to be his comprehension of reality and truth, so that he becomes one with God in his understanding of the relationships of all things and his behavior comes to be in harmony and accord with this orderly reality.

We also believe that man — imperfect in his comprehension and perspective, and burdened with sins and shortsightedness of his own making — is inevitably unable to sense the full reality. To survive in his environment, he makes judgments and evaluations which, because of his limited comprehension, are admittedly imperfect. He arms himself with personal values which, while enabling him to function in the world, may prevent him from seeing the ultimate reality, the truth which actually exists. To us, spirituality means making a continuing, conscious effort to rise above these inevitable human limitations — a maximum endeavor to comprehend the ultimate values, the truth and the reality of the orderliness of the universe — and to live in accordance with this reality.

We cannot prove the point of view we have stated. Neither can it be disproved. It is simply an act of faith. It is comforting to note, however, that research in both the physical and the social sciences has suggested the existence of order in the universe and has indicated that all things are related to one another in a nonrandom way. Moreover, none of these validated findings has in any way contradicted the teachings of the great prophets. One is justified in believing that both prophets and researchers are pointing at the same truth.

Within this view of reality we deal with *personal values, which are the goals and criteria unique to each individual. We shall talk about ethics or morality, not as ideas necessarily sacred or "right" in themselves, but merely as widely held values which, rightly or wrongly, receive widespread sanction and approval. We will hold as ultimate values those goals and criteria which seem to us to be most closely in accord with what is real. These ultimate values, which are held by every great religion and which have been advanced by each of the great prophets and religious leaders throughout recorded history, are: love of fellow man, justice in all acts among men, and the self-fulfillment of the individual through understanding and through actions that bring him closer to living in accord with reality.

Guides to Action

Systems of values (implicit or explicit) are inherent in the behavior of all persons. Also, each individual's personal values — the standards he uses in making evaluations and the goals he chooses for action — are different, in greater or lesser degree, from anyone else's set of values.

Moreover, not only do values differ from individual to individual, but also each individual's values change from one situation to the next, whether he is aware of it or not. Specific facts, persons, and events cannot be talked about or dealt with without considering the values that different persons, including ourselves, place on them. Two managers are discussing what went wrong in a production schedule. Do they trust the foreman or not? Are they interested or disinterested in the aspirations of production workers? Is their sole concern with making a good profit showing this month? And so on.

For each individual, reality is whatever his values allow him to recognize. And since each person's values are unique, his conception of the "right" thing to do will differ from others'. Nonetheless, many men assume that other persons of good intentions will see things the same way they do and brand those who disagree with them as unethical, immoral, or just plain stupid. By assuming that they can bring a set of absolute values to bear on any situation and thus reveal a course of action, they drastically oversimplify the situation, missing its impact on their interpretation of their values as well as the impact of their values on what they see before them — all of which tends to make them victims of the situation, not masters over it.

On the other hand, just recognizing that values differ from person to person and situation to situation does not provide a satisfactory guide to action either. The world we live in is so complex, and man's capacity so finite, that complete pragmatism can lead only to confusion, inconsistency, or a philosophy of expediency and caprice. What is needed is for each man to try to hold as criteria a very few ultimate values which for him represent essential truths and to cling to these criteria tenaciously and absolutely in every situation. He can then deal highly pragmatically with the inevitable conflicts of personal values inherent in any situation and work out the range of action uniquely appropriate to it, using his ultimate values as standards for judging the reality of the various courses of action.

This approach is not easy — far from it. It requires living with tremendous personal discomforts and conflicts, with a gnawing, inescapable admission of one's own fallibility and inadequacy. To be consciously aware of the inadequacies of his perceptions and still be able to take action is perhaps the most difficult position that a person can maintain.

With these assumptions and beliefs stated, we can proceed to discuss two questions of great practical importance: What values commonly held by businessmen block the growth of spirituality in business behavior? What do beliefs like those just stated mean for executive action?

Unrealistic Dreaming

Businessmen have a variety of ways of thinking about the relationships between spiritual and business considerations. For instance, some persons, including many who clearly endeavor to serve the highest concepts of spiritual values in their personal activities, contend that spiritual considerations simply cannot be given a position of major importance in business decisions. To these individuals, the suggestion that such values can be, or are, given a prominent role by management seems unrealistic dreaming at best, or, at worst, hypocritical distortion or misrepresentation. A few go even further to suggest that even if it were realistically possible to do so, it would be inappropriate (perhaps even immoral) for a businessman to employ his business position as a means to the achievement of his individual spiritual concepts.

This general view is documented in a multitude of ways. Central to each of these ways is the belief that most of the problems encountered in business can be dealt with as purely business problems without directly encountering the spiritual values that may be involved. The spiritual ramifications of a situation are not denied; they are simply not treated as factors with which the businessman can or should concern himself as an executive.

Typical Attitudes

Men who subscribe to this view back it up with statements like these:

◖ "I believe in behaving responsibly; but when the chips are really down (i.e., when the financial stakes are high and the competitive pressures are pronounced), then business profits, and hence long-term business survival, are often incompatible with spiritual considerations. The businessman has no choice but to treat the former as the dominant consideration."

◖ "Business requires competition. That's what private enterprise is all about. And the tougher the competition, the better the service that business can give and the more valuable the contributions it can make. But competition means that someone's going to be hurt. If you *really* worried about spiritual values, you couldn't bring yourself to be truly competitive."

◖ "Look, I wouldn't last six months in this business if I really asked myself whether everything I do really meets acceptable spiritual standards. Now you understand I don't prefer it this way; and, if the time ever comes when things are different, why I'll be the first to go along. But as long as my competitors think it's all right to do this, as long as my customers expect me to do that, as long as my boss tells me such-and-such, and as long as our stockholders demand what they do, and so forth and so forth, why, then I'll just have to. . . ."

◖ "A businessman is supposed to run his business profitably. A successful business in itself can be a tremendous contributor toward 'good.' But if the businessman spends his time worrying about 'doing good,' he'll divert his attention from his real purpose — he'll lose his effectiveness as a businessman. Remember what they say, 'Shoemaker, stick to your last.' A businessman should stick to business and leave to others (the government, the church, the individual) the job of setting right all of mankind's problems."

◖ "Spiritual questions involve value judgments. They hinge on questions of what's right and what's wrong — what's good and what's bad. Business has no right to exercise its power to try to further

its own particular answers to such considerations. There's nothing in my company's corporate charter about trying to push my own ideas of social, cultural, or political considerations, and certainly nothing about furthering ultimate values as such. We shouldn't get involved in this sort of thing. And certainly we shouldn't try to force our views on others."

◖ "Only a handful of companies are big enough to exert any real influence insofar as spiritual values are concerned. Even in those companies, there are only a handful of men at the very top who can make any difference. The average fellow would just be committing business suicide if he were to try. He'd lose his value to the organization."

◖ "Do you know what it is to meet a payroll? It's damn tough, and there are plenty of times when you can't take time to worry about whether a saint would approve of everything you've done. . . ."

We are all familiar with similar examples, and many more could be given. What is significant here is that few people find that such a framework gives them much real satisfaction from their work. Most adherents — particularly those to whom their religion is a deep and serious commitment — grant that they wish business life *could* be different; but they believe that, in fact, business is amoral, and they have resigned themselves to it. Many of these people find that participation in church activities, community affairs, charity work, and so on gives their lives some of the meaning which they feel is denied in their work activities, but this compartmentalization tends to add to their frustration rather than diminish it.

"Just Good Business"

Another familiar framework or rationale is that, over the long run, good ethics *is* good business. Elaboration and support of this proposition fall into a number of subdivisions. Certain of these are so closely related as to overlap. By contrast, some of the arguments advanced in support of the proposition are mutually incompatible. But for each subdivision proof can be (and usually is) advanced in the form of personalized experiences or observations.

Practical Incentives

One view is that good ethics is good business because of readily understandable *quid pro quo* concepts: a business that behaves ethically induces others to behave ethically toward it. Supporters document this with episodes (actual or hypothetical) drawn from all sectors of the business scene. For example:

• A firm exercises particular care in meeting all responsibilities to its employees. As a result, it is rewarded with an unusual degree of employee loyalty, application, and productivity. (In a familiar variation on this theme, such a firm is rewarded by a spirit of militant antiunionism on the part of its loyal, appreciative work force.)

• A supplier refuses to exploit his advantage during a sellers' market and thereby retains the loyalty (and continued business) of customers when conditions change to those of a buyers' market.

• A firm that employs handicapped persons discovers that they are actually more productive, hardworking, loyal, and so on than the nonhandicapped persons normally employed.

Another view supports the proposition that "good ethics is good business" by stressing the dangers and probable penalties inherent in unethical business behavior. This view is documented with such examples as:

• A customer is dealt with unfairly and thereafter refuses to deal with the supplier in question. Other firms, learning of the situation, also refuse to deal with the supplier because "he has shown he cannot be trusted."

• A firm allows its salesmen to disseminate misleading information about its competitors' products. This invites open retaliation by competing salesmen (who perhaps prove even more effective in their use of this technique).

• A union whose reasonable demands are rejected during a period of union weakness vengefully wrests unreasonable concessions from the company when the balance of bargaining power shifts in its favor.

Advocates of this viewpoint frequently observe that if the entire business community fails to meet the standards and the desires of society, punitive legislation will be enacted which will be far more severe than warranted. Ethical behavior on the part of business is thus advocated as a form of insurance against retaliatory acts.

Virtue Triumphs

A third view supporting the proposition that good ethics is good business explains itself in essentially mystical terms drawing on empirical evidence. For advocates of this view, the concepts of "good ultimately rising above evil" and of "right making might" (both deeply engrained in human consciousness and buttressed by legend and literature) are seen to be fully operative in business settings. A "good man" who steadfastly tries to be ethical, i.e., "to do the right thing" somehow always overtakes his immoral or amoral counterpart in the long run. Bread cast upon the waters *is* returned, even if the process is sometimes an indirect one and the waiting period is extensive.

Documentation of this view is again drawn from a variety of quarters. Frequently it is characterized by the unexpected, the unforeseen, the mysterious. To illustrate:

• A man unjustly discharged from a position in which he has given faithful service finds even greater success and satisfaction in the new job he has been forced to take.

• An associate who had persisted in hostility and obstructionism toward a "good man" suddenly sees the error of his ways, apologizes, and becomes a staunch ally.

• A firm loses an important account rather than enter into a form of reciprocity that it considers unethical. Then it unexpectedly obtains a new customer whose business fully compensates for the abandoned account.

• Or the "Executive Suite" theme — an individual who steadfastly refuses to further his career by the use of unethical tactics wins out (usually at the last split second) over those who do.

For some advocates of this school of thought, the explanation for such occurrences rests in the operation of some divine force that ultimately assures a happy ending. Its operation is not to be analyzed or understood. Rather, it is to be accepted and confidently anticipated by those who put their faith in ethical behavior.

An alternative explanation of the view that virtue ultimately triumphs suggests that when an individual operates with a sense of certainty regarding the ethical soundness of his position, his mind and energies are freed for maximum productivity and creativity. On the other hand, when practicing what he knows to be unethical behavior, an individual finds it necessary to engage in exhausting subterfuge. Furthermore, in a violent battle of conscience, his energies are diluted, his effectiveness is diminished, and his chances of ultimate success are destroyed.

Thus, given any situation in which basic capabilities and tangible resources are in even approximate balance, the individual with a sense of ethical certainty will invariably be more productive than the individual who has elected to pursue his goals unethically.

Wide Appeal of Concept

Regardless of which explanation is considered, it is not difficult to understand why the concept that good ethics is good business. has won for itself so wide a following among those who advocate conscious consideration of spiritual dimensions.

It is, in the first place, a concept that seemingly avoids any painful choice between appealing but mutually incompatible alternatives. Instead it professes to offer the vastly attractive prospect of desirable goals compounded. The businessman, it suggests, really can have "all this and heaven too." Actually, it seems to imply, the two may be more surely achieved jointly than separately. Spiritual values are not attained at the cost of business success; instead, conscious pursuit of them helps create business success.

If this is true, here, indeed, is a merchandisable product!

The appeal of the proposition is further intensified by the fact that it bypasses the troublesome question of the separability of spiritual considerations from all the other elements of a business decision. Once it is accepted that good ethics is good business, it is neither necessary nor germane to ponder whether the two can be separated. If good ethics is good business, no effective businessman would endeavor to isolate spiritual considerations from the other elements in a business situation, even were it possible to do so.

Still further appeal arises from the fact that if good ethics is good business, then spiritual behavior can be frocked in the apparently appealing garb of "hardheaded," "practical" business expediency. No longer need the businessman fear (consciously or subconsciously) that considering spiritual values in business decisions will indicate to "practical men" that he is unwilling to meet the stern realities of the business world. He need never fall into the apparently vulnerable role of an advocate of spiritual values for their own sake. Instead, he can fly the banner of the "practical man" and can stress the goal of business success as the real motive underlying his acts.

The proposition that good ethics is good business also has the important advantage of being difficult, if not impossible, to disprove. By the same token it is, of course, almost impossible to prove. But it is apparent that many businessmen find intuitive support of this proposition to be a more gracious, more comfortable, and more affirmatively human position than its rejection.

New Approach Needed

To us, neither the proposition that business and spiritual considerations are separable nor the view that good ethics is good business is a fully adequate or satisfying guide for action. Both, we feel, represent oversimplified attempts to find an easy way out of an excruciatingly complex situation.

To us, the thesis that business decisions need not reflect spiritual considerations contains the fatal flaw of unrealism. We believe that in business, as in all other human endeavors, the spiritual values of each individual involved are inextricably linked to all the other elements in the situation, including the often differing value perceptions held with equal sincerity by other people concerned. Businessmen, whether they want to or not, cannot escape involvement with spiritual values in any segment of their activities. Instead, by the very act of responding to the total context of whatever situation confronts them, they either serve or disavow spiritual values held by themselves or by others.

For us, then, the question is not *whether* a businessman must deal with spiritual values. Instead, the question is *how* the businessman can broaden his perception of reality to assure that the spiritual implications which inevitably attend his actions conform as closely as is humanly possible with his ultimate values.

The answer to this question does not lie merely in the assertion that "good ethics is good business." In our judgment, this too is an inadequate framework, and is marred by major shortcomings.

Uncertainty of Reward

We are troubled, first of all, with the implied certainty of material reward which permeates the proposition and which, we feel, constantly threatens its usefulness to those who embrace it. We grant that furtherance of spiritual values over the long run does often lead to successful business results. But does it follow that such results invariably can or ought to be anticipated, or that they should be interpreted as even partial justification for the pursuance of spiritual goals? None of the major religions says that ultimate values may always be served without cost, sacrifice, or hardship, even in the long run. Insofar as material satisfactions are concerned, man, as man, is not promised "all this and heaven too," even in exchange for the most devout human behavior. And does not the totality of business experience reveal numerous situations in which success or failure emerges both in the *presence* and in the *absence* of conscious pursuit of ethical values?

For us, therefore, the suggestion that there is some close, causal connection between business success and spiritually oriented behavior seems, at best, deceptively superficial and fraught with dangers of disillusionment for those who follow it. At worst, there may even be a danger that, through its appealing simplicity, the proposition could deaden one's sensitivity to the ethical challenges each of us continually faces. If embraced wholeheartedly and employed indiscriminately as the rationale for business decisions, the concept that good ethics is good business could lead unwittingly to acceptance of the reverse corollary that good business is good ethics — and to the deceptive assumption that men of goodwill somehow will, automatically and without conflict, serve ultimate values in their actions.

Even more devastating is the possibility that spiritual values might come to be viewed as a *means* to business success, rather than as a *goal* in themselves. If given such an interpretation, the whole proposition becomes irreverent and irreligious.

Facing Up to Conflict

We are troubled, too, by the thought that the proposition offers no helpful guidance for a businessman's conduct in the short-term decisions that continually confront him, whatever his rank or status in an enterprise. How can the belief that in the long run good ethics is good business help the manager who is responsible for immediate results, particularly if attention to spiritual values entails a risk of financial loss or even immediate failure for the individual himself, the enterprise, or both?

To us, every decision involves a conflicting set of forces. This is particularly true in business, where the individual often finds himself forced to choose among personal values and ultimate loyalties that may be in sharp conflict with each other, with the values held by others (which look "right" from their points of view), or with urgent organizational considerations. The terrible task of leadership is to live with conflicts and tensions, to make discriminating judgments where necessary, and to find mutual relationships where possible. What is crucial is that the administrator realize that he always has a *choice* of what his behavior or decisions will be — (at least, if he is willing to accept the inevitable discomforts entailed by different courses of action).

There are always a multitude of forces in any organizational framework which make conflict inevitable and negative consequences unavoidable. Someone will always be placed under tensions or restrictions, or denied things that he believes to be rightly his. Individual interests must frequently be sacrificed for the good of the larger organization.

For these reasons we do not believe that it is satisfactory either to ignore spiritual considerations in business or to try to make spiritual and business considerations identical. Both approaches are oversimplifications: the former because it requires a man who wants to serve God to compartmentalize his life; the latter because it offers no way of dealing with the conflicts which occur in every decision-making situation. Neither recognizes the inevitability of conflict or the complexity of the situation in which business decisions must be made. What, then, is a more adequate framework?

Faith in a Process

To us, a third frame of reference offers a more adequate and realistic basis for facing the awesome complexities that are invariably encountered in industry, and for bearing the inner human tensions that are inevitably experienced when an individual stands at the juncture between his own spiritual values and the demands of his daily business activities.

We do not pretend to know the ultimate course of action in any specific situation. Nor do we believe in the existence of easy, generalized solutions: each situation requires its own unique resolution. But we do have faith in a *process* by which men can perceive and act on as much of God's answer to each situation as is within their limited power of discernment.

Underlying Assumptions

This process is based on assumptions — some of them cited earlier — which we acknowledge are not within the scope of human proof. But, for us, they require no proof. They are our articles of faith.

❦ We believe that there is an *order* to the universe. We have faith that this order is God's law and that it represents the ultimate *reality*. But we also believe that man's imperfections prevent him from ever fully comprehending this reality in each specific situation that confronts him.

❦ We believe that as a result of this limited perception, finite man is constantly violating God's law in some way. Inevitably, each of us is always inadequate to the full demands of whatever situation we encounter. From each of us, then, is demanded a continuing, profound humility concerning the spiritual adequacy of our own ideas and actions.

❦ We believe that ultimate values — love of fellow man, justice in all dealings among men, and opportunity for self-fulfillment for all persons — although known to man throughout his civilized history and embraced by many of his historical religious and ethical systems, do not provide direct answers for specific situations. Instead, they must be employed as criteria by which man discerns the implications of the alternative courses of action that are available to him.

❦ We believe that every business situation, in common with all other forms of human endeavor, inevitably involves conflicts of values among the men concerned. Wherever possible, men must strive with good will for an integration of these divergent values, even though that integration may involve compromises which frustrate the individual because what he sees as right varies so sharply from what he realizes is attainable. Men must also be willing to face the tensions that result from those conflicts which prove irreconcilable, knowing that these tensions, too, are part of God's process.

❦ We believe that God works through men — others as well as ourselves. We believe that a forthright interchange of views between men, however divergent their values, provides an opportunity for more complete comprehension of God's reality than any one man can achieve alone, however sincere his motivation or intense his application. Men working together, sharing perceptions, and respecting the intrinsic worth of each other's contributions often find integrated solutions to even the most difficult situations.

Even when the conflicts of value prove irreconcilable and integration is, at least for the moment, impossible, comparisons of divergent points of view can help illuminate the probable consequences of alternative courses of action and suggest the interim solution that most effectively preserves an opportunity for integration at some future date. Men's answers will be nearer to God's reality when they emanate from a free and open exchange of views and when they embrace the broadest possible perspective of the values held by all the men involved.

Each of us, therefore, faces the obligation to seek and respect the ideas of others. Only in this way can we augment our own inevitably fragmentary grasp of God's reality. But the ultimate responsibility for decision — and for its consequences, favorable and unfavorable — must be our own.

In short, the essence of the process we advocate is that man should possess complete faith in the omniscience of the Creator and in the existence of order in His universe and constantly strive to comprehend and to act in accord with more and more of the reality in each situation, relying on free discussion with other men as a means through which he may perceive reality more fully.

Implicit in this process is the recognition that there is a spiritual significance to every phase of a man's work, be it in business or any other calling. The businessman who embraces this process must do so knowing that the way of faith is hard, rigorous, and filled with continuously humbling evidences of man's imperfection, and realizing that even when seeking to do good, finite man, with his limited perception of reality, is always inflicting some measure of evil.

Background for Decision

Those who place their faith in the process described — i.e., men who steadfastly attempt to augment their own fragmentary perception of reality by seeking and comprehending the values held by others, men who honestly attempt to integrate even the most intense value conflicts, men who accept as a normal fact of existence the personal tensions inherent in compromise and in problems yet unresolved — can forthrightly face the spiritual implications and tensions of their daily activities. Although burdened by the knowledge that their efforts have been imperfect, they will nevertheless possess the reassurance that they have tried, within the limits of human capabilities, to do God's work in the everyday world. And even more importantly, they will possess a spiritual reservoir that will enable them to continue unceasingly toward the ultimate, though unattainable, goal of perceiving and fulfilling God's reality.

Such men can bring their faith to every situation they encounter, saying:

"I need not fear any situation, any conflicts, any difference in values, or the burden of responsibility. The fact that I have not yet decided what the real problem in the particular circumstances is or that I do not have a ready-made, preconceived solution need not discourage me, for down deep in my heart I know I can draw on the resources of other men's expertness, points of view, and values to assist in reaching a balanced conclusion or plan of action.

"All I need to do is to reach out for these resources, have imagination to comprehend who might have interests or points of view to consider, possess a genuine desire to listen to their contributions with an open mind, have a capacity to articulate the other person's point of view to facilitate exchange of ideas and the consideration of potential solutions or new integrations.

"I will recognize that the foregoing sets a standard of perfection. While I do not expect perfection either in myself or in others, and realize that all of us are less than perfect, I shall be able to live with my imperfect self and my imperfect answers while endeavoring to achieve the perfect goal. I will try to avoid the sin of pride or self-righteousness. I have faith in the process, and in my ability to participate in it in an open-minded way. I have faith that through the exchange of ideas of men with different views it is practicable to achieve better answers than I can achieve alone. I will attempt to fulfill my own personal destiny and do my share of God's work in this world in this way.

"For better or for worse, I, like everyone, must realize my spiritual destiny in connection with my work. I will not find it in some ideal world, detached from reality."

HBR Classic

O. A. Ohmann

'Skyhooks'

With special implications
for Monday through Friday

Foreword

This "HBR Classic" was first published in the May-June 1955 issue of HBR. It won immediate acclaim in the business community and started off a new line of thinking about the nature of effective leadership. When Mr. Ohmann wrote the article, he was Assistant to the President of the Standard Oil Company of Ohio and worked on problems and programs for management development. Now retired from that company and living in Hendersonville, North Carolina, he continues to consult with organizations on questions of management development, and is Director of The Church Executive Development Board, Inc., in New York. Earlier in his career he was head of the Department of Psychology at Cleveland College of Western Reserve University.   *Reprint 70106*

During the last several years, while my principal job assignment has been management development, I have become increasingly impressed with the importance of intangibles in the art of administration. With the managerial revolution of the last generation and the transition from owner-manager to professional executive, there has appeared a growing literature on the science and art of administration. A shift in emphasis is noticeable in these writings over the past 30 years.

Following the early engineering approach typified by the work of Frederick Taylor and others, there next developed a search for the basic principles of organization, delegation, supervision, and control. More recently, as labor relations became more critical, the emphasis has shifted to ways of improving human relations. The approach to the problems of supervisory relationships was essentially a manipulative one. Textbooks on the techniques of personnel management mushroomed. Still later it became more and more apparent that the crux of the problem was the supervisor himself, and this resulted in a flood of "how to improve yourself" books. Meanwhile the complexities of the industrial community increased, and the discontents and tensions mounted.

It seems increasingly clear, at least to me, that while some administrative practices and personnel techniques may be better than others, their futility arises from the philosophical assumptions or value judgments on which this superstructure of manipulative procedure rests. We observe again and again that a manager with sound values and a stewardship conception of his role as boss can be a pretty effective leader even though his techniques are quite unorthodox. I am convinced that workers have a fine sensitivity to spiritual qualities and want to work for a boss who believes in something and in whom they can believe.

This observation leads me to suspect that we may have defined the basic purposes and objectives of our industrial enterprise too narrowly, too selfishly, too materialistically. Bread alone will not satisfy workers. There are some indications that our people have lost faith in the basic values of our economic society, and that we need a spiritual rebirth in industrial leadership.

Certainly no people have ever had so much,

and enjoyed so little real satisfaction. Our economy has been abundantly productive, our standard of living is at an all-time peak, and yet we are a tense, frustrated, and insecure people full of hostilities and anxieties. Can it be that our *god of production* has feet of clay? Does industry need a new religion—or at least a better one than it has had?

I am convinced that the central problem is not the division of the spoils as organized labor would have us believe. Raising the price of prostitution does not make it the equivalent of love. Is our industrial discontent not in fact the expression of a hunger for a work life that has meaning in terms of higher and more enduring spiritual values? How can we preserve the wholeness of the personality if we are expected to worship God on Sundays and holidays and mammon on Mondays through Fridays?

I do not imply that this search for real meaning in life is or should be limited to the hours on the job, but I do hold that the central values of our industrial society permeate our entire culture. I am sure we do not require a bill of particulars of the spiritual sickness of our time. The evidences of modern man's search for his soul are all about us. Save for the communist countries there has been a world-wide revival of interest in religion. The National Council of Churches reports that 59% of our total population (or 92 million) now claim church affiliation. The November 22, 1954 issue of *Barron's* devoted the entire front page to a review of a book by Barbara Ward, *Faith and Freedom.*[1]

Perhaps even more significant is the renaissance in the quality of religious thought and experience. Quite evidently our religion of materialism, science, and humanism is not considered adequate. Man is searching for anchors outside himself. He runs wearily to the periphery of the spider web of his own reason and logic, and looks for new "skyhooks"—for an abiding faith around which life's experiences can be integrated and given meaning.

Why 'skyhooks'?

Perhaps we should assume that this need for "skyhooks" is part of man's natural equipment —possibly a function of his intelligence—or, if you prefer, God manifesting Himself in His creatures. It seems to me, however, that the recent intensification of this need (or perhaps the clearer recognition of it) stems in part from certain broad social, economic, political, and philosophical trends. I shall not attempt a comprehensive treatment of these, but shall allude to only a few.

Abundance without satisfaction: I have already indicated that on the economic front we have won the battle of production. We have moved from an economy of scarcity to one of abundance. We have become masters of the physical world and have learned how to convert its natural resources to the satisfaction of our material wants. We are no longer so dependent and so intimately bound to the world of nature. In a way we have lost our feeling of being part of nature and with it our humble reverence for God's creation.

While the industrialization of our economy resulted in ever-increasing production, it also made of individual man a production number— an impersonal, de-skilled, interchangeable production unit, measured in so many cents per hour. For most employees, work no longer promotes the growth of personal character by affording opportunities for personal decision, exercise of judgment, and individual responsibility. A recent issue of *Nation's Business* quotes the modern British philosopher, Alexander Lindsay, on this point as follows:

"Industrialism has introduced a new division into society. It is the division between those who manage and take responsibility and those who are managed and have responsibility taken from them. This is a division more important than the division between the rich and poor."[2]

Certainly the modern industrial worker has improved his material standard of living at the cost of becoming more and more dependent on larger and larger groups. Not only his dignity but also his security has suffered. And so he reaches out for new "skyhooks"—for something to believe in, for something that will give meaning to his job.

1. New York, W.W. Norton & Company, Inc., 1954.

2. John Kord Lagemann, "Job Enlargement Boosts Production," December 1954, p. 36.

Retrospective commentary

It's time I level with HBR readers about how "Skyhooks" came about. In a very real sense, I did not write it. It came as a stream of consciousness—but only after I had worked very hard for several weeks at putting my ideas together. I wrote the paper mainly to clear my own thinking, and to try it out for criticism on the Cleveland Philosophical Club. After much reading and thinking, I got absolutely nowhere. In desperation I was about to abandon the idea and write on a different subject. Deep inside my consciousness I said in effect to my silent partner within, "Look, if you want me to do this, you better help." About 2 a.m. that morning the ideas flowed in a continuous stream, and I put them down in shorthand notes as fast as I could.

The word "Skyhooks" for the title came in the heat of a discussion with a group of business executives attending the Institute of Humanistic Studies at Aspen, Colorado. As we debated the limits of the rational and scientific approach to life, it occurred to me that science appears rational on the surface, but at its very foundation typically lies a purely intuitive, nonrational assumption made by some scientist. He just hooked himself on a "piece of sky out there" and hung on. It was a complete leap of faith that led him.

In my studies of exceptional executives I had found a mystery not easily explainable by rational elements. These men, too, were hanging on skyhooks of their own—hidden and secret missions which went way beyond their corporate business objectives. Sometimes the mission was a "nutsy" one. Often it had long roots back in the executive's childhood and was emotional, intuitive, beyond rationality, selfless—but it stuck. For example, it might be like John F. Kennedy's determination to become President; reportedly he was doing it for his older brother, who had the ambition to be President but never made it because he was a war casualty.

Or perhaps the mission was like that of the president of one of our largest corporations. When he was 12 years old, his father died. He promised his mother he would help her work the farm in the hills so that his eight younger brothers could go through school. This is what he continued to do all of his life—helping other young men to make something of themselves. He was a great developer of managers.

I could fill a book with such examples. Many great executives I have known have something deep inside that supports them; something they trust when the going gets tough; something ultimate; something personal; something beyond reason—in short, a deep-rooted skyhook which brings them calm and confidence when they stand alone.

There is another interesting aspect to this question. In our rational, analytical, and highly successful Western culture, we have come to place great value on the material gains which represent the end results of our achievements. This is what our kids are complaining about: that we have gone overboard on material values and made a culture of *things*. But the *results* of our strivings are dead works; the life is in the *process* of achieving, in the leap of faith. David was great not when he slew Goliath, but when he decided to try.

So it seems to me that the skyhooks mystique is also characterized by a commitment to value the *process*, the working relationships with others, the spiritual bonds growing out of the faith in the God-potential deep within another person, and the basis of genuine community. The rest is the means, not the end.

In 1955, when my article was published, the generation gap had not been invented, and Marshall McLuhan had not alerted us to the fact that "the medium is the message." Yet a quick look backward reveals the considerable impact of youth and "McLuhanism" on our history and our future. The "McCarthy Kids" have ousted a President and his party, halted the military domination of our foreign policy, radically changed our educational and religious institutions, revised industry's approach to management recruiting, and made the Peace Corps type of job competitive with the "goodies" offered by business. Generalizing about the medium having greater impact than the message, they have pointed out that our values are dictated by our social systems—especially the technological, political, and managerial systems. More important than the things we create in industry, they say, is the *way* we create them—the kind of community we establish in our working together.

Without debating the merits of "pot" versus liquor, or anarchy versus order, I believe their emphasis on social process is introducing a new dimension into our corporate life and values.

"Skyhooks" was written for myself and not for publication. For a while I refused to give anybody a copy, but under pressure I duplicated a small number of copies for my friends, and they wanted copies for their friends. When the Editor of HBR got his copy and asked, "How about publishing it?" I answered, "Only if you take it as it is; I don't want to revise it." I see little need for revising it now—except perhaps the reference (on page 108) to the increase in membership in the institutional church. The search for ultimate values and meanings is keener than in 1955, but it is apparently no longer satisfied merely by church affiliation.

Disillusionment with science: A second trend which seems to bear some relation to our urgent need for a faith grows out of our disillusionment with science. As a result of the rapid advance of science, the curtains of ignorance and superstition have been pulled wide on all fronts of human curiosity and knowledge. Many of the bonds of our intellectual enslavement have been broken. Reason and scientific method were called on to witness to the truth, the whole truth, and nothing but the truth. We were freed from the past—its traditions, beliefs, philosophies, its mores, morals, and religion. Science became our religion, and reason replaced emotion.

However, even before the atom bomb there was a growing realization that science did not represent the whole truth, that with all its pretensions it could be dead wrong, and, finally and particularly, that without proper moral safeguards the truth did not necessarily make men free. Atomic fission intensified the fear and insecurity of every one of us who contemplated the possibility of the concentration of power in the hands of men without morals. We want science to be in the hands of men who not only recognize their responsibility to man-made ethical standards (which are easily perverted) but have dedicated themselves to the eternal and absolute standards of God. Thus, while the evidence of material science has been welcomed, our own personal experiences will not permit us to believe that life is merely a whirl of atoms without meaning, purpose, beauty, or destiny.

Trend toward bigness: A third factor contributing to our insecurity is the trend toward bigness and the resulting loss of individuality. This is the day of bigger and bigger business—in every aspect of life. The small is being swallowed by the big, and the big by the bigger. This applies to business, to unions, to churches, to education, to research and invention, to newspapers, to our practice of the professions, to government, and to nations. Everything is getting bigger except the individual, and he is getting smaller and more insignificant and more dependent on larger social units. Whether we like it or not, this is becoming an administrative society, a planned and controlled society, with ever-increasing concentration of power. This is the day of collectivism and public-opinion polls. It is the day when the individual must be *adjusted to the group*—when he must above all else be sensitive to the feelings and attitudes of others, must get an idea of how others expect him to act, and then react to this.

This is the insecure world which David Riesman has described so well in his book, *The Lonely Crowd*.[3] He pictures man as being no longer "tradition directed" as was primitive man, nor as in Colonial days is he "inner directed" as if by the gyroscope of his own ideals, but today he is "outer directed" as if by radar. He must constantly keep his antenna tuned to the attitudes and reactions of others to him. The shift has been from morals to morale and from self-reliance to dependence on one's peer group. However, the members of one's peer group are each responding to each other. Obviously these shifting sands of public opinion offer no stable values around which life can be consistently integrated and made meaningful. The high-water mark of adjustment in such a society is that the individual be socially accepted and above all else that he appear to be *sincere*.

This is certainly not a favorable environment for the development of steadfast character. It is essentially a neurotic and schizophrenic environment which breeds insecurity.

This socially dependent society also offers an ideal market for the wares of the "huckster," the propagandist, and the demagogue. Lacking a religious interpretation of the divine nature of man, these merchants in mass reaction have sought the least common denominator in human nature and have beamed the movies and newspapers at the ten-year mental level. One wonders if this approach to people does not make them feel that they have been sold short and that they are capable of much better than is expected of them. Has this demoralizing exposure of the cheapness of our values not intensified our search for something better to believe in?

On top of all these disturbing socioeconomic trends came the war. This certainly was materialism, science, and humanism carried to the logical conclusion. The war made us question our values and our direction. It left us less cocksure that we were right, and more fearful of ourselves as well as of others. It made us fearful of the power which we had gained, and led us to search our soul to determine whether we had the moral strength to assume the leadership role that had been given to us. We have been humbled in our efforts to play god and are about ready to give the job back. Note, however, that this is not a characteristic reaction to war. Typically wars have been followed by a noticeable deterioration of moral standards, of traditional values, and of social institutions.

Perhaps none of these rationalizations for our return to religion is entirely valid. I suspect that the search for some kind of overarching integrative principle or idea is the expression of a normal human need. Certainly history would indicate that man's need for a god is eternal even though it may be more keenly sensed in times of adversity. A religion gives a point of philosophical orientation around which life's experiences can be organized and digested. Without the equivalent, a personality cannot be whole and healthy. Short-term goals which need to be shifted with the changing tide do not serve the same integrative function as do the "skyhooks" which are fastened to eternal values. I do not personally regard the current religious revival as a cultural hangover, nor as a regression. Being a mystic I prefer instead to view the need for such a faith as the spark of the Creator in us to drive us on to achieve His will and our own divine destiny.

Why Monday through Friday?

If we may grant for the moment that modern man *is* searching for deeper meanings in life, we may then ask: What has this to do with industry?

3. New Haven, Yale University Press, 1950.

If he needs "skyhooks," let him get them in church, or work out his own salvation. The business leaders of the past insisted that "business is business" and that it had little bearing on the individual's private life and philosophy.

There are several reasons why "skyhooks" must be a primary concern of the business administrator:

☐ For the individual the job is the center of life, and its values must be in harmony with the rest of life if he is to be a whole and healthy personality.

☐ This is an industrial society, and its values tend to become those of the entire culture.

☐ The public is insisting that business leaders are in fact responsible for the general social welfare—that the manager's responsibilities go far beyond those of running the business. They have delegated this responsibility to the business executive whether he wishes to play this role or not.

☐ Even if the administrator insists on a narrow definition of his function as merely the production of goods and services as efficiently as possible, it is nevertheless essential that he take these intangibles into account, since they are the real secrets of motivating an organization.

☐ Besides all this the administrator needs a better set of "skyhooks" himself if he is to carry his ever-increasing load of responsibility without cracking up. The fact that so many administrators are taking time to rationalize, defend, and justify the private enterprise system is an outward indication of this need for more significant meanings.

Anything wrong with capitalism?

We may ask, then: What specifically is wrong with our capitalistic system of private enterprise? What is wrong with production or with trying to improve our present standard of living? What is wrong with a profit, or with private ownership of capital, or with competition? Is this not the true American way of life?

Nothing is necessarily wrong with these values. There are certainly worse motives than the profit motive. A refugee from communism is

reported to have observed: "What a delight to be in the United States, where things are produced and sold with such a nice clean motive as making a profit."

I am not an economist, and it is beyond the scope of this article to attempt a revision of our economic theory. I am tempted, however, to make a couple of observations about these traditional economic concepts:

1. That while the values represented by them are not necessarily wrong, they are certainly pretty thin and do not challenge the best in people.

2. That many of the classical economic assumptions are outmoded and are no longer adequate descriptions of the actual operation of our present-day economy.

For example, the concept of economic man as being motivated by self-interest not only is outmoded by the best current facts of the social sciences, but also fails to appeal to the true nobility of spirit of which we are capable.

The concept of the free and competitive market is a far cry from the highly controlled and regulated economy in which business must operate today. General Motors does not appear to want to put Chrysler out of business, and apparently the union also decided to take the heat off Chrysler rather than to press its economic advantage to the logical conclusion. The assumption that everyone is out to destroy his competitors does not explain the sharing of technology through trade associations and journals. No, we also have tremendous capacity for cooperation when challenged by larger visions. We are daily denying the Darwinian notion of the "survival of the fittest" —which, incidentally, William Graham Sumner, one of the nineteenth-century apologists for our economic system, used for justifying unbridled self-interest and competition.

Certainly the traditional concept of private ownership of capital does not quite correspond to the realities of today's control of large blocks of capital by insurance companies and trusteed funds.

The notion of individual security

through the accumulation of savings has largely given way to the collectivist means of group insurance, company annuities, and Social Security.

The concept that all profits belong to the stockholders is no longer enthusiastically supported by either the government or the unions, since both are claiming an increasing cut.

And so, while we may argue that the system of private enterprise is self-regulatory and therefore offers maximum individual freedom, the simple, cold fact is that it is in ever-increasing degree a managed or controlled economy—partly at the insistence of the voters, but largely as the result of the inevitable economic pressures and the trend toward bigness.[4]

Regardless of the rightness or wrongness of these changes in our system of enterprise, the changes have been considerable, and I doubt that classical economic theory can be used as an adequate rationale of its virtues. I am therefore not particularly optimistic about the efficacy of the current campaign to have businessmen "save the private enterprise system and the American way of life" by engaging in wholesale economic education, much of which is based on outmoded concepts.

Much as economic theory needs revision, I fear that this is not likely to cure our ills. Nor do I believe that profit-sharing or any other device for increasing the workers' cut (desirable as these efforts may be) will give us what we really want. It is, rather, another type of sharing that is needed, a sharing of more worthy objectives, a sharing of the management function, and a sharing of mutual respect and Christian working relationships.

Goals and purposes: What is wrong is more a matter of goals and purposes—of our assumptions about what we are trying to do and how we can dignify and improve ourselves in the doing. There is nothing wrong with production, but we should ask ourselves: *Production for what?* Do we use people for production or produc-

4. See John Kenneth Galbraith, *American Capitalism* (Boston, Houghton Mifflin Company, 1952).

tion for people? How can production be justified if it destroys personality and human values both in the process of its manufacture and by its end use? Clarence B. Randall of Inland Steel, in his book, *A Creed for Free Enterprise*, says:

"We have come to worship production as an end in itself, which of course it is not. It is precisely there that the honest critic of our way of life makes his attack and finds us vulnerable. Surely there must be for each person some ultimate value, some purpose, some mode of self-expression that makes the experience we call life richer and deeper." [5]

So far, so good, Mr. Randall. But now notice how he visualizes industry making its contribution to this worthy objective:

"To produce more and more with less and less effort is merely treading water unless we *thereby release time and energy for the cultivation of the mind and the spirit* and for the achievement of those ends for which Providence placed us on this earth." [6]

Here is the same old dichotomy—work faster and more efficiently so that you can finish your day of drudgery and cultivate your soul on your own time. In fact he says: "A horse with a very evil disposition can nevertheless pull the farmer's plow." No, I am afraid the job *is* the life. *This* is what must be made meaningful. We cannot assume that the end of production justifies the means. What happens to people in the course of producing may be far more important than the end product. Materialism is not a satisfactory "skyhook." People are capable of better and want to do better. (Incidentally, I have the impression that Mr. Randall's practices line up very well with my own point of view even if his words do not.)

Perhaps we should ask: What is the really important difference between Russian communism and our system? Both worship production and are determined to produce more efficiently, and do. Both worship science. Both have tremendously improved the standard of living of their

people. Both share the wealth. Both develop considerable loyalties for their system. (In a mere 40 years since Lenin started the communist revolution a third of the world's people have come to accept its allegiance.) True, in Russia capital is controlled by the state, while here it is theoretically controlled by individuals, although in actual practice, through absentee ownership, it is controlled to a considerable extent by central planning agencies and bureaus, both public and private.

No, the real difference is in the philosophy about people and how they may be used as means to ends. It is a difference in the assumptions made about the origin of rights—whether the individual is endowed with rights by his Creator and yields these only voluntarily to civil authority designated by him, or whether rights originate in force and in the will of the government. Is God a myth, or is He the final and absolute judge to whom we are ultimately responsible? Are all standards of conduct merely man-made and relative, or absolute and eternal? Is man a meaningless happenstance of protoplasm, or is he a divine creation with a purpose, with potential for improvement, and with a special destiny in the overall scheme of things? These are some of the differences—or at least I hope that they still are. And what a difference these intangible, perhaps mythical "skyhooks" make. They are nevertheless the most real and worthwhile and enduring things in the world. The absence of these values permitted the Nazis to "process" people through the gas chambers in order to recover the gold in their teeth.

The administrator contributes

This, then, is part of our general cultural heritage and is passed on to us in many ways. However, it really comes to life in people—in their attitudes, aspirations, and behaviors. And in a managerial society this brings us back to the quality of the individual administrator. He interprets or crystallizes the values and objectives for his group. He sets the climate within which these values either *do* or *do not* become working

realities. He must define the goals and purposes of his group in larger and more meaningful perspective. He integrates the smaller, selfish goals of individuals into larger, more social and spiritual, objectives for the group. He provides the vision without which the people perish. Conflicts are resolved by relating the immediate to the long-range and more enduring values. In fact, we might say this *integrative function* is the core of the administrator's contribution.

The good ones have the mental equipment to understand the business and set sound long-term objectives, but the best ones have in addition the philosophical and character values which help them to relate the overall goals of the enterprise to eternal values. This is precisely the point at which deep-seated religious convictions can serve an integrative function, since they represent the most long-range of all possible goals.[7] Most really great leaders in all fields of human endeavor have been peculiarly sensitive to their historic role in human destiny. Their responsibility and loyalty are to some distant vision which gives calm perspective to the hot issues of the day.

This function of the administrator goes far beyond being a likable personality, or applying correct principles of organization, or being skillful in the so-called techniques of human relations. I am convinced that the difficulties which so many executives have with supervisory relationships cannot be remedied by cultivation of the so-called human relations skills. These difficulties spring, rather, from one's conception of his function or role as a boss, his notion about the origin and nature of his authority over others, the assumptions he makes about people and their worth, and his view of what he and his people are trying to accomplish together. To illustrate:

If, for example, my personal goal is to get ahead in terms of money,

5. Boston, Little, Brown and Company, 1952, p. 16.

6. Ibid.

7. For further elaboration, see Gordon W. Allport, *The Individual and His Religion* (New York, The Macmillan Company, 1953).

position, and power; and if I assume that to achieve this I must best my competitors; that the way to do this is to establish a good production record; that my employees are means to this end; that they are replaceable production units which must be skillfully manipulated; that this can be done by appealing to the lowest form of immediate selfish interest; that the greatest threat to me is that my employees may not fully recognize my authority or accept my leadership—if these are my values, then I am headed for trouble—all supervisory techniques notwithstanding.

I wish I could be quite so positive in painting the picture of the right values and approaches to management. I suspect there are many, many different right answers. No doubt each company or enterprise will have to define its own long-term purposes and develop its own philosophy in terms of its history, traditions, and its real function in our economy. I am also certain that no one philosophy would be equally useful to all managers. The character of an organization is, to a large extent, set by the top man or the top group, and it is inevitable that this be the reflection of the philosophy of these individuals. No one of us can operate with another's philosophy. I have also observed that in most enterprises the basic faith or spirit of the organization is a rather nebulous or undefined something which nevertheless has very profound meaning to the employees.

A successful executive: Recognizing then the futility of advocating any one pattern of values, it occurs to me that it might, however, be suggestive or helpful if I told you something of the philosophy of one extremely successful executive whom I have pumped a good deal on this subject (for he is more inclined to live his values than to talk about them):

As near as I can piece it together, he believes that this world was not an accident but was created by God and that His laws regulate and control the universe and that we are ultimately *responsible to Him*. Man,

as God's supreme creation, is in turn endowed with creative ability. Each individual represents a unique combination of talents and potentials. In addition, man is the only animal endowed with freedom of choice and with a high capacity for making value judgments. With these gifts (of heredity and cultural environment) goes an obligation to give the best possible accounting of one's stewardship in terms of maximum self-development and useful service to one's fellows in the hope that one may live a rich life and be a credit to his Creator.

This executive also assumes that each individual possesses certain God-given rights of self-direction which only *the individual* can voluntarily delegate to others in authority over him, and that this is usually done in the interest of achieving some mutual cooperative good. The executive therefore assumes that his *own* authority as boss over others must be exercised with due regard for the attendant obligations to his employees and to the stockholders who have temporarily and voluntarily yielded their rights in the interest of this common undertaking. (Notice that he does not view his authority as originating with or derived from his immediate superior.) This delegated authority must, of course, be used to advance the common good rather than primarily to achieve the selfish ambitions of the leader at the expense of the led.

He further assumes that the voluntary association of employees in industry is for the purpose of increasing the creativity and productivity of all members of the group and thus of bringing about increased benefits to all who may share in the ultimate use of these goods and services. What is equally important, however, is that in the course of this industrial operation each individual should have an opportunity to develop the maximum potential of his skills and that the working relationships should not destroy the individual's ability to achieve his greatest maturity and richness of experience. As supervisor he must set the working conditions and atmosphere which will make it possible for his employees to achieve

this dual objective of increasing productivity and maximizing self-development.

These goals can best be achieved by giving employees maximum opportunity to exercise their capacity for decision making and judgment within their assigned area of responsibility. The supervisor is then primarily a coach who must instruct, discipline, and motivate all the members of the group, making it possible for each to exercise his special talent in order to maximize the total team contribution. Profits are regarded as a measure of the group's progress toward these goals, and a loss represents not only an improper but even an immoral use of the talents of the group.

There is nothing "soft" about his operation. He sets high quality standards and welcomes stiff competition as an additional challenge to his group. He therefore expects and gets complete cooperation and dedication on the part of everyone. Incidentally, he views the activity of working together in this manner with others as being one of life's most rewarding experiences. He holds that this way of life is something which we have not yet fully learned, but that its achievement is part of our divine destiny. He is firmly convinced that such conscientious efforts *will* be rewarded with success. He manages with a light touch that releases creativity, yet with complete confidence in the outcome.

This is probably a poor attempt at verbalizing the basic philosophy which this man lives so easily and naturally. I hope, however, that it has revealed something of his conception of his role or function as an executive, and his view of what he and his organization are trying to do together. With this account of his values I am sure that you would have no difficulty completing the description of his administrative practices and operating results. They flow naturally from his underlying faith, without benefit of intensive training in the principles and art of administration.

As you would suspect, people like to work for him—or with him. He attracts good talent (which is one of the real secrets of success). Those with shoddy values, selfish ambitions, or character defects do not survive—the organization is self-pruning. Those who remain develop rapidly because they learn to accept responsibility. He not only advocates but practices decentralization and delegation. His employees will admit that they have made mistakes, but usually add with a grin that they try not to make the same one twice. People respond to his leadership because he has faith in them and expects the best in them rather than the worst. He speaks well of the members of his organization, and they appear to be proud of each other and of their record of performance. He takes a keen interest in developing measurements of performance and in bettering previous records or competitive standards. He feels that no one has a right to "louse up a job"—a point on which he feels the stockholders and the Lord are in complete agreement.

While he does not talk much about "employee communications" or stress formal programs of this type, his practice is to spend a large proportion of his time in the field with his operating people rather than in his office. He is "people oriented," and he does a particularly good job of listening. The union committee members have confidence in his fairness, yet do a workmanlike job of bargaining. In administering salaries he seems to be concerned about helping the individual to improve his contribution so that a pay increase can be justified.

In his general behavior he moves without haste or hysteria. He is typically well organized, relaxed, and confident, even under trying circumstances. There is a high degree of consistency in his behavior and in the quality of his decisions because his basic values do not shift. Since he does not operate by expediency, others can depend on him; and this consistency makes for efficiency in the discharge of delegated responsibility. Those operating problems which do come to him for decision seem to move easily and quickly to a conclusion. His long-term values naturally express themselves in well-defined policies, and it is against this frame of reference that the decisions of the moment easily fall into proper perspective.

In policy-level discussions his contributions have a natural quality of objectivity because "self-concern" does not confuse. Others take him at face value because his motives are not suspect. When differences or conflicts do arise, his approach is not that of compromise; rather, he attempts to integrate the partisan views around mutually acceptable longer-range goals. The issues of the moment then seem to dissolve in a discussion of the best means to the achievement of the objective. I have no doubt that he also has some serious problems, but I have tried to give a faithful account of the impression which he creates. There is a *sense of special significance* about his operation which is shared by his associates.

This is the key

It is precisely this "sense of special significance" which is the key to leadership. We all know that there are many different ways of running a successful operation. I am certainly not recommending any particular set of administrative practices—although admittedly some are better than others. Nor am I suggesting that his set of values should be adopted by others, or for that matter could be. What I am saying is that a man's real values have a subtle but inevitable way of being communicated, and they affect the significance of everything he does.

These are the vague intangibles—the "skyhooks"—which are difficult to verbalize but easy to sense and tremendously potent in their influence. They provide a different, invisible, fundamental structure into which the experiences of every day are absorbed and given meaning. They are frequently unverbalized, and in many organizations they defy definition. Yet they are the most real things in the world.

The late Jacob D. Cox, Jr., formerly president of Cleveland Twist Drill Company, told a story that illustrates my point:

Jimmy Green was a new union committee member who stopped in to see Mr. Cox after contract negotiations had been concluded. Jimmy said that every other place he had worked, he had always gone home grouchy; he never wanted to play with the children or take his wife to the movies. And then he said, "But since I have been working here, all that has changed. Now when I come home, the children run to meet me and we have a grand romp together. It is a wonderful difference and I don't know why, but I thought you would like to know." [8]

As Mr. Cox observed, there must be a lot of Jimmy Greens in the world who want an opportunity to take part freely in a cooperative effort that has a moral purpose.

8. *Material Human Progress* (Cleveland, Cleveland Twist Drill Company, 1954), p. 104.

- Sundays *and* weekdays —
- At home *and* at work —
- In principle *and* in practice —

Can the Businessman Apply Christianity?

By Harold L. Johnson

Some critics maintain that the fundamental religious tradition in this country — Judaeo-Christianity — is simply not applicable to the day-to-day problems of a business office. While these people may agree with the position taken by Thomas C. Campbell, Jr., in his article on "Capitalism and Christianity" in HBR July–August 1957, to the effect that there is no inherent *conflict* between the values of religion and the values of an economic system, they claim that the individual businessman can find no *guidelines* in the specific doctrines on which most of our nation's religious creeds are based.

This may seem surprising in the face of what has been characterized as a "spiritual reawakening" in the United States today. After all, the United States is generally regarded as a Christian nation. Our coins declare "In God We Trust," and public school classes and even football games often open with prayer. Most Americans express a belief in some kind of God; and if church membership is any evidence, the country surely should be classified as Christian. Over 100 million of the population, or about 60% of the total, are members of churches or synagogues. Furthermore, the percentage of the population with church membership has risen to the highest on record in the postwar "return" to religion.

Nevertheless, as one study indicates, "religion plays little part, or at least at the conscious level, in the decisions" made by individuals [1]; and many churchgoers seem unaware of the relevance of their religion to the problems and decisions which confront them daily. Similarly, students of American business in analyzing the "American business creed" have concluded that "the creed bows to the importance of religion, admits seeking religious guidance, but continues to be a predominantly secular ideology." [2]

Operating Guide

To my mind, this is most unfortunate because Christian doctrines do, in fact, offer a perspective from which to view modern commercial life, and this perspective *can make a difference* in the decisions and actions of businessmen. They are relevant in that they can help him choose the "best" (not necessarily the "correct") alternative in a given situation. Some theologians call this the "always dramatic interaction between God and man," while an occasional businessman points out that religion is not just a Sunday matter but an operating guide in the complexities of daily living. [3]

I want to demonstrate this point by taking several basic articles of doctrine and relating them to business life. In doing so, I shall reflect my own experience and my own convic-

[1] Marquis W. Childs and Douglass Cater, *Ethics In A Business Society* (New York, New American Library of World Literature, 1954), pp. 173-174.

[2] Francis X. Sutton et al., *The American Business Creed*

(Cambridge, Harvard University Press, 1956), p. 269.

[3] See O. A. Ohmann, " 'Skyhooks' (With Special Implications for Monday Through Friday)," HBR May–June 1955, p. 33.

Reprint 57505

tions, but many of the ideas expressed stem from the thinking and discussion in which I participated at a two-week seminar at the Harvard Business School. Here, under the sponsorship of the Danforth Foundation, businessmen, educators, and religious leaders have been brought together during the last two summers for the specific purpose of tackling business-religious problems on the realistic basis of actual case situations. To me, just this demonstration of the fact that men feel the need to increase understanding in this area is itself of the highest significance.

No Clear Blueprint

The application of religion's ultimate insights to specific situations is, of course, a tremendously difficult task. There are no blueprints, no simple rules to go by. Christianity does not present the executive with a tool kit of easy-to-use rules and precepts by which problems can be solved. The doctrines are not bound up in a simple list of "dos" and "don'ts" somewhat in the style of a book of etiquette, which if followed will result in harmonious, gentlemanly relations within and without a business.

But it does offer a *frame of reference,* a universe view, which instead of giving peace of mind and easy success in human relations often breaches the barricade of self-assurance, focuses on difficulties, and erases naive hopes of business progress ever onward, ever upward.

This frame of reference is constructed from specific Christian ideas. Accordingly, let us look at several of these articles of doctrine — the concepts of God, creation, man, sin, forgiveness, and Christian vocation — and indicate how each furnishes insights into problems and actions confronting businessmen.

The Concept of God

One of the distinguishing features of Western civilization is a belief in the order and plan of the universe, which comes, Christians and Jews affirm, from God. But what other factors enter into the Judaeo-Christian understanding of the nature and character of the Supreme Being? While mystery shrouds this question, so that we "see only darkly," most of us in some

sense agree that God is a personal, transcendent Being whose nature is revealed to us in the life of Jesus.

The words *personal* and *Being* are extremely significant, for they are used to imply, not an anthropomorphic concept, but rather that God is closely connected with human life. They mean that God exists, not as a process working through history — though God does work in history — but as a reality that *cares for* and *is concerned about* the past, present, and future of human existence. The God of Christian and Jew is an Almighty Father who exists and who loves all his children with a divine passion: "Praise the Lord, all nations! . . . For great is his steadfast love toward us; and the faithfulness of the Lord endures forever." [4]

God is also transcendent. He is the Absolute, above and beyond human processes and problems. "With men it is impossible, but not with God; for all things are possible with God." [5] As the Supreme Reality, God stands at the center of existence, the Ultimate by which all things are judged and evaluated.

Temperature Test

But what is the significance of these observations concerning God for the businessman? Very simply, they place everything human under the rule of God, warning against the idolatry of putting the business firm, the nation, "free private enterprise," or the career at the center of life. With such a perspective, all things pertaining to business stand under the judgment of God as *limited* goals and loyalties.

If, however, we accept the definition of religion as "man's profoundest solicitude about the things he counts most valuable," [6] then in all honesty it must be stated that for many businessmen the worship of God is not the center or focus of their religion. According to one leading churchman, the "god" of an individual can be determined by the use of a "temperature test"; that is, *the* concept, goal, or loyalty which gets people most excited, wrought up, and agitated is *their* "Supreme Being." [7] Application of such a test undoubtedly would reveal a variety of personal idols for business executives: the enterprises for which they have labored for years, the economic order which has given them

[4] Psalms 50:14-15. (All scriptural citations will be from the Revised Standard Version of the *Holy Bible* unless otherwise noted.)

[5] Mark 10:27.

[6] Ralph Barton Perry, quoted in Alexander Miller, *The Renewal of Man* (Garden City, New York, Doubleday & Co., 1955), p. 43.

[7] James Luther Adams, "A Faith for Free Men," *Together We Advance,* edited by S. H. Fritchman (Boston, The Beacon Press, 1946), pp. 45–65.

and their nation so much in material goods, or the goal of becoming the most noted men in their industries.

Many investigators have testified to the company-centered frame of reference so common among executives today. As Howard R. Bowen has put it in his *Social Responsibilities of the Businessman*:

"It [the corporation] is an object which has needs and aspirations, which experiences many of the vicissitudes of life, and to which one can give selfless devotion and unswerving loyalty. Moreover, the manager thinks of the corporation as having a kind of immortality in that it goes on — or should go on — indefinitely into the future. He thinks of his own leadership of it as temporary. One of his deepest concerns is to see that it prospers under his care. . . . This description of the manager's attitude suggests an almost mystical relationship between him and the corporation." [8]

With the Judaeo-Christian view of God, the totality of individual *and social or institutional* existence comes under judgment and evaluation. Even the economic system of "free business enterprise" — or any other economic order for that matter — falls under the scrutiny and creative criticism of a biblical perspective. This questioning of "free enterprise" is particularly pertinent for these times, for while some businessmen appear to put the corporation at the center of their personal faith, others seem to worship the economic system. Their creed embraces a complex of beliefs, which laud individualism, private property, competition, and a relatively laissez-faire economic order. Judging by the temperature test, the "devils" of this creed are high taxes, government encroachment, and creeping socialism.

Faith in the corporation, in one's career, or in free enterprise, of course, is no more clearly antireligious than the communists' fanatical abjuration of everything except materialism. Both are idolatrous; both commit the fundamental sin of the Judaeo-Christian faith — putting man and man's values in the place of God.

Needless to say, businessmen are not the only individuals ignoring the biblical admonition, "Thou shalt have no other gods before me"; for self-centeredness is a universal human characteristic.

All of us, then, must answer the same dread question: "What has *first* priority for me?" or "In this particular pricing or personnel or financing decision, what is my *ultimate* criterion — my own career, the enterprise, the system, or what?" The Christian concept of God provides real help as we formulate a reply.

The Doctrine of Creation

The doctrine of creation is of profound interest, for it supports the position that God may be found in the issues and problems of economic life. According to the writer of Genesis, "In the beginning God created the heavens *and the earth*. . . . And God saw everything that he had made, and behold, it was very good." [9] The biblical view of creation, then, is not that things of the spirit or of heaven are "good" while material things are "evil," as in the thinking of ascetic mysticism. There is not a gulf between things of the spirit or of God and the world which he created. God, on the contrary, created *both* heaven and earth and found *both* good. Furthermore, according to the Scriptures, God instructed man to subdue the earth and to have dominion over it. [10]

The Christian perspective, then, does not treat material goods and services — the peculiar domain of the businessman — as inherently evil and sinful. In fact, God gave specific instructions to man for the use and development of goods and services.

Many religious critics, however, have couched their onslaught against a business civilization in the terms of antimaterialism, implying that religious and spiritual values are somehow incompatible with new automobiles, television sets, and fresh-frozen lobster claws. [11] Even businessmen seem often to feel that because they deal particularly with the material, worldly goods of this life, *ipso facto* they fall short of the Kingdom of God. But, as Alexander Miller makes abundantly clear, Christianity and Judaism are not world-renouncing religions. He states:

"[There is in the Hebrew attitude] . . . a lip-smacking, exuberant delight in the ingenious beauty and variety of the created world; in wine and milk, oil-olive and honey. It is a world whose paths drop fatness, where the little hills rejoice on every side. Such a world has a place for heroism, but none for asceticism." [12]

[8] New York, Harper & Brothers, 1953, p. 87.
[9] Genesis 1:31 (italics added).
[10] Genesis 1:28.

[11] See J. D. Glover, *The Attack on Big Business* (Boston, Division of Research, Harvard Business School, 1954).
[12] Alexander Miller, op. cit., p. 54.

Corporation executives are counseled, consequently, by the doctrine of creation that they are doing work which does not inevitably have the taint of sin — that in their production, pricing, and sales decisions they *may* be doing the will of God.

Another aspect of the doctrine of creation which is significant for Christian executives is the concept of stewardship. As a matter of fact, "the most radical theory" of property known stems from the Christian view of creation.[13] According to this view man owns nothing. As presented in a recent National Council of Churches statement, "All resources of the earth . . . are gifts of God . . . and God is the only absolute owner."[14] The "temporal owner" of labor, capital, or natural resources, accordingly, is a trustee or steward of such property for God and for his fellow man. The businessman, while given rights and powers to use resources by earthly laws of contract and sales, is responsible to others for the actions and policies of the enterprise which he helps administer.

This concept of Christian stewardship provides part of the religious underpinnings for the philosophy of "social responsibility" that many businessmen espouse. This approach to business affairs requires managers to weigh the impact of their policies on the many interest groups, including the community at large, which are affected by the enterprise. The stewardship concept ties this "balancing of interests" to responsibility to God and, as a consequence of that responsibility, also to fellow man.

The Nature of Man

The nature of man as postulated by Christian doctrine is highly relevant to the problems of the administrator. According to Christian tradition, man is a complex of conflicting, opposing attributes. He is capable of approaching the infinite; yet he is sinful. He is created in the image of God; yet he is inherently imperfect. Jehovah and Satan both are part of his being. Let us look first at the God-like side.

Man the Angel

The Genesis story tells us that "God created man in his own image, in the image of God he created him."[15] The story makes clear, in addition, that man is worthy — and able — to commune and converse with God. The whole flow of the Scriptures emphasizes this close linkage between human beings and Ultimate Reality. The significance of man in Christian belief is, perhaps, best typified in the famous Old Testament song:

"When I look at thy heavens, the work of thy fingers, and the moon and the stars which thou hast established; what is man that thou art mindful of him, and the son of man that thou dost care for him? *Yet thou hast made him little less than God,* and dost crown him with glory and honor. Thou hast given him dominion over the works of thy hands."[16]

Thus one side of the Christian view of man declares that man is full of dignity and able to do extraordinary things, even though he is a finite being. As one writer states:

"Man, in the Christian view, has not been placed in the universe as one thing among other things. He is not, for weal or woe, installed in a ready-made world; he co-operates in its genesis."[17]

But what significance does this observation have for the businessman of today? It suggests that the real explanation for the remarkable modern developments in science, technology, and administration lies in the fact that God made men able to exert such force in the universe. This view suggests, more specifically, that men have been equipped with the physical, intellectual, and moral capacities for solving the involved economic and business problems that face them.

How often do we stand appalled at the size of the task which confronts us? And how frequently does our very anxiety about our competence to handle it — alone or in cooperation with others — weaken or even wash out our efforts? Braced by an innate confidence in the power of human beings, and therefore in our own power, we can face complex decisions boldly and make them effectively.

Further, a basic confidence in our fellow man, coupled with a continuing effort to judge just where his greatest competencies lie, provides a frame of reference for personnel deci-

[13] Quoted from the commentary by F. Ernest Johnson in Howard R. Bowen, op. cit., p. 244.

[14] *Christian Principles and Assumptions for Economic Life,* statement adopted by the General Board of the National Council of the Churches of Christ in the U.S.A.,

September 15, 1954 (New York, 1954), p. 2.

[15] Genesis 1:27.

[16] Psalms 8:3–6 (italics added).

[17] J. H. Oldham, *Work in Modern Society* (New York, Morehouse-Gorham Co., Inc., 1950), p. 36.

sions. Executives are constantly called on to take gambles in situations where a man must be chosen to do a job. It is helpful to have a guideline: "Play it safe; do not trust the man," or "Believe in him, and he will measure up." Christian doctrine urges us to err on the side of confidence, not mistrust. As Donald K. David, former dean of the Harvard Business School, has observed:

"Without delegation so extensive that it involves real risk — the placing of bets on people's ability — individuals in an organization cannot develop the competence which makes delegation possible. We begin to believe that delegation better serves its purpose when we take chances on subordinates than when we hesitate for fear they will fall short."[18]

Finally, confidence in his fellows encourages a man to make vast concessions of personal pride and status in his effort to understand another's viewpoint. Needless to say, this does not involve the obligation to agree with his antagonist; indeed, the clearer his understanding grows, the more he may disagree. However, the thrust of his effort will be to understand, to consider, and to judge fairly.

Man the Devil

The Christian understanding of man does not end, however, with a being possessing tremendous creative capacities; it goes on to encompass a being with an inevitable tendency "to sin and fall short of the glory of God."

For the Christian, sin is the "moral evil that lies at the juncture of nature and Spirit."[19] This is not the black-and-white perspective, referred to above, which summarily tags all material matters evil and all spiritual things divine; nor is it equivalent to the oft-stated modern idea that there is no sin. In some current ideology, all the difficulties and calamities of the world are said to arise simply from ignorance or misshapen institutions. This modern rationale optimistically contends that all problems can be removed by education, moralizing, or revisions in the institutional framework of society.

The dualistic viewpoint offers no hope whatever for those of us who are involved deeply in the material aspect of living. The Christian view, on the other hand, places sin at the spiritual core of man. In Reinhold Niebuhr's words:

"But man is destined, both by the imperfections of his knowledge and by his desire to overcome his finiteness, to make absolute claims for his partial and finite values. He tries, in short, to make himself God."[20]

This Christian admission that man is sinful, and inevitably trying to puff up his own importance, serves as a warning to ambitious executives who are advancing through the hierarchy of an industrial organization to positions of responsibility and prestige. Almost inevitably, such individuals will assume exaggerated views of their abilities, judgments, and contributions to the enterprise of which they are a part. These inflated self-appraisals may be a particular occupational disease of men in positions of responsibility, and cannot help but affect their behavior and their decision making.

But the doctrine of sin issues a warning to managers at all levels that their self-interest and pride are often woven into the fabrics of their judgments and policies even though they may firmly believe their policies to be objective and impartial:

❡ Plant managers may suggest a program of expansion and modernization, characterizing it as essential for company health, when the strength of their interest actually stems from their desire to enlarge their own areas of control.

❡ Other company executives may stress that their "socially responsible" philosophy works to the general benefit; yet basically such a philosophy may be a subtle device to maintain economic power in their own hands by extending their influence and decision-making power into so many nonbusiness areas that they become benevolent dictators.

❡ Other managers may support mammoth advertising expenditures and rapid model changes as "in the public interest" since they foster a high level of employment and national income, while the real objective may be to reduce competition and increase company net revenue.

❡ Corporations may give funds to charitable or educational institutions and may argue for them as great humanitarian deeds, when in fact they are simply trying to buy community good will.

A Clouded Future

The concept of sin, furthermore, cautions against an easy optimism that business enterprises are going to solve all their problems, establishing "big happy families" of employees,

[18] *The Management Team,* edited by Edward C. Bursk (Cambridge, Harvard University Press, 1954), p. 4.
[19] Reinhold Niebuhr, *An Interpretation of Christian Ethics* (New York, Meridian Books, Inc., 1956), p. 81.
[20] Ibid., p. 82.

employers, consumers, and suppliers. Failures, mistakes, and antagonisms, according to a Christian calculation, will always characterize company operations despite "human relations" or "social responsibility" or "professional management," or any other expanding concept. Of course, new ways of looking at and doing things may lessen tensions and reduce problems to more manageable proportions. But no manager should expect, even subconciously, that they will give him a problemless world.

The excessive optimism of many business executives crops up in the widely held, somewhat mystical, belief that free enterprise, if left alone, will build a "heavenly city" on earth and produce a steadily expanding standard of living for all. By the same token, some businessmen talk as though each American family will have three cars in every garage, color television, electronic cooking, and a helicopter in the back yard if only it will accept, unchallenged, "sensible business leadership." And indeed there seems to be a considerable amount of evidence to support this point of view. The Christian concept of man, however, balances these calculations of progress ever onward with the warning that incomplete knowledge, self-centeredness, and faulty institutional patterns mean that the future, though it can be better than the present, holds continued conflict, problems, and stupidity.

Finally, the businessman who understands the doctrine of sin will not be so shocked and self-righteous when he perceives the "taint of corruption" in others, because he will know it exists in his own heart as well. He will be less resentful of the checks and balances against his own power, economic and otherwise, in modern society and will accept the need for "countervailing power," competition, or government action to help him keep his own company in line. He will be cautious about attacking the other party in labor negotiations as "selfish" or "hypocritical," because he will be conscious of these same weaknesses in his position. Incidentally, if more controversies with unions were carried out in that way, we might not usher in a new era of brotherly love, but tensions would be lowered and solutions more easily found.

The Doctrine of Forgiveness

The biblical picture of man as a creature of basic contradictions means that he will inevitably sin and cannot, by his own efforts, keep himself from so doing. Alone, human beings are unable to cure this disease of the spirit. As Alexander Miller states, "The human dilemma . . . calls not for a resolve but for a rescue." [21]

The Christian believes that this rescue is effected by the forgiving love of God as witnessed in the life and death of Jesus Christ. "But God shows his love for us in that while we were yet sinners Christ died for us." [22] The doctrine of forgiveness also suggests that, as God forgives human beings, so should they forgive one another. But not everyone can forgive; the gift can be given only by —

". . . those who know that they are not good, who feel themselves in need of divine mercy, who live in a dimension deeper and higher than that of moral idealism, feel themselves as well as their fellow man convicted of sin by a holy God and know that the differences between the good man and bad man are insignificant in his sight." [23]

The concept of forgiveness has many applications for the business manager beyond the obvious one of overlooking or forgetting the errors and slights of others which are so much a part of the business day.

It provides a constant reminder that men cannot be expected to make basic changes in their methods and attitudes without help from the outside. It does little good to tell a subordinate, "You simply *must* be more careful about the figures in your reports"; part of the executive's task is to help the man improve, by training, by closer supervision, or even — if the situation seems hopeless and yet the man is too valuable to lose — by moving him over into a job that he can handle.

Faith and hope in divine forgiveness offer an additional insight to businessmen in the throes of decision making. How often managers have to devise solutions to problems with only incomplete and often erroneous data available! How often an administrator is all too conscious of conflicting goals and of conflicting group interests!

Even with today's advanced analytical tools, uncertainty remains a basic characteristic of business operations. Furthermore, moral dilemmas cannot be fed into an electronic data-processing machine; in many situations all the available alternatives seem to have serious ethical

[21] Alexander Miller, op. cit., p. 59.
[22] Romans 5:8.
[23] Reinhold Niebuhr, op. cit., pp. 203–204.

deficiencies which do not yield to a slide rule. For example:

❧ In deciding whether to lay off a portion of a labor force, managers are acutely aware that keeping the men employed may endanger the financial health of the entire organization, jeopardizing the economic interests of customers, suppliers, other employees, stockholders, and the community at large. At the same time, they well appreciate the hardships that will be visited on the men who are let go.

❧ In the presentation of information about a product for advertising purposes, executives may be concerned about statements which are factually or legally correct but are designed to mislead the potential customer and stimulate him to think something which is not true. Company officials may fear, on the other hand, that if such advertising practices are not used, revenues will decline to the point where many individuals depending on the sales success of the company are likely to suffer.

Thus, businessmen contend constantly with problems in which every available proposal is obviously less than perfect. In these circumstances, the concept of a forgiving God is sorely needed. As Miller states:

"And since our grasp of the faith is always unsure and our mastery of the facts always partial and limited; since we can neither assess our motives with confidence nor calculate consequences with certainty, we are cast in the end always on the forbearance and forgiveness of God." [24]

Administrators and other men of decision consequently find the doctrine of forgiveness a peculiar blessing. While reliance on a forbearing Ultimate to pardon faulty human actions easily can serve as a rationalization for shallow, selfish decisions, it does give men the courage to attempt the formation and execution of policies about complex matters. The alternatives to this approach to problem solving are twofold: (1) Businessmen can withdraw from points of decision — which is impossible, after all, for they cannot abdicate altogether from the human race. Or (2) they can cynically ignore their spiritual deficiencies, shortages of information, and conflicting goals, and use their power to make their decisions stick. Neither of these alternatives is a live option for managers imbued with a Christian outlook on life.

Christian Vocation

The doctrine of Christian vocation is based on the "call" issued to man by a forgiving and merciful God "to repentance and faith and to a life of fellowship and service in the Church." [25] It is a call to rebirth and transformation, assuring mortals that the Ultimate will accept them into His Kingdom and save them from the self-centeredness of mortal perspectives and motivations. "Behold your God will come with vengeance with the recompense of God. He will come and save you." [26] [God] saved us and called us to a holy calling, not in virtue of our works but in virtue of his own purpose and the grace which he gave us in Christ Jesus." [27]

While this summons to salvation may have otherworldly implications, it is clearly a challenge to change in orientation and attitude here and now. "The kingdom of God is not coming with visible display, and so people will not say, 'Look! Here it is,' nor 'There it is,' for the kingdom of God is within you." [28] It is clear, furthermore, that the call is not to any particular occupational position such as sales manager, plumber, or accountant, but rather to a personal revolution which puts God at the center of existence:

"The Bible knows no instance of a man's being called to an earthly profession or trade by God. St. Paul, for example, is called by God to be an apostle, he is not 'called' to be a tent-maker. . . .
"We cannot with propriety speak of God's calling a man to be an engineer or a doctor or a schoolmaster. God calls doctors and engineers and schoolmasters to be prophets, evangelists, pastors and teachers as laymen in His Church. . . ." [29]

The first aspect, then, of a conception of Christian vocation is a sense of reformation of "one's whole heart and mind and soul into a new relationship with God who continually seeks us out." [30]

With rebirth as a saved person, according to the Christian, comes a tremendous sense of

[24] Alexander Miller, op. cit., p. 101.
[25] Alan Richardson, *The Biblical Doctrine of Work* (London, Student Christian Movement Press, Ltd., 1952), p. 35.
[26] Isaiah 35:46.
[27] I Timothy 1:9.

[28] Luke 17:20-21, *The New Testament, A Private Translation in the Language of the People*, translated by Charles B. Williams (Chicago, Moody Press, 1949).
[29] Alan Richardson, op. cit., pp. 35, 36.
[30] Albert Terril Rasmussen, *Christian Social Ethics* (Englewood Cliffs, N. J., Prentice-Hall, Inc., 1956), p. 266.

gratitude and, consequently, a sense of responsibility to God for this salvation. Miller describes this aspect of the doctrine of Christian vocation as follows:

"The man who acknowledges himself debtor to God is committed to serve him in the midst of the world. He accepts a new *Stand* — a new status of responsibility — in relation to other men. He is not only called into the community of God's debtors, but he is called to serve God in the total community of mankind. . . . He may be at once a church official, citizen, a cobbler, and the father of a family. This matrix of obligation defines the form of his earthly vocation as it derives from his heavenly citizenship, his status as a forgiven sinner." [31]

Thus while the Christian is not called to be a cobbler or a corporation vice president, the free gift of the Kingdom of God prompts gratitude and responsibility, which overflow into his "earthly" work as a citizen, company official, and father. The impact of the call to God's Kingdom is felt thereby in the social, political, and economic relationships in which he lives.

A second meaningful feature of the doctrine of vocation relates to work as the divine ordinance for man. Before "the fall of man into sin," according to the Genesis story, man was to "fill the earth and subdue it; and . . . have dominion over . . . every living thing that moves upon the earth." [32] Man was put in the Garden of Eden "to till and keep it." [33] As Richardson notes, biblical writers expound "the notion of man's ordinary, everyday, routine labour" as "the normal, fitting and inevitable lot of mankind." [34] Richardson concludes, "The teaching of the Old Testament on the subject of work may be generally summed by saying that it is a necessary and indeed God-appointed function of human life." [35]

The two Reformation thinkers, Luther and Calvin, further emphasize the importance of work, stressing that even mundane labor may be a place for service to God and man. Luther agreed, "a cobbler, a smith, and a farmer, each has the work of his trade, yet they are all alike consecrated priests and bishops." [36] Professor Rasmussen in summarizing the Reformation contribution to the doctrine states that "all work — worthy of doing at all — is a responsible ministry, elevated to an ordination of service to God and to neighbor." [37]

How does this idea of Christian vocation apply to the executive? There are many ways; here are several of them:

❡ The concept of vocation imposes a special set of motivations on business managers. Service to God and consequently service to the many individuals affected by the enterprise is the Christian mainspring of action, rather than accumulations of status, prestige, dollars, or power.

Since one task is as important as another from the Christian viewpoint of vocation, the businessman is obligated to respect the work of factory, mine, and office, as well as his own function. Further, he should make an effort to endow it with dignity and social usefulness.

The social necessity of many executive positions is readily apparent to most observers, for the coordination, management, and planning of enterprise forms an essential part of large-scale industrial operations. But a similar sense of dignity and importance is usually denied to those who work on small parts of a productive process, tabulating figures in a ledger or performing a single act on an assembly line.

The doctrine of vocation implies, then, that the business manager has the responsibility to show individuals the worthwhileness of their labor. And, further, he ought to be actively concerned about upgrading it, making it more interesting, providing the maximum opportunities for personal fulfillment both in the job itself and in the work environment.

❡ It raises disturbing questions about some types of business activity which, perhaps, cannot qualify as work consecrated to God and to fellow man. The element of dignity and social utility of labor may be difficult to uncover in some types of advertising, for instance, which are based on the assumption that human beings are stupid and gullible. Advertising stressing "extraordinary" differences between brands of gasoline or of cigarettes in the face of laboratory evidence that such differences do not exist hardly comes under the heading of social usefulness. Advertising practices and rapid model obsolescence which accentuate acquisitive and conspicuous consumption tendencies of Americans, likewise, may not qualify as important work, even though such practices may be cloaked in arguments about the "public interest."

❡ Still another implication from this doctrine of Christian vocation strikes one with real force: God

---

[31] Alexander Miller, op. cit., p. 148.
[32] Genesis 1:28.
[33] Genesis 2:15.
[34] Alan Richardson, op. cit., p. 21.

[35] Ibid., p. 23.
[36] Martin Luther quoted in Albert Terril Rasmussen, op. cit., p. 267.
[37] Albert Terril Rasmussen, op. cit., p. 268.

cares not whether a man is an executive or a laborer. His primary concern is with what *kind* of man he is, on and off the job. Does he let his business so absorb him that he is no longer a father, a friend, or a citizen? Does he treat people as human beings, or building blocks? Does he brush aside the ordinary standards of courtesy because he is "too busy to think about that kind of thing"? Maybe he can accept the excuse that "my job is so important — everything else will have to be secondary." Maybe even his family and friends will say, "Well, that's just the way he is, and, after all, he is so talented that it's all right." But the doctrine of Christian vocation raises real questions as to whether God uses these same scales.

Conclusion

As stated at the outset, the task of this article is to demonstrate that there can be important connections between Christian concepts and the activities of business enterprise. Christianity, it seems to me, offers a most fruitful frame of reference by which to view the realities of business activities. Executives equipped with such a perspective do many things differently from those not so equipped; a major difference between a Christian and a non-Christian approach, as many writers have noted, is a difference in attitude and depth of understanding in confronting all the perplexities of business affairs.

Businessmen holding this viewpoint would, for example, be less likely to commit the idolatry of worshiping the business enterprise, economic system, or career as the ultimate of existence. Thoroughgoing humility rising out of a realization of one's grievous shortcomings balanced by freedom from anxiety stemming from an awareness of judgment *and forgiveness* by a Being beyond the level of man would also characterize the Christian administrator.

One point should be made in this connection: the Judaeo-Christian outlook is made up of a network of interrelated doctrines. One concept is insufficient without the support of the others. The doctrine of man as the image of God without the concept of God offers an exaggerated understanding of the capabilities of man; and the idea of sin without forgiveness would make business executives either cynics or prime candidates for mental institutions.

This interlocking set of beliefs, though not a formal code of laws, offers the businessman an attitude, a way of looking at the world and its problems, a set of values which can be far more revolutionary in its effects than any blueprint for an institution or daily calendar of business activities.

If the business manager will rid himself of the notion that the doctrines of the church — any church — offer him nothing but vague ideas about human relationships, and sit down with the theologian to explore the teachings of his faith, he will find vast quantities of material out of which he can construct a map for his business life. If he takes the time and trouble to probe such apparently abstract ideas as the nature of God and man, the doctrines of forgiveness, sin, and creation, he will find them rich in implications and applications.

Working in concert with theologians, and perhaps collegiate schools of business (both cooperatively and separately), he can make ever more clear and more concrete the relevance of a Judaeo-Christian perspective to business administration.

3 Running the business right

John J. Fendrock

Crisis in conscience at Quasar

A provocative case of ethics
at Quasar Stellar Company underscores
a difficult management problem

Foreword

This case history, based directly on an actual situation, emphasizes the complex and arduous problem of ethics—business and personal—facing managers today. Undoubtedly, ethical conduct has always been a problem of some proportion, but in today's competitive business environment perhaps it is even more so. The case raises the issue of the correct course of action for managers who are confronted with accepting questionable conduct of their superiors by being expect-ed either to agree to it or to close their eyes to it.

Mr. Fendrock is Vice President of Avion Electronics, Inc. in Paramus, New Jersey. His experience includes directing operations for Avion, which specializes in military electronics and sophisticated electronic systems for NASA's space program involving the Gemini and Apollo craft; consulting in the United States and in Europe; and doing advanced studies in the management sciences at Stevens Institute of Technology.

The increasingly competitive business environment has resulted in a condition in which many managers are being subjected to tests of conscience for which they are ill prepared—indeed, for which there may be no preparation. It has become increasingly difficult for them to act their individual parts well, and still retain free and clear consciences.

The thesis of this article is that modern-day managers are often faced with situations where they are required to commit themselves, either openly or tacitly, to an action they may not agree with. They may be participating, willingly or unwillingly, in activities that are morally and ethically cloudy; questionable from a business point of view; and, perhaps, of doubtful legality.

The subject here is not the case of an act that is patently illegal; or where the responsibility is specific and detailed; or where the facts are clear-cut and defined. Rather, the issue under scrutiny involves unclear, undefined areas of activity where, by association, an individual is involved in a course of action that he *believes*—not necessarily *knows*—is wrong.

Readers are invited to send in their views on this provocative case history, set forth below, which tackles one of the more complex and difficult problems facing managers today.

The case setting

Universal Nucleonics Company, the parent company for a number of wholly owned subsidiaries, suddenly found itself in the embarrassing posi-

Reprint 68203

tion of having to report that its earnings for the year would be substantially lower than had been announced at the end of the previous quarter. Shortly thereafter, a statement appeared in the "Who's News" section of *The Wall Street Journal* reporting that Quasar Stellar Company, one of Universal's subsidiaries, had a new president and a new vice president of finance (replacing the former controller).

As time went on, the financial community learned that Universal had discovered that one of its subsidiaries had been withholding the truth, purposely distorting the facts, or other-

structure at Quasar, no feedback had been received independently of the president-controller monthly statement; whether any of the other executives were involved in the reports either knowingly or unknowingly, willingly or unwillingly; and, finally, what steps could be taken to prevent a recurrence of the situation in the future.

Fact-finding team

To resolve these questions, Universal's executive committee decided that a direct approach

Exhibit I. Organization chart of Quasar Stellar Company

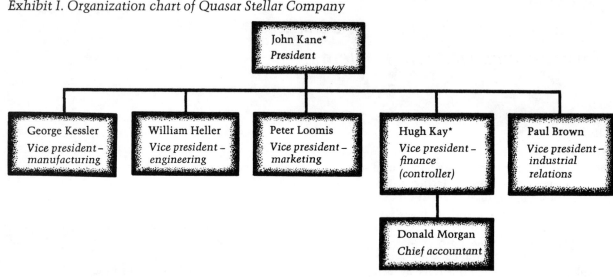

*Now replaced by new man.

wise misrepresenting the situation at hand in its monthly reports to corporate headquarters. By the time Universal had realized the actual condition of Quasar's financial situation, it was too late to correct it without affecting the reported year-end earnings of the parent company.

The two individuals most directly concerned at Quasar—John Kane, president, and Hugh Kay, controller—had both "resigned." It was generally agreed by the board of directors that there would be no public announcement as to the reasons for the resignations. Privately, however, one director stated flatly that out-and-out fraud was involved; another, more in tune with the times, said that the situation was directly attributable to the pressures to make good and the tendency to have a positive outlook on the outcome of all individual company problems.

Corporate headquarters was vitally interested in finding out why, given the organizational

should be taken. The executive vice president and the vice president of industrial relations for the corporation would conduct a series of interviews with the Quasar Stellar personnel who might have been involved. Both men were well qualified to appraise the situation. Jim Bowden, the executive vice president, was both an operating and a financial man, having spent a number of years in each area. Hubert Clover, vice president of industrial relations, was a former professor of industrial psychology at one of the leading business schools.

It was further agreed that each executive would interview different men, compare notes, and then speak with each other's interviewees if the situation so warranted. After studying the organization chart (see *Exhibit I*), and the company's "Manual of Responsibilities," they decided it would be best to talk to Peter Loomis, vice president-marketing; George Kessler, vice president-manufacturing; and William Heller, vice president-engineering.

Loomis' session

The scene opens in a small conference room at Quasar Stellar Company. The first man to be interviewed is Peter Loomis, vice president-marketing, who is known to be outspoken, demanding, and intensely loyal. Loomis is greeted by Hubert Clover.

Clover: Pete, as you know, the purpose of our chat is to see if we can learn something from this unfortunate episode that can help to prevent such an occurrence in the future. I would like to get your version of what has happened and any suggestions you may be able to offer as to what can be done to help our planning.

Loomis (defensively): Well, Hubert, you know I thought very highly of John. I'm certain you are aware that he hired me for this job. I don't mind admitting that I think the decision to fire him was unwarranted and ill advised.

Clover: If there is one thing I am certain of, Pete, it is that there is no question of your loyalty to John. I hope that won't bias your outlook. As for John's resignation, perhaps the best I can say is that on the basis of all facts available, the board decided this was the only logical course of action. And if. . .

Loomis (interrupting): Let me set the record straight on two points. My loyalty to John was based on respect for his abilities—not on personal grounds. And I'm not disagreeing with you, either on the basis of the facts available at the time or on those turned up by the investigation, that the action was not warranted. But I also feel that there was too hasty a collection of facts and an overreaction resulting in his dismissal. What I'm saying is that had a more thorough and penetrating investigation been made, the conclusions would probably have been different.

Clover (attempting to lead the interview back): I understand your point, Pete, but what are some of the additional facts that you think could have influenced the decision differently?

Loomis: You are most likely aware that the failure to receive the Apollo and LEM contracts had significant effects on the overall picture. But when John informally notified headquarters that our chances of receiving these two jobs were less than 50-50, he was told he was just being pessimistic. It was quite evident to him that the board of directors felt these were two prestige jobs that we simply had to get. The trouble was that while we dissipated our efforts on trying to land these low-probability programs, a half-dozen other less known, but perhaps more lucrative, opportunities slipped by.

Clover: You say John told headquarters about this. Have you any idea why the so-so probabilities and the alternatives were not openly presented and discussed at the appropriate company board meeting?

Loomis: To be frank, the 50-50 chance was an after-the-fact estimate. When the decision was made to pursue the two jobs, because of the pressure from headquarters and knowing what the work could mean to Quasar, I was undoubtedly too optimistic myself. A staff meeting was held in which the two marketing efforts were reviewed in detail.

Clover: Who attended that meeting?

Loomis: As I recall, there was George Kessler, Bill Heller, Hugh Kay, John, and myself.

Clover: Was it unanimously agreed that you should go after the two contracts?

Loomis (shaking his head): Oh, no! Bill felt very strongly that we should. He thought that the engineering department could gain a heck of a lot by being involved—state-of-the-art stuff. George was against the effort. He argued that production would be severely affected, because these projects would require such a long-term engineering effort before production could start. He wanted more immediate work that would occupy his work force. Hugh was with George. Not only was he worried about overhead and profits, but he had a "gut feeling" that our chances were less than what I forecast. He was right, of course. John was in favor of pursuing the contracts only if we had about a 75% chance of capturing each. John tossed the ball to me when he asked what our chances of getting the jobs were. At the time, I indicated that while I couldn't stick my neck out to 75%, I was willing to guess it would be much closer to 75%

than to, say, 50% or even 60%. Considering the attitude at headquarters, the stakes, and my projection, we finally decided to go after both.

Clover: Are you saying that you didn't really feel that your chances were as close to 75% as you indicated?

Loomis: I believe they weren't. But that isn't to say that I didn't feel they could or should have been.

Clover: How long had you been with the company when this meeting took place, Pete?

Loomis: Just about nine months. I'm quite sure I know the reason for your question. Actually, I was not as familiar with the company as I should have been to express so strong an opinion on such an important matter.

Clover: Obviously, you showed a good deal of enthusiasm. . .

Loomis (interrupting again): And, I'm afraid you'll have to agree, naiveté. Remember, however, that this is—or at least was—a gung-ho operation. I was anxious to earn my spurs. Those contracts would have put us on the map and made Quasar and Universal household words.

Clover: I can certainly understand your decision to go after the big fish, but, once you found that you were out of fishing water, why was headquarters not kept informed of the deteriorating market picture? Wouldn't that have been the logical thing to do?

Loomis: Logical, yes, but hardly practical. In retrospect, that is probably what we should have done, but let's go back six months. That's when our fears of a drop in production began to inject themselves. Hugh's warnings about profitability were proving to be only too accurate, and there was nothing that could be pulled in at the last minute to bridge the gap.

Clover: Yes, but you must have known very early that your odds were way off.

Loomis (after a pause): Well, perhaps I did not emphasize that fact strongly enough. I assure you, however, that both George and Hugh did, since their operations were directly and indirectly involved.

Clover (bothered by Loomis' evasiveness): How, then, was the decision reached not to inform headquarters of this situation? Didn't it bother you to think that there might be adverse effects on employment?

Loomis: Once the decision was made to go after the two projects, any reversal could only result in a loss of face and prestige. Like the gambler at the roulette wheel, we plunged deeper—with about the same odds—and lost. I must confess that I had my moments of doubt about our course of action. It was quite clear that people could get hurt, but that too is all part of the game. Frankly, at no time did it occur to me that I had a greater responsibility than the one I had to John. Perhaps this is wrong, but I have always felt that I owe more loyalty to my supervisor than to the company. And besides, I'm not certain to what degree personal morality should enter into business decisions.

Clover: Pete, let me ask you one final question. What do you think we might do to prevent this sort of thing from happening again in the future?

Loomis: Frankly, I feel that headquarters should give us more independence. For example, if headquarters had not exerted pressure on us to pursue these two contracts, we might have followed a different course. To me, what happened was that headquarters decided on a set course of action, passed the word down, and then—when it became impossible for us to follow through—they looked for scapegoats. Both John and Hugh were sacrificed because of poor headquarters policy.

Clover (rising): Thanks for a frank and open presentation of your thoughts on the situation, Pete. By the way, Jim Bowden may or may not wish to speak with you, depending on how things go in general. In any event, we'll let you know later. Once again, thanks for your ideas.

Loomis: Thanks for asking. I honestly thought this might just be allowed to die on the vine without anyone looking deeper into it.

Follow-up questions

Hubert Clover brooded over his interview with Loomis, scanning his notes in a manner that suggested more sorrow and disappointment than thought. He then decided to summarize his observations and to recommend that Bowden not interview Loomis. But, after reviewing the results of Clover's conversation, Bowden concluded that there was one more thing he wanted resolved: Why had not Loomis, in routine fashion, been put in a position to send a report back to headquarters that would have been at variance with the official statement? Later that afternoon, the two men got together. After exchanging the usual pleasantries and engaging in small talk related to the previous interview, Bowden asked the specific question he had in mind.

Bowden: The one thing that puzzles me, Pete, is why you were not able to transmit your misgivings about the possibility of receiving the two contracts directly to the corporate vice president of marketing.

Loomis: Your question, Jim, implies that I was *unable* to do this. Actually, it was always possible, but I was not *required* to do it. However, I was expected to give my observations to John and to support him in any decision he made as to how the information was to be handled.

Bowden: Your answer implies to me that you were fully aware that two distorted monthly reports were sent to corporate headquarters. Am I correct in this assumption?

Loomis: From what I have said to both you and Jim, there is no doubt that your conclusion is correct. And, to be honest, I was completely aware of the distortions in the reports. I can only repeat what I said earlier this afternoon to Hubert: my loyalty is to my supervisor, and I always support him in his use of information in any way he sees fit.

Kessler's interrogation

The next man to be interviewed was George Kessler, vice president-manufacturing, who was an old-timer by Quasar standards, having been at Quasar for 15 years. He was known for his outspokenness, integrity, and forcefulness. Clover and Bowden decided that Bowden should conduct the interview with Kessler because there existed a somewhat close relationship between them. As a former operations man, Bowden had taken a direct interest in manufacturing, and he had developed a healthy respect for Kessler.

Bowden greeted Kessler, and the two exchanged a few pleasantries.

Bowden: I guess we could keep up the chitchat all day, George, but I'm afraid we've got to get down to business. A fellow in your position must have seen what was coming—how in hell could you let it happen?

Kessler: I would rather continue reminiscing about old times than get into this. To answer your question, Jim, I saw what was coming; but, to turn the question back to you, how could I possibly have prevented it?

Bowden: All right, George, you couldn't have stopped it. Really, what I am asking is this: Seeing what was happening, wasn't there something you could have done to raise the storm signals?

Kessler: You know me well enough to realize that I am not one of the gung-ho types. While I had tremendous respect for John's ability to analyze a situation, I always suspected that he had a streak of the gambler in him. Let's face it; if he had pulled those two jobs out of the hat, he would have been Universal's brightest star.

Bowden: Getting back to the point, George, wasn't there some way for you to signal headquarters of what was happening?

Kessler (frowning): You insist on pursuing this point, don't you? Jim, you know as well as I do that I answered directly to John. I'm not going to beat a dead horse; but, without going into details, I think I expressed my views strongly on the approach we were taking. Certainly, I was concerned about a number of things. . .the number of old-time employees who were going to take a beating if this thing fizzled, as it did; what might actually happen to the company overall; and what I owed to myself as well as to John. Taking all these points into consideration, I did what I thought was morally and managerially right, and I don't say that lightly. In expressing my doubts so forcefully, perhaps I did a disservice to everyone I tried to help.

Bowden: In what way do you think you performed a disservice?

Kessler: In short order, I found myself outside of the actual development of the monthly reports. The result was that any influence I might have exerted in determining what information was to be generated for headquarters was cancelled out.

Bowden (nodding): I appreciate your dilemma, George, and I also respect the position you took. But don't you feel that there might have been some way to get this back to our office?

Kessler: In weighing my responsibility to the company, corporate headquarters, employees, self, and supervisor, I may possibly have erred in following too narrow a path. It seemed to me at the time, and I feel the same way even now, that with the organizational structure we have, my only approach was to try to change things through the existing framework. My efforts failed. Perhaps I should have been more adventurous and requested—demanded, if you will—an audience with you fellows. But I am certain that if a similar situation arose again, I still would not do this.

Bowden: Then let me ask you what you think can be done to prevent this from happening in the future.

Kessler: To me, there must be an approach that will allow for greater communication between headquarters and the company office. Perhaps the answer lies in having an executive committee sign the monthly report; or possibly having each committee member prepare a short concurrence or dissent report of his own, after the pattern of the Supreme Court; or even a more direct approach of having each manager give an independent report to his respective staff contact at corporate headquarters. The fact is, so long as we have a characteristic line and staff organizational structure, we can only follow the channels of communication that the chief executive officer decides on. No self-respecting manager would consider surreptitiously reporting behind his superior's back.

Bowden (rising and extending a handshake): George, thanks for your observations. I like your suggestion of a concurrence or disagreement by an executive committee. I hope the next time we have a little get-together it can be under more pleasant circumstances.

Heller's interview

To some extent, the interview had merely reinforced Bowden's estimation of Kessler. However, he couldn't help but feel a sense of frustration that a man of Kessler's caliber did not find a way to communicate his misgivings to those who could have done something about the developing Quasar problem.

After reading Bowden's notes, Clover concluded there was no need for him to talk with Kessler. Instead, he decided to carry on with the next interview. The final man singled out was William Heller, vice president-engineering, an intense, serious-minded, pipe-smoking engineer whose forte was considered to be R&D, not administrative work. He too was a long-term employee, having been with Quasar over ten years. Clover met him at the door of the conference room and, with a wave of his hand, motioned Heller to a chair.

Clover: I suppose the idea of sitting down to discuss this problem is not the most appealing thing to you, Bill. I hope it won't be as painful as realizing that an R&D project is going sour.

Heller: Since your call a few minutes ago was not completely unexpected, I prepared for this by fixing myself an extra tightly packed pipe of tobacco. It will give me more time to think about your questions.

Clover: What can you contribute to our understanding of the things that happened here, and do you have any suggestions as to how they might be prevented in the future?

Heller: I wonder if you could narrow your question somewhat. Exactly what would you like me to address myself to?

Clover: The specific problem, Bill, is this. Do you have an idea why Quasar's deteriorating condition was not reported back to headquarters? Of greatest interest, of course, is the overall condition of the plant operation, but the decline in engineering activity is something you can probably elaborate on in detail. Any light you can shed will be useful.

Heller: While you have become more specific, I still have a wide-open field. Probably I should first outline what happened to engineering, and from this we might then be able to work into the bigger picture. How does that appeal to you?

Clover (nodding): That would be a good start.

Heller: About a year ago, it became obvious that our engineering activity, including both research and development and general engineering, was going to decline. The decision was made that a joint effort with marketing would be undertaken. After a series of meetings, it was decided to pursue actively and aggressively two relatively large contracts.

Clover: Those would be the Apollo and LEM contracts. *(Heller nods assent.)* When you say it was decided that those two contracts would be pursued, what did this imply?

Heller: It meant that a radically new—for us—course of action was decided on. Always in the past we had operated as a subcontractor to primes on large systems. However, John and Pete took the stand that we were in a position to enter the systems area itself. Frankly, while I had initial skepticism about this approach, John portrayed the picture in optimistic terms. He was convinced that the contracts would be awarded more on the basis of marketing activity than on the engineering proposal, and he was equally confident that Pete's personal contacts would help us in capturing this work. Apparently John knew, or he felt he knew, that Pete had influence with the right people where those two contracts were involved. Thus, while in the past we had been merely keeping our fingers in the pie and hoping to get a piece of the action, it was decided at that point we would go the whole hog after them.

Clover: And you agreed with this approach?

Heller: As I indicated, initially I was skeptical. Our organization is simply not capable of coping with proposals of this size. However, after John and Pete argued their case so persuasively, I was fully in favor of the decision. Actually, I knew it involved a lot of risk, but Quasar stood

to benefit greatly if it worked out, and so I went along with them on it.

Clover: What did you think the chances were of getting those contracts, Bill?

Heller (pausing to light his pipe): To me, our chances were less than those expressed by Pete, who, as I recall, said he figured them to be closer to 75% than to 60% or so. Frankly, I would have guessed 60% to be the upper limit on our chances for each contract. However, even at that, it seemed like a good risk because, if we had captured but one of them, engineering would have benefited greatly.

Clover: And how about the rest of the plant operations?

Heller: Here, unfortunately, I was shortsighted. While the engineering activity would benefit, in retrospect the company as a whole could conceivably lose if only one, or perhaps even if both contracts were awarded to Quasar. I might add that this point was brought out strongly by George and Hugh. To offset this argument, however, it was pointed out that while a temporary downturn might occur, in about two years Quasar would be hard pressed to satisfy the requirements for the projects. In addition, Quasar would become so well known that interim work would be easy to come by.

Clover: Might it not also have worked to Quasar's disadvantage? How can you assume that other companies would be willing to give you work, knowing that it would be short-term and that you certainly would give attention to your own contracts once it was time to begin production?

Heller: Yes, it was an optimistic outlook and probably very shortsighted from a total company point of view.

Clover: Even assuming that the decision was a good one when made, why didn't someone recognize it was the wrong course before the entire operation went sour?

Heller (puffing on his pipe for a moment): Now you are in an area that is too deep for me. Once it was decided on to pursue those contracts, my group concentrated its efforts on the technical proposal. We are extremely thin in this area.

Therefore, our R&D activity was almost totally devoted to the proposal. Let me add that for approximately a 3-month period, 10- to 12-hour days and 7-day weeks were common for my staff.

Clover: But this very activity reduced your effectiveness on current work, did it not, and resulted in costly overruns and delays on contracts already in the house?

Heller: Unfortunately, yes, but that was not totally unexpected. We attempted to minimize the overruns and delays, but some were certainly inevitable. Since we were trying to maintain our staff, a lot of the added cost went into overhead and project charges as we stockpiled personnel during the initial period when the decline began to manifest itself. Of course, we had to face facts later and let some people go when it became apparent that the plans were not working out.

Clover: At that point, why didn't the company reverse itself, abandon its course, and go after some short-term subcontract work? And why didn't you get back to headquarters with your problem?

Heller: At that point, both John and Pete felt retreat would be impossible. Frankly, I supported them against my better judgment, both because I could see no way to change their attitude, and because I had an obligation to do my utmost in attempting to rectify the situation. Now, then, your other question as to why headquarters was not informed is difficult for me to answer. What can I say?

Clover: I would like a frank comment on this point, Bill.

Heller (knocking the ashes from his pipe): Both John and Pete stood high in my book. I don't pretend to be a business manager; rather, I am an engineering manager. The tangibles of engineering are something I grasp and manipulate readily, but the intangibles of business are quite another thing. In retrospect, it's easy to criticize past decisions, but I respect the decisions that were made then. I personally felt there was an obligation to the parent company, but even though I disagreed with the principle of not reporting the situation to headquarters, I accepted it as a business decision.

Clover: Then you were aware, were you not, that the reports sent to headquarters distorted conditions at Quasar to such an extent that the status of projects was inaccurately reported, actual and projected earnings were blatantly inflated, and the entire status of the operation was totally misrepresented? How could you have accepted such a situation?

Heller: If only I could answer you in a manner that might express my feelings at the time. Was I aware of what was going on? Yes, of course, I was. But I didn't *want* to know about it. I will go so far now as to say that I tried *not to know* what was being done. Realistically, once I accepted the basic decision to ride the thing out, I felt stuck with the consequences. There was nothing, as I saw it, that I could do to alter the course taken.

Clover: Bill, did you have any opportunity to bring this to the attention of headquarters?

Heller: Formally, no, of course not. No mechanism existed, or perhaps should ever exist, for circumventing top management. On a few occasions I might have had the opportunity to mention to the corporate vice president of engineering what was happening, but I certainly would not do that.

Clover (shaking his head slowly): I think you will agree such a situation should never be allowed to exist. Can you offer any suggestions as to how information of such importance to the welfare of both the company and the corporation could be made available to top management without violating any precepts—actual or imaginary?

Heller: I have given considerable thought to this point. I honestly feel that what gets reported back to headquarters can only reflect what the president sees fit. I would hit the ceiling if I found out one of my project managers was reporting directly or indirectly to the president. By the same token, the president shouldn't have to guard against insurgency in his ranks. The corporation might use an internal audit team composed of knowledgeable personnel to make frequent checks on various phases of the operation. Apart from that, I've no suggestion.

Clover: Bill, your pipe's been cold and empty long enough. Thanks for your comments. Hopefully, we won't need another one of these sessions with you.

Morgan's opinions

Clover discussed his report with Bowden, and they agreed that another interview with Heller was unnecessary. Then they went over the results of all three interviews in depth. When they had finished, they decided to pursue two additional questions from two other specific areas: (a) Why did the accounting people not find a way to report to headquarters? (b) What was the quality of the morale of the personnel during this period?

Accordingly, Donald Morgan, chief accountant, and Paul Brown, vice president-industrial relations, were invited to sit down with Bowden and Clover, respectively, in two simultaneous sessions. Since both corporate fact finders felt that too much briefing might tend to "lead" the interviews and stifle response, they agreed that the only statement they would make at the start would be to the effect that efforts were being made to prevent a repetition of the Quasar situation in the future.

Bowden: Don, you certainly are aware of the upheaval here at Quasar, and I suspect you know pretty well the reasons for it.

Morgan: Yes, I have a good idea of what's what.

Bowden: I wonder if you would care to express your opinions on two specific points. First, why was it not possible to have the information fed back to corporate headquarters once the deteriorating situation began and, second, what might be done to prevent what happened from taking place again?

Morgan: As standard company policy on reports, we generate our financial statements from whatever information is given to us. Our statements, in turn, are sent to the controller's office, and he does what he sees fit with them. Should we receive instructions from his office to reorganize, let's say, or otherwise manipulate the reports, there is very little we can do but follow instructions. This is particularly true when matters of judgment are involved. Let me give you a for-instance: if a project is reported as being behind schedule by the program manager and, after review by the controller's office it is de-cided that it is not all that far behind, naturally adjustments are made. Or, say, an expected contract has not yet been received, but management decides to open up a project number anyway and begins accepting charges in anticipation of receiving the job; this too is done. So far as I can see, this is nothing more than exercising management prerogative. I will summarize my position by saying that I do pretty much what I am told. Sometimes I may not like it, but my job is not to set policy or to question decisions. Rather, it is to follow instructions.

Brown's observations

At that point, Bowden decided that he had heard enough and abruptly ended the interview. Meanwhile, Clover was undertaking his interview with Paul Brown.

Clover: Paul, can you give any insight into the state of morale during the period when Quasar was apparently falsifying reports to the home office and after it became apparent that a serious problem existed?

Brown: For a while, everybody acted as if they were on "pot"; everyone was filled with high expectations. To be sure, there were a couple of exceptions. But, in rapid fashion, things began to settle down and disillusionment set in. Many people sensed that there was trouble ahead and that nothing was being done. After a month or two, the exodus began, and, as you know, it still hasn't ceased. I know that some of the managers tried their best to hang onto their key people, but as usual it was just this caliber of individual who could read the writing on the wall and got out while the getting was good. I'm equally certain that a number of the other top people would have left except for loyalty to the company and their fellow employees, their years of company service, and/or other factors. My only other observation on this is that I hope our new president and controller have been selected more for solid, long-range accomplishments than for flashy, short-term results.

The interviews having been concluded, Clover and Bowden are now faced with drafting a series of recommendations on the individuals interviewed and the steps to be taken by Universal Corporation.

Thinking Ahead

The courts are saying that matters traditionally considered an organization's own business may be the public's as well

A new generation of employees and the courts are questioning yet another of management's prerogatives. Once, differences of opinion between an employee and his or her employer concerning policies and practices were resolved within the organization. It was the manager's place to arbitrate and the employee's to accept the manager's decision. The only proper course of action for an employee who could not abide by the decision was to resign. To take his case outside the organization or to go over his superior's head in any way was at least improper and perhaps disloyal. Whistle blowing, then, was a disgraceful act deserving outright dismissal. But today's employee is claiming his right to speak out if his conscience so dictates. Here the author assesses the current status of laws applicable to such dissent in public and in private organizations. But, he suggests, by enabling the employee to express his views without compromising his employer's public integrity, management can do much to improve employer-employee relationships and thus obviate the need to blow the whistle.

The author is assistant professor of business, government, and society in the Graduate School of Business Administration at the University of Washington. He is a member of the California Bar Association.

Reprint 75412

Kenneth D. Walters

Your employees' right to blow the whistle

A recent manifestation of the perpetual tug-of-war between employees and employers is the new phenomenon known as whistle blowing. A whistle blower has been called a "muckraker from within, who exposes what he considers the unconscionable practices of his own organization."[1] Having decided at some point that the actions of the organization are immoral, illegal, or inefficient, he or she acts on that belief by informing legal authorities or others outside the organization. Such a public denunciation of policies or practices that an employee deems intolerable has been characterized as a deed of "courage and anguish that attend[s] the exercise of professional and personal responsibility."[2]

Organizations have always had to contend with outside muckrakers and critics, but the current movement emphasizes the responsibility of inside critics to uncover and report organizational misconduct. Within the last three years several books that emphasize the importance and frequency of employee whistle blowing have been written.

The first published and still the best general treatment is the report, *Whistle Blowing*, edited by Ralph Nader, Peter J. Petkas, and Kate Blackwell. This report describes the dilemmas faced by employees in deciding to tell the public about their companies' defective products, concealed hazards, pollution, corruption, or law breaking. Nader insists that "loyalties do not end at the boundaries of an organization."[3] The defense of "just following orders" was rejected at Nuremberg, he argues. In addition to spelling out the rationale underlying the whistle-blowing ethic, the report also contains a series of cases in which employees have blown the whistle. According to a reviewer in the *Wall Street Journal*, this report "probably deserves far wider readership at all levels of the corporate ladder than it is likely to get."[4]

A. Ernest Fitzgerald, the Pentagon cost specialist who revealed cost overruns in the production of C-5A transport

Author's note: The research assistance of Victoria Broadhead is gratefully acknowledged.

1. Footnotes are listed at the end of this article on page 143.

planes and whose job was therefore abolished, wrote *The High Priests of Waste*.[5] He recounts numerous official attempts to hush up what he calls bureaucratic bungling, chiseling, waste, collusion, and fraud on the part of defense contractors. As a result of taking legal action, he has been reinstated to his position.

In *Blowing the Whistle: Dissent in the Public Interest*, Charles Peters and Taylor Branch present several case studies of government employees who have revealed organizational abuses or deceptions.[6] Peters and Branch, editors of *Washington Monthly*, see whistle blowing as a notable new development in the history of American reform movements.

Louis McIntire, who worked as a chemical engineer for Du Pont, claims he was fired for writing *Scientists and Engineers: The Professionals Who Are Not*,[7] a fictional account of a chemical corporation's attitude toward its professional employees.

In *Advise and Dissent: Scientists in the Political Arena*, Joel Primack and Frank von Hippel urge scientists to assume a wide variety of professional and ethical responsibilities, including whistle blowing.[8]

The whistle blower: Judas Iscariot or Martin Luther?

Reflecting a radical departure from long-held organizational beliefs, the basic assumption behind this new genre of literature is that employees who disagree with organizational policy on grounds of conscience are obliged not to quit their jobs but to remain in their organizations and act as forces for change from within. This stance is very different from the traditional role of the employee whose "preeminent virtue is loyalty" and whose "principle is 'your organization, love it or leave it'."[9] Some businessmen hold to this traditional view and strongly oppose any effort to dilute the undivided loyalty expected from employees. In 1971, James Roche, then chairman of the board of General Motors Corporation, warned against

what he considered to be the insidious effects of whistle blowing:

"Some critics are now busy eroding another support of free enterprise—the loyalty of a management team, with its unifying values of cooperative work. Some of the enemies of business now encourage an employee to be disloyal to the enterprise. They want to create suspicion and disharmony, and pry into the proprietary interests of the business. However this is labelled—industrial espionage, whistle blowing, or professional responsibility—it is another tactic for spreading disunity and creating conflict."[10]

Roche's views reflect the fact that from the time we are children we are taught the value of "playing on the team." Learning to get along by showing loyalty to others is a vital social lesson, especially in a society where more and more earn their livelihood in an organizational environment. This institutional loyalty, coupled with a general loathing for traitors and tattletales, casts the whistle blower more in the role of Judas Iscariot than in that of Martin Luther. Peters and Branch have remarked that "in fact, whistle blowing is severely hampered by the image of its most famous historical model, Judas Iscariot. Martin Luther seems to be about the only figure of note to make much headway with public opinion after doing an inside job on a corrupt organization."

Some organization theorists seem to agree that employees should have undivided loyalty to their employers. Paul R. Lawrence says, "Ideally, we would want one sentiment to be dominant in all employees from top to bottom, namely a complete loyalty to the organizational purpose."[11] Harold J. Leavitt comments that Likert's ideal organization has loyal employees who see no conflicts between personal goals and organizational purposes.[12] In his critique of organization theory, Robert Presthus appears to regret but to admit that "organizational logic . . . has been essentially authoritarian."[13]

Other theorists stress the idea that employees in a free society should not

be obligated to restrict their loyalty to only one institution or cause. Clark Kerr advocates allowing plural loyalties as a necessary guarantee against totalitarianism: "A pluralistic system assumes a 'pluralistic person,' that is, one who is willing to work with divided loyalties and set his own pattern of activities, rather than have it set for him by a single external institution."[14] Kerr's fears have proved to be well-founded. We have recently been reminded of the consequences of following a Nixonesque pattern of demanding complete loyalty from subordinates. It is one thing to expect employees to commit themselves to pursuing broad organizational objectives; it is quite another to see the contract of employment as a Faustian bargain in which employees suspend all critical judgment to serve their superiors.

The informer in public organizations

Advocates of whistle blowing point out the need for legal protection of critics within an organization. In "Whistle Blowing and the Law," Arthur S. Miller, a specialist in constitutional law, notes that the present legal system offers little protection to such informers.[15] While it is true that most employees undertake to blow the whistle at their own risk, a fact that has received little notice is that employees in public organizations do have substantial legal protection in this regard. It arises from the First Amendment's provision that government may not deny citizens freedom of speech. Although current legal protection for whistle blowers extends mainly to employees in government organizations, managers in private organizations as well should be aware of these new legal trends. Whistle blowers in private organizations are steadily gaining legal support and may someday enjoy essentially the same rights as employees in government organizations.

In *Pickering* v. *Board of Education* in 1968, the U.S. Supreme Court established legal protection for certain kinds of whistle blowing by public employees. In a letter to the editor of a local newspaper, Pickering, an Illinois high school teacher, criticized the school board for its policies, particularly for its allocation of funds to athletic programs. Pickering was fired for this act of disloyalty, which the school board found "detrimental to the efficient operation and administration of the schools of the district." Pickering sued, alleging a right to free speech. The U.S. Supreme Court found that Pickering's "right to speak on issues of public importance may not furnish the basis for his dismissal from public employment." The right to raise such an issue publicly is protected by the First Amendment:

"The question whether a school system requires additional funds is a matter of legitimate public concern on which the judgment of the school administration, including the School Board, cannot, in a society that leaves such questions to popular vote, be taken as conclusive. On such a question free and open debate is vital to informed decision making by the electorate."

The Court went on to say that teachers like Pickering have special competence and interest in speaking out on issues that affect the organizations for which they work:

"Teachers are, as a class, the members of a community most likely to have informed and definite opinions as to how funds allotted to the operation of the schools should be spent. Accordingly, it is essential that they be able to speak out freely on such questions without fear of retaliatory dismissal." [16]

A survey of cases involving public employees since the *Pickering* case shows that nearly all whistle blowers who have been punished for their outspoken views do win their cases when they challenge such punishment in court.[17] The courts appear to be agreeing with an assessment that Peters and Branch have made, which is that the "strength on which whistle blowers have relied is basically that they have

been judged *right* by most of the people who have studied the conflicts from outside the battle area." Such a consensus seems rather ironic if we contrast it with the specter of treachery that shadows whistle blowers. The nearly unanimous conclusion that they "did the right thing" perhaps testifies to the morality of the positions they have taken.

Disloyalty or legitimate dissent?

As Peters and Branch point out, not all organizational loyalty is bad, and not all whistle blowing is good. What factors, then, should determine whether an employee who protests company practices should be protected against sanctions that are imposed by the organization?

Perhaps the best way to answer this question is to look at the legal cases that have arisen from public employees' criticizing their bosses. The courts have outlined some general guidelines that are helpful in distinguishing between whistle blowing that deserves protection and that which does not. It should be stressed that these rules currently apply only to whistle blowers in government and public organizations, but some legal scholars believe that similar rules will soon be applied to organizations in the private sector, a matter I will examine later in this article.

Motive: The employee's motive for blowing the whistle has been an important factor used by the courts in determining whether or not the employee's freedom of speech should be protected. Usually an informer attempts to publicly expose misconduct, illegality, or inefficiency in an organization.

Several cases fit this pattern. In *Rafferty* v. *Philadelphia Psychiatric Center*, for instance, Mrs. Rafferty, a psychiatric nurse, was fired following the publication of a news article in which she was quoted as being critical of patient care and medical staff behavior at the state mental hospital where she was employed. Her comments caused great controversy at the hospital, and

the staff appeared to resent her statements. The court concluded, however, that Mrs. Rafferty "was engaging in precisely the sort of free and vigorous expression that the First Amendment was designed to protect." [18]

In *Muller* v. *Conlisk*, a policeman discovered that other policemen had taken stolen property they had recovered in the course of their duties into their own use. He reported this fact to his superiors, waited, and saw no indication that they were investigating the charge. Finally, he appeared on a television news program and suggested that the fact he had reported was being covered up. He was fired for making "derogatory comments reflecting on the image or reputation of the Chicago Police Department." The court ordered him reinstated on the ground that the rule prohibiting derogatory comments was "unconstitutionally overbroad," and that the First Amendment protects "some speech by policemen which could be considered 'derogatory to the department'." [19]

Sometimes the issues addressed may seem so trivial that they can hardly be characterized as whistle blowing. Nevertheless, superiors who are the objects of even mild criticism sometimes react (or overreact) defensively, and then the courts are forced to step in and protect the employee's freedom of speech.

For example, in *Downs* v. *Conway School District*, an elementary school teacher with over 25 years of experience publicly voiced concern over the use of an open incinerator on the playground during school hours. She also assisted students in composing a letter to the school cafeteria director that requested that raw instead of cooked carrots be served occasionally. For these and other similarly innocuous activities, the superintendent decided not to recommend Mrs. Downs for renewal of her teaching contract. The court found that "the superintendent demanded blind obedience to any directive he gave, whether illegal, unconstitutional, arbitrary or capricious." It ruled that Mrs. Downs's activities were constitutionally protected by the First Amendment:

"When a School Board acts, as it did here, to punish a teacher who seeks to protect the health and safety of herself and her pupils, the resulting intimidation can only cause a severe chilling, if not freezing, effect on the free discussion of more controversial subjects."[20]

Internal channels: Does it make a difference if whistle blowing takes place inside or outside an organization? Perhaps the employee owes his or her employer enough loyalty to try to work first within the organization to attempt to effect change. This is a sound general rule to follow, but the Supreme Court in the *Pickering* case did not sanction organizational rules requiring that employees always resort first to internal grievance procedures:

"There is likewise no occasion furnished by this case for consideration of the extent to which teachers can be required by narrowly drawn grievance procedures to submit complaints about the operation of the schools to their superiors for action thereon prior to bringing the complaints before the public."

In fact, employees usually do seek change within the organization first. Perhaps this is an indication that most employees appreciate the harm that could be done to the organization if every problem were aired publicly before attempts to solve it inside were made.

The organization's internal environment for free speech should be a key consideration in deciding whether employees must exhaust internal channels of communication before they seek outside help. In general, employees will probably tend to go through organizational channels before going public if they have not had too much trouble with bureaucratic red tape in the past, if their superiors have demonstrated some empathy with them for legitimate grievances in the past, and if the employees perceive their superiors to be more or less colleagues. Whistle blowers are most likely to go directly to the public when their earn-

est criticisms are met with bureaucratic runarounds, deaf ears, or hostility.

The subject matter of the grievance may also determine whether it is reasonable to expect employees to resort to internal grievance channels before going public.

In *Tepedino* v. *Dumpson*, social investigators in the New York City Department of Welfare wrote a letter to an HEW official in Washington. In it, they criticized existing procedures and asked for information they had been unable to receive from superiors. The suspended employees' superior argued before the New York Court of Appeals that the social investigators had violated the grievance procedure mandated by the department. The court held that in many cases it is reasonable that employees be required to follow grievance procedures, but that the nature of some grievances are such that they need not be raised through established procedures: "The subject matter of the letter, critical though it may have been of the Welfare Department's operations, could not be appropriately raised or dealt with through its grievance machinery." The court distinguished between "individual problems of employees" and "broad issues" and ruled that the latter need not be carried through grievance procedures.[21]

One can also foresee cases in which whistle blowers should not be required to go through internal channels when time is important. They may be warning against an imminent danger, and, by the time they have gone through a complex and time-consuming bureaucratic maze, the harm of which they warn may have already occurred.

Another problem is that the requirement that all employees go through organizational channels before speaking in the forum of their choice conflicts with the constitutional principle that prior restraints on speech are "impermissible with but the narrowest of exceptions."[22]

One can see that it is impossible to lay down a simple yet fair rule on the issue of whether employees must ex-

haust internal remedies before making public allegations. Each case must be examined on its own merits. This matter will be clarified further as the courts look at a wider variety of cases raising the issue.

Organizational friction: One of the major concerns of the courts in adjudicating whistle-blowing cases has been the question of harm done to personal relationships in an organization because of such actions. Aside from the aspect of possibly damaged public relations, the organization must often deal with upset working relationships between the informer and his or her co-workers and superior.

The Supreme Court in *Pickering* noted that the public statements were "in no way directed towards any person with whom appellant would normally be in contact in the course of his daily work as a teacher" and "thus no question of maintaining either discipline by immediate superiors or harmony among co-workers [was] presented." Pickering's relationships with the school board and the superintendent were "not the kind of close working relationships for which it can persuasively be claimed that personal loyalty and confidence are necessary to their proper functioning." The Court therefore held Pickering's speech to be protected but warned that "significantly different considerations" could apply if "the relationship between superior and subordinate is of such a personal and intimate nature that certain forms of public criticism of the superior by the subordinate would seriously undermine the effectiveness of the working relationship between them."

The problem that must be squarely faced in deciding whether speech that disrupts personal relationships should be protected is that, in virtually all whistle-blowing cases, these relationships are already upset to one degree or another. The very nature of whistle blowing implies the presence of conflict or disagreement. A comment by the California Supreme Court in *Adcock* v. *Board of Education* recognizes this fact and points out that all organizational conflict is not necessarily dysfunctional:

"Disharmony and friction are the healthy but natural results of a society which cherishes the right to speak freely on a subject and the resultant by-products should never prevent an individual from speaking or cause that individual to be penalized for such speech."[23]

Because of this unavoidable friction in relationships, the real task of the courts is to balance the benefits from the employee's freedom of speech (which are often quite substantial in whistle-blowing cases) with the costs or harm from the speech. Only after this careful weighing of the employee's and the employer's interests do the courts reach a decision.

In both the *Downs* and the *Rafferty* cases, the courts obviously felt that the whistle blowers had not harmed their organizations seriously but had performed a public service. In *Rafferty*, one of the alleged reasons for the nurse's discharge was the "staff anxiety" created by her public criticism of hospital conditions. The court found this anxiety to have been overstated by the employees and not an acceptable reason for firing Mrs. Rafferty. And in *Downs*, although the superintendent and the school board were upset by what they regarded as Mrs. Downs's impertinence, the court felt that for her not to have warned of the open incinerator on the school grounds "would be violative of her moral, if not legal, duty to protect the health and safety of her students."

Courts have sometimes ruled that the employer's assertion that working relationships have been seriously harmed have simply not been proved from the facts. In *Dendor* v. *Board of Fire and Police Commissioners*, a fireman said that the village's fire marshal did not know how to manage the fire department and predicted that his lack of direction would "end in disaster." The employer discharged Dendor because his continued presence "would be seriously detrimental to the discipline, morale, and efficiency of the Fire Department." But the court said that the employer "has the burden of proving that the forbidden speech rendered the

speaker unfit for public service or so adversely affected the public service involved that it justifies impairment of free speech." The employer, the court said, "did not find, and describe by such finding, the kind of harm inflicted on the village fire department by Dendor's derogatory statements."[24]

Other courts have concluded that the disharmony resulting from an employee's speaking out is the result of "over-sensitivity to criticism" on the part of the superior or "bureaucratic paranoia."[25]

Discretion: There are other factors that courts will obviously have to consider as new whistle-blowing cases arise. Whether the allegations are true or false is certainly relevant, as is the degree of care exercised in gathering the data on which the charges are based. A negligent dissenter who harms an organization by recklessly making serious charges that are false does not deserve to be protected.

A further factor to consider is confidentiality. On the one hand, unauthorized disclosures of confidential information obviously cannot be permitted every time an employee personally feels the public would benefit from having such information. On the other hand, organizations should not be allowed to hide a multitude of sins under the guise that the matters are proprietary or confidential. Individual cases will have to determine the delicate balance between revealing misconduct and maintaining legitimate requirements of confidentiality.

When whistle blowers lose

We have already suggested that a whistle blower who seriously damages personal relationships in an organization by saying things that have no countervailing benefit to the organization or to society would probably not be given legal protection. We also saw that some situations may require that a critic exhaust internal remedies before going outside the organization. No court, however, has actually held that a whistle blower's freedom of

speech would be unprotected in such situations.

In only two cases have the courts held that the public employee's criticisms were not protected by the First Amendment. In *Kelly* v. *Florida Judicial Qualifications Commission*, the Florida Supreme Court split four to three over whether a Florida district court judge could be disciplined for criticizing his fellow judges in public for their alleged failure to establish procedural reforms in judicial administration. Saying that he was motivated by personal vanity and political ambition rather than by genuine concern for the public interest, the majority upheld the censure of Judge Kelly. In essence, the majority seemed to feel that Judge Kelly lacked the true whistle-blowing ethic—a desire to improve the performance and quality of public service. The dissenting judges disagreed with the majority's finding that Judge Kelly was motivated by self-interest.[26] The *Kelly* case illustrates that determining an employee's motive can be a difficult but critical task, since it differentiates the true whistle blower from the employee whose real object is harassment or blackmail.

In *Watts* v. *Seward School Board*, a teacher publicly criticized the school administration in an open letter to the school board and as a result was not rehired.[27] The case is interesting in that its facts are quite similar to the landmark *Pickering* case, decided by the U.S. Supreme Court. The Supreme Court of Alaska distinguished Watts's case from Pickering's (unpersuasively, a dissenting judge said) when it noted that the teacher's letter in *Watts* was not met with "massive apathy and total disbelief" by the general public as in *Pickering* but became a very disruptive force in this small Alaskan community.

Whistle blowing in private organizations

As we have seen, employees in public organizations can generally engage in open dissent within certain reasonable limits. The issue remaining is: What will be the future for whistle blowers who work for private organizations? Speculation on future trends and laws is risky, but certain forces that could greatly expand the legal rights of whistle blowers are already at work.

Professor Thomas I. Emerson, perhaps the nation's foremost First Amendment scholar, has made the following observation:

"A system of freedom of expression that allowed private bureaucracies to throttle all internal discussion of their affairs would be seriously deficient. There seems to be general agreement that at some points the government must step in. In any event the law is moving steadily in that direction."[28]

Another legal scholar, Phillip I. Blumberg, has explored in detail the current law on the employee's duty of loyalty to the employer. Blumberg predicts that whistle blowing "will become an area of dynamic change in the corporate organization and in time will produce significant change in established legal concepts."[29]

A complete discussion of the legal trends to which Professors Emerson and Blumberg refer is impossible here, but I can briefly cite three of them:

Collective action: First, if unionism spreads to new employee groups, one can expect that legal protection for whistle blowers will include these groups. Union contracts generally specify that employees may only be discharged for just cause or good cause. Whistle blowing is not usually considered to be just cause for firing. Edward A. Gregory, a perennial thorn in General Motors' flesh for his whistle blowing on auto design safety, credits his union with protecting him from attempted disciplinary actions by General Motors.[30]

A second but related development involving collective employee action is the banding together of employee groups who refuse to work for organizations that condition employment on the sacrifice of basic rights. This appears to be a course of action appealing particularly to professional and scientific employees. For example, the American Chemical Society is proposing to set up a legal aid fund for members who are punished for criticizing their organizations' policies and to institute sanctions against offending employers.[31] The Federation of American Scientists has a similar program and goal.[32]

Rights of employment: Another trend that in the long run may produce more fundamental changes in employee rights is the movement of courts away from the time-honored rule that an employee who has no formal contractual rights to employment may be fired for any reason or for no reason, within the limits of statutory law (for example, civil rights laws). This rule has been uniformly applied in all states and has been described by Lawrence E. Blades as "what most tends to make [the employee] a docile follower of his employer's every wish."[33]

But in Petermann v. International Brotherhood of Teamsters an employee fired for testifying against his employer (a labor union) at a legislative hearing was found to have been unlawfully discharged. The court ruled that the firing was "against public policy" even though there was no formal contract of employment.[34] And in 1974 the New Hampshire Supreme Court in Monge v. Beebe Rubber Co. ruled that a married employee with three children could recover damages when she claimed she was fired because she refused to go out on a date with her foreman. The court declared:

"We hold that a termination by the employer of a contract of employment at will which is motivated by bad faith or malice or based on retaliation is not in the best interest of the economic system or the public good and constitutes a breach of the employment contract."[35]

The decisions in the Petermann and the Monge cases do not seem revolutionary given the facts involved, but the basic rationale underlying the decisions reveals the willingness of some courts to examine the circumstances surrounding discharges of nonunion employees, an inquiry that the courts previously have studiously avoided in all cases. Petermann and Monge may be harbingers of future employee claims that whistle blowing is not a ground for discharge and that discharge of a whistle blower can be "against public policy."

Regulatory provisions: A final legal development is the appearance of specific statutory provisions that prohibit employers from discharging or disciplining an employee who discloses conduct that the statute forbids. An example of this kind of provision is Section 110(b) of the Coal Mine Safety Act:

"No person shall discharge or in any other way discriminate against or cause to be discharged or discriminated against any miner or any authorized representative of miners by reason of the fact that such miner or representative (A) has notified the Secretary or his authorized representative of any alleged violation or danger, (B) has filed, instituted, or caused to be filed or instituted any proceeding under this Act, or (C) has testified or is about to testify in any proceeding resulting from the administration or enforcement of the provisions of this Act."[36]

Making whistle blowing unnecessary

How can an organization work with its employees to reduce their need to blow the whistle? Here are five procedures that might be kept in mind:

☐
First, managers should assure employees that the organization will not interfere with basic political freedoms. Management theorists have increasingly stressed that organizations should encourage an open environment in which employees freely express their often controversial views.

☐
Second, the organization's own grievance procedures should be streamlined so that employees can get a direct and sympathetic hearing for issues on

which they are likely to blow the whistle if their complaints are not heard quickly and fairly. Much whistle blowing occurs only because the organization is unresponsive to early warnings from its employees. A sincere commitment to an "open door" policy makes much whistle blowing unnecessary.

□

Third, the organization should take a look at its concept of social responsibility. Too often social responsibility is seen as being limited to corporate gifts to charity parceled out by top management and the board of directors. But the organization's interface with society is far more complex than this, and employees at all levels have a stake in the organization's social performance. Keeping the internal channels of communication open, not only on personal issues affecting employees but also on these larger questions of corporate social policy, decreases external whistle blowing.

□

Fourth, organizations should formally recognize and communicate to employees a respect for the individual consciences of employees. Jay W. Forrester has proposed that the modern enterprise "should develop around a 'constitution' that establishes the rights of the individual and the limitation of the power of the organization over him." [37]

□

Fifth, the organization should recognize that dealing harshly with a whistle-blowing employee could result in adverse public reaction and publicity. Respecting an employee's right to differ with organizational policy on some matters, even if the law does not currently require it, may be in the best interests of the organization in the long run.

References

1. Charles Peters and Taylor Branch, *Blowing the Whistle: Dissent in the Public Interest* (New York: Praeger, 1972), p. 4.

2. Ralph Nader, Peter J. Petkas, and Kate Blackwell, eds., *Whistle Blowing, The Report of the Conference on Professional Responsibility* (New York: Grossman, 1972), p. 10.

3. Ibid.

4. Richard Martin, "Why People Inform on Their Bosses," *Wall Street Journal*, 17 October 1972.

5. A. Ernest Fitzgerald, *The High Priests of Waste* (New York: Norton, 1972).

6. Peters and Branch.

7. Louis V. McIntire and M.B. McIntire, *Scientists and Engineers: The Professionals Who Are Not* (Lafayette, La.: Arcola Communications, 1971).

8. Joel Primack and Frank von Hippel, *Advise and Dissent: Scientists in the Political Arena* (New York: Basic Books, 1972).

9. Nader et al., p. 26.

10. James M. Roche, "The Competitive System, To Work, To Preserve, and To Protect," *Vital Speeches of the Day*, 1 May 1971, p. 445.

11. Paul Roger Lawrence, *The Changing of Organizational Behavior Patterns, A Case Study of Decentralization* (Boston: Division of Research, Harvard Business School, 1958), p. 208.

12. Harold J. Leavitt, "Applied Organizational Change in Industry," in *Handbook of Organizations*, ed. James G. March (Chicago: Rand McNally, 1965), p. 1156.

13. Robert Presthus, *The Organizational Society* (New York: Vintage Books, 1962), p. 321.

14. Clark Kerr, *Labor and Management in Industrial Society* (Garden City, N.Y.: Anchor Books, 1964), p. 17.

15. Arthur S. Miller, "Whistle Blowing and the Law," In *Whistle Blowing*, ed. Nader et al., p. 25.

16. Pickering v. Board of Education, 391 U.S. 563 (1968).

17. Tepedino v. Dumpson, 249 N.E. 2d 751 (1969); Muller v. Conlisk, 429 F.2d 901 (1970); Brukiewa v. Police Commissioner of Baltimore, 263 A.2d 210 (1970); Downs v. Conway School District, 328 F.Supp. 338 (1975); Donahue v. Staunton, 471 F.2d 475 (1972), *cert. den.* 93 S.Ct. 1419 (1973); Turbeville v. Abernathy, 367 F.Supp. 1081 (1973); Dendor v. Board of Fire and Police Commissioners, 297 N.E. 2d 316 (1973); Rafferty v. Philadelphia Psychiatric Center, 356 F.Supp. 500 (1973); Adcock v. Board of Education, 513 P.2d 900 (1973). The current United States Supreme Court has also recently upheld the whistle-blowing concept in Perry v. Sindermann, 408 U.S. 593 (1972), where a college professor alleged that his termination was the result of testimony he gave before the state legislature and other public criticism of the school administration.

18. Rafferty v. Philadelphia Psychiatric Center, 356 F.Supp. 500 (1973).

19. Muller v. Conlisk, 429 F.2d 900 (1970).

20. Downs v. Conway School, 328 F.Supp. 338 (1971).

21. Tepedino v. Dumpson, 249 N.E. 2d 751 (1969).

22. Board of Education v. West Hempstead, 311 N.Y.S.2d 708, 710 (1970).

23. Adcock v. Board of Education, 513 P.2d 900 (1973).

24. Dendor v. Board of Fire and Police Commissioners, 297 N.E.2d 316 (1973).

25. Roberts v. Lake Central School Corporation, 317 F.Supp. 63 (1970); Murray v. Vaughn, 300 F.Supp. 688, 705 (1969).

26. Kelly v. Florida Judicial Qualifications Commission, 238 So.2d 565 (1970).

27. Watts v. Seward School Board, 454 P.2d 732 (1969).

28. Thomas I. Emerson, *The System of Freedom of Expression* (New York: Vintage Books, 1970), p. 677.

29. Phillip I. Blumberg, "Corporate Responsibility and the Employee's Duty of Loyalty and Obedience," *Oklahoma Law Review*, August 1971, p. 279.

30. "Lonely Causes: For Edward Gregory, General Motors Corp. Is Employer and Target as Assembly-line Inspector, He Publicly Raises Issues About Standards, Defects," *Wall Street Journal*, 31 December 1973.

31. Nicholas Wade, "Protection Sought for Satirists and Whistle Blowers," *Science*, 7 December 1973, p. 1002.

32. "New Ethical Problems Raised by Data Suppression," *Federation of American Scientists Professional Bulletin*, November 1974, p. 1.

33. Lawrence E. Blades, "Employment at Will vs. Individual Freedom: On Limiting the Abusive Exercise of Employer Power," *Columbia Law Review*, December 1967, p. 1405.

34. Petermann v. International Brotherhood of Teamsters, 344 P.2d 25 (1959).

35. Monge v. Beebe Rubber Co., 316 A.2d 549 (1974).

36. Coal Mine Safety Act, §110(b), Public Law 91-173.

37. Jay W. Forrester, "A New Corporate Design," *Industrial Management Review*, Fall 1965, p. 14.

Problems in Review

David W. Ewing

Case of the rogue division

What tack should a company take when it is the subject of a scandal?

The scene is the office of E.J. ("Brad") Bradenhoff, president of North Central Power Company, a division of Trans-National Power Corporation.
With Bradenhoff are Alvin H. Tillman, director of public relations; Beverly Walensa, director of personnel; Richard Rinehart, chief legal counsel; and Louis Hyde, vice president of Trans-National. Hyde has just arrived from corporate headquarters in Pittsburgh.

Rumors of improper business conduct move through the grapevine like fire through August wheat, yet company executives are often slow in responding to them. The media, of course, are quick to bite at news of payoffs, kickbacks, and suicides. If caught off guard, companies can feel pressed to defend themselves before they have even established whether the allegations are true.

The top managers of one U.S. corporation found themselves struggling to save face for the organization, which was at the center of a scandal involving legislators and rate-making officials. Disguised in the case presented here, the company's situation tests the thinking and judgment of even the most experienced business leaders. HBR asked three executives— Joseph T. Nolan, Donald N. Scobel, and Douglas S. Sherwin—to discuss their reactions to the company's predicament. Read the case and compare your diagnosis and prescription with those of the three commentators.

Mr. Ewing is managing editor of HBR. He is the author of 'Do It My Way or You're Fired!' (John Wiley & Sons, 1983) and of numerous articles, including "How to Negotiate with Employee Objectors" (HBR January-February 1983). Mr. Nolan is Monsanto's vice president for public affairs. Mr. Scobel is director and founder of the Creative Worklife Center in Mentor, Ohio and was formerly manager of employee relations development for the Eaton Corporation. Mr. Sherwin is board chairman of Duraco Products, Inc. in Streamwood, Illinois and until recently was president of Phillips Products Company, Inc., a subsidiary of Phillips Petroleum (Duraco was organized to acquire Phillips Products from Phillips).

Reprint 83303

Hyde: Brad, why don't you bring me up to date on the bidding. I've only heard bits and pieces about this thing, and being in Europe most of the past month doesn't help.

Bradenhoff: About eight months ago, Lou, I heard about improprieties in some of the district offices. I can't say it was the first time I had heard the rumors, because it wasn't. But in my year here I've had a lot to learn, and I had other problems to work out first. So I asked Rich to investigate. His people went about it as discreetly as they could, but the upshot was they found a mess in one district. It happens to be the Reardon-St. Thomas district up to the north, Lou. Well, there were payoffs to city and town officials, contracts with relatives, some pretty extravagant entertainment going on— you name it, they found it. So I suspended Martin Adams and Gordon Gilby, the two managers who were most involved. After further investigation, I terminated Adams, and then he brought suit against us.

Hyde: This was after Gilby—

Bradenhoff: After Gilby committed suicide, yes.

Hyde: That was when the media got excited.

Bradenhoff: And then Adams, you see, began talking to reporters, claiming he was being made the scapegoat. That fueled the fire.

Hyde: This story from the *Herald*, now. Is this the kind of thing the papers are saying?

Adams Says North Central Ordered Payoffs, Favors

Midwest City – A former employee of North Central Power Co. charged today that he had been ordered to make payments to designated political candidates and do favors for members of the state legislature.

"I dared to resist corporate rapacities," stated Martin Adams, who was fired from his job as Midwest district manager in June. "I didn't like what they were doing, and they decided the best way to shut me up was to get rid of me."

Adams claimed that he and other executives at the department head and division levels were given pay raises that included $1,500 a year to cover political contributions. Also, he said that the company routinely asked managers to make out false expense vouchers so that illegal payments could be made to legislators and municipal officials.

One city mayor, he said, sold more than $80,000 of supplies to the company after presiding over power rate hearings and voting for an increase. A city councilman, said Adams, did more than $165,000 of business with an affiliate of North Central.

Gordon Gilby, Adams's boss and a vice president of the company, also was a victim of the company's retaliation, Adams claimed. Gilby committed suicide last May 19. His estate is joining suit with Adams in charging the company with slander.

The legislature has appointed a subcommittee to look into charges that the company influenced legislators and rate-making officials. The subcommittee will begin hearings Wednesday.

When contacted, officers of Trans-National Power, the parent organization in Pittsburgh, offered no comment.

Bradenhoff: That's typical, yes. I don't believe Adams has told them much that they haven't reported.

Hyde: Pretty one-sided, isn't it? I would've expected better than this from the press out here, but maybe I'm naive. Everybody's so antibusiness these days.

Walensa: Actually, the press has treated us OK. In general, anyway.

Bradenhoff: It's just that you've got that combination of suicide, which was front-page news because of who Gilby was – his family and everything – and Adams taking potshots at us at every chance –

Tillman: And with rates going up all the time, who likes a power company?

Hyde: So when the trial starts, I suppose that'll light a fire under it all over again.

Bradenhoff: We're in a very awkward position, you know. In order to defend ourselves, we've got to demonstrate what Rich found in his investigation of Adams and Gilby. All of which of course plays right into the hands of the reporters.

Hyde: What's the worst that can happen? Just so there won't be any surprises.

Bradenhoff: What do you think, Rich? What's the worst that can happen?

Rinehart: The Adams-Gilby suit is for slander, and $6.5 million is being asked in damages. It will be alleged by plaintiff Adams that his termination was a retaliatory act because of his knowing too much, with the further motive of discreditation. It will be asserted by Adams that the investigation of his and Gilby's activities was initiated upon our being apprised of their critical stance, a kind of de facto whistleblowing, if you will, and that Gilby *in extremis* –

Hyde: Holy cow, what language is this? I'm a country boy from Radcliff, Kentucky and all this day facto and streemus business –

Walensa: Rich is our scholar. How many years of Latin did you have at Princeton, Rich?

Rinehart: Please, Pennsylvania.

Hyde: Anyway, you were saying about Gilby?

Rinehart: The suicide was committed in acute anguish.

Tillman: Brought on by Gilby's fears that the company was out to get him, Rich means.

Hyde: Thank you. So Gilby – or rather, Gilby's widow – and Adams, they're going to be telling us we sat on them to make them swallow the whistle?

Bradenhoff: Right. I mean wrong, because of course it isn't true; we didn't do that. The fact is we didn't start the probe until rumors came to us about their improprieties. And at the time we had no knowledge that Adams was critical of the company.

Hyde: Can that timing be established?

Rinehart: I believe it can be documented, yes. No word of criticism was heard from Gilby, so far as we know, until the writing of his suicide note. As for the plaintiff, Adams, to the best of our knowledge, no allegations against the company were made until after his termination by Brad, which was later still.

Hyde: And Mrs. Gilby, the widow, is suing for the same thing as Adams?

Rinehart: In essence, yes, although more damages are claimed by her. In addition, the same or similar witnesses will be offered by both plaintiffs. It is anticipated that testimony will be concerned largely with the attempted influence by management in respect to rate-making officials and legislators. This, it is alleged, Adams and Gilby were threatening to disclose and were therefore penalized.

Hyde: Former employees testifying against us? I don't like the sound of that.

Rinehart: The irony is that comparable testimony will be proffered by our own witnesses, only with regard to the plaintiffs' malfeasance, not management at large.

Hyde: Slander is it? Why not just damages for the suspension?

Bradenhoff: It's a kind of Catch-22, Lou. To investigate the rumors about Adams and Gilby's conduct, we had to ask many employees about their activities. So the grapevine got to work, you know. There was no way to keep it from buzzing. Most everyone learned early on that Adams and Gilby were under suspicion. So the whole investigation was loaded like a pistol.

Rinehart: When Adams was terminated, after the Gilby suicide, the implication clearly was "guilty as charged." Adams is an ambitious man. As he sees it, his career is ruined.

Hyde: So you'll be parading witnesses at the trial, Rich, who will lay this out? And what's the bottom line? I mean, what side of the law are we trying to land on?

Rinehart: Essentially, what is said by the law is that if North Central did what would have been done by any reasonable employer in similar circumstances, it is on solid ground.

Hyde: And you're not worried about proving that?

Rinehart: I believe it can be documented that our inquiries were discreet, appropriate, timely, and when the evidence was in, our actions could only be called judicious. Not to have acted would have been a breach of responsibility.

Hyde: Will it be a long trial?

Rinehart: According to our best estimate, on the order of two to four weeks.

Hyde: Two to four weeks! Two to four weeks of parading witnesses in and out to testify about kickbacks, payoffs, sex —

Tillman: Why didn't we try to settle?

Rinehart: As you know, I took a strong position against that. A settlement would have been tantamount to a tacit admission of guilt, in the public mind if not legally, and *a fortiori* a generous settlement, as demanded by the plaintiffs.

Hyde: Does this man ever speak in ordinary words?

Bradenhoff: Only when he scuffs a golf shot.

Walensa: Anyway, settling out of court tends to leave people in the dark about what really happened.

Tillman: Pittsburgh doesn't want a settlement either? I mean, would a settlement be in the realm of possibility there?

Hyde: As I understand it, Rich convinced Pittsburgh not to go that route. But of course it's never too late; we could change our minds. You *could* still ask for a postponement and dicker for a settlement, right, Rich?

Rinehart: But why let such a dangerous precedent be set? And as I have already said, we will not be let off cheap by these plaintiffs. At the least, a demand of two million will be made.

Hyde: I'm not recommending a settlement. I'm just saying that theoretically it's a possibility.

Tillman: Two million, that's not so bad. I mean, two million might be cheap compared to what we lose in rate increases. Can you imagine the effect on the legislature and rate commission of two to four weeks of dragging out the dirty linen in court? Officials wined and dined, weekends at hunting lodges at company expense, women, business contracts — why, we'll be lucky to get a tenth of the increase we ask for! The repercussions will last for years!

Bradenhoff: Just off the cuff, every percentage in rate increase is worth three-quarters of a million dollars to us every month. Now, we're asking for 11% more in April and hoping to get at least half of it. So that settlement cost could be paid for quickly.

Hyde: That's one of the interesting things, you know. You've put your finger on something that fascinates me, Al. Here we've got this rogue division, this renegade company. Over at headquarters, hell, they've worried about it for ages. But the earnings! Damn, if only the other divisions could earn like this one has.

Rinehart: Thanks to the state.

Hyde: What do you mean, "Thanks to the state"?

Rinehart: A decentralized state agency, conflicting jurisdictions between state and municipal, gaps in control, regulation *de minimis* —

Hyde: Regulation what?

Rinehart: Minimal regulation.

Tillman: It may not be so loose after the trial. I've got a feeling there's going to be a lot of tightening up by the legislature after this imbroglio.

Hyde: If we've got such a strong case, Rich, why can't we knock it out in a week, get it over with?

Rinehart: Because at least a week will be consumed by the plaintiffs in setting forth their side, and about a week will be required by us in defense presentation. It's a case of double whistleblowing, you might say, and in addition to establishing that the requirements of just cause were met by the company, the equitableness of our procedure must be proved. Also, there are some complexities. When a quarter of a million was spent by Gilby to remodel his offices — that was accomplished, by the way, by dividing the contract into small jobs that did not have to be reviewed by the controller — several thousand dollars' worth of improvements were included by Gilby for his home in Maplewood. Actual payment for the home improvements was performed by the architect; then Gilby had an equivalent sum added to the architect's fee. Our case is documented, but the details must be set forth one by one, and more time will be consumed in cross-examination.

Tillman: We spend years building up good relations with the legislature, then a shoot-out like this happens. Pow! Everything gone. Any time the rate commission goes along with us after this, they'll be suspect. Did we buy them out again? What favors did we give them? There goes all that hard-earned trust!

Bradenhoff: I don't think it's as bad as all that, Al. Don't forget that we've got an asset of 37,000 employees living in cities and towns around the state. They're voters, they're buyers, and what's more, they can be spokespeople. Now, I've seen it happen, because we did it back when I was in Des Moines, you know. We educated the employees and told them what our problem was, and they went out like battalions. They rang doorbells, they took speaking engagements, they went to hearings. We can do that here. We have people who can go to Rotary clubs and speak. We have people who can write for their local newspapers. Some of them would appear on talk shows. We're not helpless, that's what I'm saying. We can fight.

Walensa: Sounds terrific. But how do you start the ball rolling?

Bradenhoff: With information. You always start with information.

Tillman: Like, every day we could summarize the previous day's proceedings in court. One page of facts, a copy on every desk. Every day we could set the record straight, put what Adams says in one column and refute it with the truth in the next column. Salvo! We could send our fact sheets to the legislators, to the media. Every employee would go out armed with a good summary, and whoever they talk to, they would have the answer at their fingertips.

Bradenhoff: Bev, show Lou that employee summary you made up. Lou, that shows part of my problem— how do you get a little discipline when the troops are spread out in 63 different places? But there's a plus side, too. See, we've got people in most every club and association and bowling league you ever heard of. Call it people power or whatever you want, there's a lot of weight there.

Rinehart: It's not all that transparent to me. Can we be assured that all of those 37,000 are waiting for marching orders, ready to go out and spread the word? If you want the truth, a lot of them regard anything from management with great skepticism. Why not let our talking be done for us by the verdict? Let our day in court be had and many doubts will be put to rest. What is more, a large proportion of employees are in distant and outlying cities and towns, with their own problems to worry about.

Tillman: That's fine if you can get people to withhold judgment, but they won't. Every day this goes on, more bombardment from the media— parties, payoffs, hanky-panky. Why, already Channel Three's putting together a show on suicide, and you know what they'll focus on? The Gilby case. They'll intimate that he killed himself in despair when he learned the company would discredit him in order to shut him up. And somebody from *Time* called me about it this morning. I'm telling you, it's very hairy!

Bradenhoff: Al's our excitable one.

Hyde: It's no wonder. We're sitting on a volcano.

Bradenhoff: Still, we've got options, influence, and don't forget those employees, Lou.

Hyde: But how can you get them to think with us? Being a country boy myself, I know what it's like to be remote. "Man," you say to yourself, "I'm way out here, and there's nobody going to tell *me* what to do."

Bradenhoff: Well, we're going to work on it. One of the things I came here for is to put more coherence in this outfit, knit it closer together.

Hyde: Bev, you've been quiet.

Walensa: I was just wondering. I worry about trying to manage the news. I kind of agree with Rich that what we say is suspect. But I also agree with Al that we don't want to leave a vacuum for the media to fill. It'll be all sensationalism coming from them.

Hyde: So?

Walensa: Why not put the complete record of the previous day's trial on every person's desk in the morning? No editing, no commentary, nothing. Just give it to them, lock, stock, and barrel.

Tillman: Are you joking?

Walensa: I didn't mean to be.

Tillman: What about all the testimony that's not true? And what about the embarrassments—people who got promoted by Adams and Gilby for sexual favors, people who saw what was going on and looked the other way? They'll all be named in the proceedings, weird accusations and all. Let all that hang out?

Hyde: We've got to be careful of morale. Let's not hurt too many feelings.

Bradenhoff: If we're the subject of such hot news, maybe we could get Channel Three to put one of our people on every few days and give our side of the story.

Hyde: That sounds kind of defensive. I wonder if it'd be convincing.

Tillman: Whatever we do, we seem to lose. Adams and Mrs. Gilby clobber us when they open the case, our own witnesses clobber us when we give our side. Coming and going, we get it.

Walensa: I still think that if we could inform every employee completely and be credible, it could be a learning experience.

Hyde: We'll learn how to eat crow.

Bradenhoff: Intellectually I agree with Rich, you know, but emotionally I can't. I can't resign myself to sitting here watching it happen. And I get a feeling the public will respect us more if we fight.

Walensa: Yes, but there really isn't any way to win it, is there? Except legally, maybe. So all we can do is work ahead for the next round.

Tillman: The trouble is it's good managers who were the wrongdoers. Hell's bells, Gilby was a fair-haired boy. They said he could go to the top, if he wanted to. And Adams worked his way up from scratch. He started as a cost analyst and ended up running the whole northern area. It's not a case of those guys always wearing the black hats.

Hyde: Well, there's a bunch of alternatives for you, Brad, but they all seem to lead downhill, as they are. Do you want to keep your head below the grass or get out and fight? Well, each way there are implications. I don't have to go back till tonight, so you don't have to decide anything right now, but I've got to have something to tell Pittsburgh. I don't say they're going to argue with you, just that they're breathing a little hard out there wondering what's going to happen. So that's what I've got to know. What do you say we meet here again this afternoon at, oh, about 4 o'clock?

Query to readers: *Putting yourself in the shoes of E.J. Bradenhoff, what would you tell Lou Hyde you plan to do? After you have decided, compare your opinions with those that follow.*

In general, the three executives invited by HBR to comment on the case agree that:

☐   Top management has failed to do its job well.

☐   The heads of North Central Power should investigate their own possible contribution to the imbroglio before trying to make corrections in policy and structure.

☐   Management should level immediately with the public about what has happened and why.

☐   However it acts with regard to the current situation, the company will take a beating. Yet management can take many steps to prevent a recurrence of such a crisis. These steps range from enacting codes of conduct for employees to setting up better accounting systems.

Because our three commentators are lucid and articulate, I shall let them do most of the "talking" from here on. They take strong stands on this case, and HBR readers should find their comments rewarding.

Taking the blows

The ebullient Joseph T. Nolan makes a forceful case for management's leveling right away with the public:

"New York retailer Nathan Ohrbach said it best. 'I've got a terrific gimmick,' he confided to his advertising colleagues. 'Let's just tell the truth.' That's not only the best course for North Central Power Company but very likely the only one left.

"An out-of-court settlement of the lawsuits would not put off the day of reckoning since a state legislative subcommittee is planning to open public hearings momentarily. Besides, Martin Adams has already gone public with his version of events and can be expected to say even more.

"As Watergate demonstrated so clearly, the best way to prolong an unpleasant situation like this is to follow the 'limited hangout' strategy – to tell only part of the story. North Central should come clean and offer its wholehearted cooperation to authorities to track down any wrongdoing.

Joseph T. Nolan

...there is no way to avoid criticism.

"Telling the truth should come easy for Brad Bradenhoff. After all, he has been president of North Central for barely one year. When he heard rumors of improprieties in the district offices, he launched an investigation. As soon as he had the facts, he took the initiative in suspending those managers who were implicated.

"What he should do now is make a forthright statement to the effect that as a matter of policy North Central does not condone payoffs or special deals with public officials and that it has established strict internal controls to prevent a recurrence of such practices.

"Bradenhoff should acknowledge right up front that the company made some mistakes in the past. He should take the blame for not communicating his policy as effectively as he could have. And he should start immediately to make sure all managers understand that the company is committed to achieving its commercial objectives in a manner fully consistent with the applicable laws and regulations of the state and communities in which it does business.

"This ought to be done *not* through a shower of memoranda but through personal visits to all company locations. What better opportunity to enlist the support of North Central's 37,000 employees around the state?"

Nolan harbors no illusions that such a full-disclosure stance will be painless. He continues:

Donald N. Scobel

...mass control is a vestige of serfdom.

"Will the company come up for criticism as a result of the public hearing and court trial? Certainly. Given the facts of the case, there is no way to avoid such criticism. All Bradenhoff can hope to do is limit the damage.

"If the damage control techniques are handled well, the harm to North Central's reputation should be both moderate and short-lived. A few years ago, when scores of U.S. companies were accused of making improper payments abroad, the ones that fared best were those that readily admitted their guilt, promised to make amends, and followed through on those promises. That's what North Central should do now."

Donald N. Scobel takes a dim view of Brad Bradenhoff's role to date. Putting himself in Bradenhoff's position, Scobel says he would resign:

"I would not be able to live with my ineptness in this case. When I first heard the rumors about the Reardon-St. Thomas district, I perceived it mostly as a legal problem. I failed to involve my human resource management experts. Then when the evidence came in, I blindly accepted it without asking questions or sensing the broader implications. Still I did not seek other perspectives. I suspended a vice president and one of his employees without giving them the chance to explain things – no chance for a hearing, no chance to refute the evidence.

But my greatest sin was when Gilby took his life; I let Rinehart convince me this was de facto proof of guilt and crassly terminated Adams. That is when I laid the company open for public scrutiny.

"I paid no attention to Gilby's complaints about North Central in his suicide note. I still didn't foresee the broader implications. Not even a man taking his life shook me into giving Adams a chance to defend himself. I went ahead and fired him knowing full well that he could bring suit against the company and make this a public issue.

"Adams worked for Gilby. His easiest defense would be that he did nothing that wasn't approved or even ordered by his now deceased boss. Yet even in today's discussion, I'm not asking why Adams isn't taking this simple defense.

"Adams has joined Gilby's widow in the suit to say that both of them were scapegoats for a general company malignancy. Would Adams take this far harder tack if he had no evidence at all? As Bradenhoff I would say, 'I am sorry, Mr. Hyde, but my mismanagement and insensitivity to human resource affairs has already caused this company far more damage than the alleged acts of Gilby and Adams. I urge that we try to settle this out of court in order to give the company time to get its house in order under a little less public limelight. As a first step in that building process, I urge you to accept my resignation. I cannot stay on. I feel I even have a death on my hands.'"

It's unlikely, however, that the real Bradenhoff will take this suggestion, says Scobel. A division president in a no-win situation who opines that "the public will respect us more if we fight" isn't about to say farewell. Accordingly, Scobel puts it up to Louis Hyde, the corporate vice president:

"So that leaves it up to Mr. Hyde. Now if I were he, I wouldn't be feeling so hot either, but accountability in this case does rest more squarely on the president of North Central Power. Assuming I have the authority, and in keeping with my country-boy vernacular, my first inclination would be to 'fire Bradenhoff's ass.'

"But that would be denying Bradenhoff what he wrongly denied

others—due process. I would ask him to take a week off and think about his future with the company. If he still wanted to stay, I would try to work out an arrangement whereby both perspectives could be presented to an impartial outsider with the assurance that the company would give substantial weight to his or her recommendation."

Although, as Nolan points out, the possibility of a settlement seems to have been ruled out, Douglas S. Sherwin agrees with Scobel that a strong effort should be made to reopen this route. Sherwin argues:

"Litigation will be painful, embarrassing, and very expensive for all parties. Whenever I am angry about something and think of suing, I am rescued by remembering Judge Learned Hand's caution about lawsuits, 'As a litigant, I should dread a lawsuit beyond almost anything else short of sickness and death.'

"No one can emerge a winner from this suit. That fact offers hope that the parties can find a way to meet their objectives without exposing themselves to the drawbacks of a court trial.

"The company should try to settle the case out of court not to cover up any questionable practices that the trial might disclose but to minimize further impairment of the company's ability to serve its customers, employees, and investors.

"A straight financial settlement is one option the company could consider. But if it can understand the needs that led Adams and Mrs. Gilby to sue, North Central may be able to combine certain other benefits with financial concessions as an alternative to a purely financial settlement.

"Mrs. Gilby, for example, probably wants to divert blame from her husband so as to preserve his (and her) name, to replace lost family income, and to salve her anger over the loss of her husband. Her chances of winning the suit, however, appear minimal, and if she loses, her legal expenses will be high. In any event, all the illegal and unethical actions her husband committed will be dragged through the court and his reputation will be permanently soiled. His estate might even be subject to a stockholders' suit to recover the company funds he diverted to the Gilby residence.

Douglas S. Sherwin

...take a stand on the right side.

"Adams's interests are probably to restore his income, resume his rising career, and salvage as much of his reputation as possible. His suit has only moderate probability of success and, if lost, would be very costly. In addition, the trial would make his unethical actions a matter of public record—damaging his reputation. If testimony reveals illegal acts, he might subsequently be indicted on civil or criminal charges.

"The company could offer to say whatever positive things it could about Mr. Gilby, underwrite his spouse's legal costs to date, and out of appreciation for his service to the company, set up an annuity for Mrs. Gilby. It could offer several conciliatory benefits to Adams, such as extending his salary and providing him with an office and a secretary for a year or more while he seeks new employment, underwriting career counseling services and professional resumé preparation, paying his attorney's fees to date, and agreeing to emphasize to prospective employers the talents that enabled him to work his way up to executive status."

Getting the house in order

Turning now to actions that would help in the longer run, our commentators strongly urge North Central Power's management to begin with a hard look at its role in the scandal. Sherwin has this to say:

"The company must first get the facts about its own involvement and activities. For instance, is it unequivocally and incontrovertibly true that the company began the probe only when it heard the rumors of improprieties? Were the improprieties limited to the Reardon-St. Thomas district? What basis in fact did the criticisms contained in Gilby's suicide note have? Is there any evidence or potential testimony that Adams resisted corporate rapacities? Did the company in fact give pay raises that included amounts to cover political contributions? Did it ask managers to make out false expense vouchers to cover illegal payments to legislators and municipal officials? Did the company in fact get unjustifiably large increases from the regulatory bodies?

"The answers to these and other questions will determine the company's posture. For example, demonstrating that the probe came after the rumors would undercut Adams's claim that the dismissal was retaliatory. And if the improprieties were found to be limited to the Reardon-St. Thomas district, the activities in that district could be portrayed as an aberration.

"On the other hand, proof that the company gave pay raises to cover political contributions and asked managers to fill out false vouchers for that purpose would be taken as prima facie evidence that the leadership would support other attempts by its executives to influence rate making. The company needs to establish the absolute truth of these matters; it cannot stand any surprises."

Sherwin also thinks that North Central is guilty of several significant leadership failures. To set its own house in order, management needs to know why it made so many mistakes:

☐   "By declining to offer comment when given the opportunity by the newspaper, the company betrayed its lack of foresight and preparation.

☐   "When Bradenhoff took over the division's presidency, he should have received or written a statement of the goals of the division and the business areas in which high performance was necessary to meet these goals. It would have enabled him to get on top of his job faster.

☐   "The company allowed the investigation of improprieties to drag on for eight months before dealing with the matter.

☐   "The fact that Bradenhoff suspended two employees and fired Adams after Gilby had committed suicide without beforehand assessing the probable consequences of these acts suggests that the company's leadership appointed a man who was not yet ready for the assignment or that it failed to alert him to the most sensitive aspects of the new assignment. It should have been understood that the subordinate manager was to seek higher management's counsel when unusual situations arose.

☐   "Management must discipline employees who have committed improper acts. But first it must articulate what constitutes improper behavior. That was Gilby's responsibility to Adams, Bradenhoff's to Gilby, Hyde's to Bradenhoff—and this duty extends right up to the directors of the company. This is especially important in regulated industries because of the sensitive and temptation-laden relationships with government officials.

☐   "Where were the auditors? Were they inept or were their reports quashed?

☐   "One has to question what it is about the climate that could induce a manager with Gilby's prospects to resort to such measures. Perhaps there was a precedent for Gilby's behavior."

On a broader scale, Sherwin takes corporate management to task for its apparent obsession with profits:

"Trans-National Power simply loves the profits that were coming out of the division and, if it didn't know, didn't *want* to know how they were being generated. The pursuit of profit is an indispensable internal discipline in giving private business its unique capability for economic performance. Profit is the objective investors have in risking their capital; profit commensurate with the risk undertaken is their just reward.

"But the objectives employees have in giving the company their energies and ideas and the objectives customers have in providing revenues out of which come wages and profits have to be met as well. It is only by giving equal regard to all these objectives that a manager can in fact maximize profit for the investors. For if profits are sought at the expense of employees or customers, they will in the long run, just as they have in this case, jeopardize justifiable profits for investors in the future."

Scobel believes that management must change some of its assumptions about employees. The dialogue shows him that the executives are embracing such questionable ideas as that:

1   "Employees have a pawn-like company loyalty that can be executively marshaled.

2   "Management can be prosecutor, investigator, and judge of its own employees without internal checks, balances, or due process.

3   "In the handling of human resource problems there is no real need to drive hard for truth.

4   "High levels in the organization are hardly at all accountable for the behavior of lower levels."

This executive group has some major self-corrections to make, Scobel argues. As he points out:

"Almost a third of the dialogue in this case is on the subject of manipulating employee thoughts and actions. Though some participants resist the notion, the president and PR director feel that they can move the masses with a flick. They perceive themselves as living in the Orwellian 1984. This notion of mass control is actually a vestige of serfdom.

"Another problem: most of the executives feel that decision responsibility rests at high levels yet that accountability for misjudgment or misconduct belongs down there someplace (or even out there someplace with an overzealous government, biased media, or an uninformed public). Misconduct is acknowledged, but how does it arise? What is the perceived policy or expectation? In what milieu does it flourish? The executives in this case can't face the question, Does some of the responsibility for this dilemma rest with the seats of organizational direction?

"A most perplexing part of this dialogue for me is how uninterested these executives seem to be in searching out truth in the broader sense. There is nothing very probing in vice president Hyde's inquiries. The dialogue invites an almost endless list of questions.

"Did anyone investigate the complaints against the company expressed in Gilby's suicide note? What is the validity of Adams's accusations quoted in the newspaper?

"What is the status of the legislative subcommittee investigation? Is it likely to press forward?

"Rinehart says Adams will focus on broad management efforts to influence rate-making officials. How broad? What evidence might he have?

"Why has headquarters worried about this 'rogue' and 'renegade' division for years?

"Has anyone tried to find out if similar problems exist in other districts?

"The list could go on and on, but it is clear that the participants are not curious. They blithely accept the premise that truth is precisely what lawyer Rinehart and his investigators say it to be. They have locked themselves into their own parochial version of truth, which they must now defend unswervingly."

Preventing a recurrence

What steps and changes in policy and organization would help North Central Power avoid getting caught in no-win situations like this one?

Nolan thinks management should issue a code of conduct for employees. He looks to Bradenhoff to do this by supplementing his personal visits to company offices with a written statement:

"Bradenhoff should promulgate a new policy statement on business conduct that prohibits the use of company funds for any unlawful purpose and requires every key employee to annually sign a certificate of compliance with this policy."

Scobel urges the company to establish mechanisms allowing employees to speak up and defend themselves when attacked. He decries the lack of any procedure for clearing the air and resolving suspicions:

"The 'discreet' inquiry into rumored improprieties was cursory at best. There is no evidence that any employee, including Gilby and Adams, had any chance to respond to the contentions of fellow employees. There was no hearing, no protection against partiality, very little evidence of factual corroboration, no opportunity for cross-questioning, and no seeking of an impartial opinion. Even the contention that a quarter of a million dollars was sneaked through in small contracts begs more questions than the investigation answers.

"In today's world, organizations need internal mechanisms for due process. If companies are not motivated by the fairness of due process, they should at least realize that employees have many avenues for disputing employer acts and that the old system for unilateral investigations and judgments is no longer viable. This case makes that clear."

Sherwin calls for revisions in accounting control and the board of directors:

"The company should review and provide for the adequacy of its system of internal accounting and management controls. It should immediately develop and issue a 'code of ethical behavior' to its managers. The company should undertake a careful review of the composition, size, and structure of its board of directors to determine whether it needs, among other things, additional outside directors and an audit committee of board members. There is a lot being written these days about the governance of corporations, and the company should incorporate the best of it into its bylaws and policies."

Sherwin believes further that management should work with state officials in scrutinizing the rate-making process and considering possible reforms:

"The case testimony suggests that profits and prices *are* higher than normal. The crucial question is why. It is conceivable that the employees' improprieties were an insignificant factor compared with the effects of the decentralized state agency, the conflicting jurisdictions between state and municipal responsibilities, loopholes in control, and so forth. If that is the case, the legislative subcommittee members should focus their attention and recommendations on correcting these structural problems.

"The company should make conciliatory moves toward citizen and consumer groups. In addition to detailing for them the steps it is taking to prevent a recurrence of improper acts by its employees, the company can legitimately point out that to a large extent its employees were in effect lured by the uneven administration of the rate-making process and the islands of arbitrary power they had to deal with. Since consumer groups are mainly interested in the service they get for their money, they are likely to prefer a general solution of the problem to ad hoc punishment of the company.

"By instigating a program to repair structural defects in the regulatory process, the company may be paving the way for a reduction in rates for itself. But the company should take a stand on the right side. To avoid punitive prices, it must be willing to settle for fair prices. When the company can no longer reap profits not warranted by the risks to which the investors' capital is exposed, as it had been doing by taking advantage of structural defects in the rate-making process and the cupidity of public servants, it will redirect its efforts to more responsible avenues for increasing its economic performance."

Finally, perhaps the executives in our case could turn the traumatic trial proceedings to the company's long-term advantage. The testimony—even the most compromising sections of it—might be converted to a forceful educational tool. Scobel says:

"I only hope Hyde and Bradenhoff have the good grace to follow Beverly Walensa's advice and keep employees fully and truthfully informed and at least start to build a credibility base for tomorrow. She is right when she says there isn't any way to win except legally, maybe. She speaks with integrity but doesn't seem to have Bradenhoff's ear. Obviously, she was not asked to play much of a role in this important human resource problem. The investigation, the discussion with headquarters, and probably the decision making were handled mostly by the chief counsel."

I would go further. I wonder if Walensa wasn't working on a potent idea when Tillman discouraged her. She was suggesting it might be useful to let every employee have the whole record every day of the previous day's proceedings in court, dirt and all. If, as Bradenhoff and Hyde maintain, management wants to develop higher standards for employees in this rogue division, that trial record could have a chastening effect. Reading the daily transcripts, employees could see for themselves the embarrassment, humiliation, compromises, and other costs that accumulate in an overly "permissive" environment.

"I don't want to end up in a transcript like this" would be a normal reaction. Management ought then to get plenty of cooperation in attempts to institute codes of conduct, as Nolan suggests, sharper accounting systems, as Sherwin suggests, and corporate due process, as Scobel suggests.

Further, daily distribution of the trial record would arm employees with all the information pro and con so that they would never be at a disadvantage in discussing the event with outsiders. I wonder if there is anything quite so denigrating to employees as to have to learn from the media what is going on in their own organization. The message from top management seems to be all too clear: "You only work here." ▽

Theodore Levitt

The morality (?) of advertising

In curbing the excesses of advertising,
both business and government must distinguish
between embellishment and mendacity

Foreword

The present controversy over the regulation of advertising may well result in restrictive legislation of some kind, but it is by no means clear how this should be set up. This article presents a philosophical treatment of the human values of advertising as compared with the values of other "imaginative" disciplines. It is designed to provoke thought about the issues at stake.

A familiar author to the HBR audience, Mr. Levitt is Professor of Business Administration at the Harvard Business School. His article "Why Business Always Loses" (March-April 1968) won the McKinsey Award for that year, and "The New Markets—Think Before You Leap" (May-June 1969) won a John Hancock Award for Excellence for 1969. Recently published is his *The Marketing Mode* (New York, McGraw-Hill Book Company, Inc., 1969). *Reprint 70411*

This year Americans will consume about $20 billion of advertising, and very little of it because we want it. Wherever we turn, advertising will be forcibly thrust on us in an intrusive orgy of abrasive sound and sight, all to induce us to do something we might not ordinarily do, or to induce us to do it differently. This massive and persistent effort crams increasingly more commercial noise into the same, few, strained 24 hours of the day. It has provoked a reaction as predictable as it was inevitable: a lot of people want the noise stopped, or at least alleviated.

And they want it cleaned up and corrected. As more and more products have entered the battle for the consumer's fleeting dollar, advertising has increased in boldness and volume. Last year, industry offered the nation's supermarkets about 100 new products a week, equal, on an annualized basis, to the total number already on their shelves. Where so much must be sold so hard, it is not surprising that advertisers have pressed the limits of our credulity and generated complaints about their exaggerations and deceptions.

Only classified ads, the work of rank amateurs, do we presume to contain solid, unembellished fact. We suspect all the rest of systematic and egregious distortion, if not often of outright mendacity.

The attack on advertising comes from all sectors. Indeed, recent studies show that the people most agitated by advertising are precisely those in the higher income brackets whose affluence is generated by the industries that create the ads.[1] While these studies show that only a modest group of people are preoccupied with

[1] See Raymond A. Bauer and Stephen A. Greyser, *Advertising in America: The Consumer View* (Boston, Division of Research, Harvard Business School, 1968); see also Gary A. Steiner, *The People Look at Television* (New York, Alfred A. Knopf, Inc., 1963).

advertising's constant presence in our lives, they also show that distortion and deception are what bother people most.

This discontent has encouraged Senator Philip Hart and Senator William Proxmire to sponsor consumer-protection and truth-in-advertising legislation. People, they say, want less fluff and more fact about the things they buy. They want description, not distortion, and they want some relief from the constant, grating, vulgar noise.

Legislation seems appropriate because the natural action of competition does not seem to work, or, at least not very well. Competition may ultimately flush out and destroy falsehood and shoddiness, but "ultimately" is too long for the deceived—not just the deceived who are poor, ignorant, and dispossessed, but also all the rest of us who work hard for our money and can seldom judge expertly the truth of conflicting claims about products and services.

The consumer is an amateur, after all; the producer is an expert. In the commercial arena, the consumer is an impotent midget. He is certainly not king. The producer is a powerful giant. It is an uneven match. In this setting, the purifying power of competition helps the consumer very little—especially in the short run, when his money is spent and gone, from the weak hands into the strong hands. Nor does competition among the sellers solve the "noise" problem. The more they compete, the worse the din of advertising.

A broad viewpoint required

Most people spend their money carefully. Understandably, they look out for larcenous attempts to separate them from it. Few men in business will deny the right, perhaps even the wisdom, of people today asking for some restraint on advertising, or at least for more accurate information on the things they buy and for more consumer protection.

Yet, if we speak in the same breath about consumer protection and about advertising's distortions, exaggerations, and deceptions, it is easy to confuse two quite separate things—the legitimate purpose of advertising and the abuses to which it may be put. Rather than deny that distortion and exaggeration exist in advertising, in this article I shall argue that embellishment and distortion are among advertising's legitimate and socially desirable purposes; and that illegitimacy in advertising consists only of falsification with larcenous intent. And while it is difficult, as a practical matter, to draw the line between legitimate distortion and essential falsehood, I want to take a long look at the distinction that exists between the two. This I shall say in advance—the distinction is not as simple, obvious, or great as one might think.

The issue of truth versus falsehood, in advertising or in anything else, is complex and fugitive. It must be pursued in a philosophic mood that might seem foreign to the businessman. Yet the issue at base *is* more philosophic than it is pragmatic. Anyone seriously concerned with the moral problems of a commercial society cannot avoid this fact. I hope the reader will bear with me—I believe he will find it helpful, and perhaps even refreshing.

What is reality?

What, indeed? Consider poetry. Like advertising, poetry's purpose is to influence an audience; to affect its perceptions and sensibilities; perhaps even to change its mind. Like rhetoric, poetry's intent is to convince and seduce. In the service of that intent, it employs without guilt or fear of criticism all the arcane tools of distortion that the literary mind can devise. Keats does not offer a truthful engineering description of his Grecian urn. He offers, instead, with exquisite attention to the effects of meter, rhyme, allusion, illusion, metaphor, and sound, a lyrical, exaggerated, distorted, and palpably false description. And he is thoroughly applauded for it, as are all other artists, in whatever medium, who do precisely this same thing successfully.

Commerce, it can be said without apology, takes essentially the same liberties with reality and literality as the artist, except that commerce calls its creations advertising, or industrial design, or packaging. As with art, the purpose is to influence the audience by creating illusions, symbols, and implications that promise more than pure functionality. Once, when asked what his company did, Charles Revson of Revlon, Inc. suggested a profound distinction: "In the factory we make cosmetics; in the store we sell hope." He obviously has no illusions. It is not cosmetic chemicals women want, but the seductive charm promised by the alluring symbols with which these chemicals have been surrounded—hence the rich and exotic packages in which they are sold, and the suggestive advertising with which they are promoted.

Commerce usually embellishes its products

thrice: first, it designs the product to be pleasing to the eye, to suggest reliability, and so forth; second, it packages the product as attractively as it feasibly can; and then it advertises this at-

tractive package with inviting pictures, slogans, descriptions, songs, and so on. The package and design are as important as the advertising.

The Grecian vessel, for example, was used to carry liquids, but that function does not explain why the potter decorated it with graceful lines and elegant drawings in black and red. A woman's compact carries refined talc, but this does not explain why manufacturers try to make these boxes into works of decorative art.

Neither the poet nor the ad man celebrates the literal functionality of what he produces. Instead, each celebrates a deep and complex emotion which he symbolizes by creative embellishment—a content which cannot be captured by literal description alone. Communication, through advertising or through poetry or any other medium, is a creative conceptualization that implies a vicarious experience through a language of symbolic substitutes. Communication can never be the real thing it talks about. Therefore, all communication is in some inevitable fashion a departure from reality.

Everything is changed ...

Poets, novelists, playwrights, composers, and fashion designers have one thing more in common. They all deal in symbolic communication. None is statisfied with nature in the raw, as it was on the day of creation. None is satisfied to tell it exactly "like it is" to the naked eye, as do the classified ads. It is the purpose of all art to alter nature's surface reality, to reshape, to em-

bellish, and to augment what nature has so crudely fashioned, and then to present it to the same applauding humanity that so eagerly buys Revson's exotically advertised cosmetics.

Few, if any, of us accept the natural state in which God created us. We scrupulously select our clothes to suit a multiplicity of simultaneous purposes, not only for warmth, but manifestly for such other purposes as propriety, status, and seduction. Women modify, embellish, and amplify themselves with colored paste for the lips and powders and lotions for the face; men as well as women use devices to take hair off the face and others to put it on the head. Like the inhabitants of isolated African regions, where not a single whiff of advertising has ever intruded, we all encrust ourselves with rings, pendants, bracelets, neckties, clips, chains, and snaps.

Man lives neither in sackcloth nor in sod huts —although these are not notably inferior to tight clothes and overheated dwellings in congested and polluted cities. Everywhere man rejects nature's uneven blessings. He molds and repackages to his own civilizing specifications an otherwise crude, drab, and generally oppressive reality. He does it so that life may be made for the moment more tolerable than God evidently designed it to be. As T.S. Eliot once remarked, "Human kind cannot bear very much reality."

... into something rich and strange

No line of life is exempt. All the popes of history have countenanced the costly architecture of St. Peter's Basilica and its extravagant interior decoration. All around the globe, nothing typifies man's materialism so much as the temples in which he preaches asceticism. Men of the cloth have not been persuaded that the poetic self-denial of Christ or Buddha—both men of sackcloth and sandals—is enough to inspire, elevate, and hold their flocks together. To amplify the temple in men's eyes, they have, very realistically, systematically sanctioned the embellishment of the houses of the gods with the same kind of luxurious design and expensive decoration that Detroit puts into a Cadillac.

One does not need a doctorate in social an-

thropology to see that the purposeful transmutation of nature's primeval state occupies all people in all cultures and all societies at all stages of development. Everybody everywhere wants to modify, transform, embellish, enrich, and reconstruct the world around him—to introduce into an otherwise harsh or bland existence some sort of purposeful and distorting alleviation. Civilization is man's attempt to transcend his ancient animality; and this includes both art and advertising.

. . . and more than 'real'

But civilized man will undoubtedly deny that either the innovative artist or the *grande dame* with *chic* "distorts reality." Instead, he will say that artist and woman merely embellish, enhance, and illuminate. To be sure, he will mean something quite different by these three terms when he applies them to fine art, on the one hand, and to more secular efforts, on the other.

But this distinction is little more than an affectation. As man has civilized himself and developed his sensibilities, he has invented a great variety of subtle distinctions between things that are objectively indistinct. Let us take a closer look at the difference between man's "sacred" distortions and his "secular" ones.

The man of sensibility will probably canonize the artist's deeds as superior creations by ascribing to them an almost cosmic virtue and significance. As a cultivated individual, he will almost certainly refuse to recognize any constructive, cosmic virtues in the productions of the advertisers, and he is likely to admit the charge that advertising uniformly deceives us by analogous techniques. But how "sensible" is he?

And by similar means . . .

Let us assume for the moment that there is no objective, operational difference between the embellishments and distortions of the artist and those of the ad man—that both men are more concerned with creating images and feelings than with rendering objective, representational, and informational descriptions. The greater virtue of the artist's work must then derive from some subjective element. What is it?

It will be said that art has a higher value for man because it has a higher purpose. True, the artist is interested in philosophic truth or wisdom, and the ad man in selling his goods and services. Michelangelo, when he designed the Sistine chapel ceiling, had some concern with the inspirational elevation of man's spirit, whereas Edward Levy, who designs cosmetics packages, is interested primarily in creating images to help separate the unwary consumer from his loose change.

But this explanation of the difference between

the value of art and the value of advertising is not helpful at all. For is the presence of a "higher" purpose all that redeeming?

Perhaps not; perhaps the reverse is closer to the truth. While the ad man and designer seek only to convert the audience to their commercial custom, Michelangelo sought to convert its soul. Which is the greater blasphemy? Who commits the greater affront to life—he who dabbles with man's erotic appetites, or he who meddles with man's soul? Which act is the easier to judge and justify?

. . . for different ends

How much sense does it really make to distinguish between similar means on the grounds that the ends to which they are directed are different—"good" for art and "not so good" for advertising? The distinction produces zero progress in the argument at hand. How willing are we to employ the involuted ethics whereby the ends justify the means?

Apparently, on this subject, lots of people are very willing indeed. The business executive seems to share with the minister, the painter, and the poet the doctrine that the ends justify the means. The difference is that the businessman is justifying the very commercial ends that his critics oppose. While his critics justify the embellishments of art and literature for what these do for man's spirit, the businessman justifies the embellishment of industrial design and advertising for what they do for man's purse.

Taxing the imagination to the limit, the businessman spins casuistic webs of elaborate transparency to the self-righteous effect that promotion and advertising are socially benign because they expand the economy, create jobs, and raise living standards. Technically, he will always be free to argue, and he *will* argue, that his ends

become the means to the ends of the musician, poet, painter, and minister. The argument which justifies means in terms of ends is obviously not without its subtleties and intricacies.

The executive and the artist are equally tempted to identify and articulate a higher rationale for their work than their work itself. But only in the improved human consequences of their efforts do they find vindication. The aesthete's ringing declaration of "art for art's sake," with all its self-conscious affirmation of selflessness, sounds hollow in the end, even to himself; for, finally, every communication addresses itself to an audience. Thus art is very understandably in constant need of justification by the evidence of its beneficial and divinely approved effect on its audience.

The audience's demands

This compulsion to rationalize even art is a highly instructive fact. It tells one a great deal about art's purposes and the purposes of all other communication. As I have said, the poet and the artist each seek in some special way to produce an emotion or assert a truth not otherwise apparent. But it is only in communion with their audiences that the effectiveness of their efforts can be tested and truth revealed. It may be academic whether a tree falling in the forest makes a noise. It is *not* academic whether a sonnet or a painting has merit. Only an audience can decide that.

The creative person can justify his work only in terms of another person's response to it. Ezra Pound, to be sure, thought that ". . . in the [greatest] works the live part is the part which the artist has put there to please himself, and the dead part is the part he has put there . . . because he thinks he *ought* to—i.e., either to

get or keep an audience." This is certainly consistent with our notions of Pound as perhaps the purest of twentieth-century advocates of art for art's sake.

But if we review the record of his life, we find that Pound spent the greater part of his energies seeking suitable places for deserving poets to publish. Why? Because art has little merit standing alone in unseen and unheard isolation. Merit is not inherent in art. It is conferred by an audience.

The same is true of advertising: if it fails to persuade the audience that the product will fulfill the function the audience expects, the advertising has no merit.

Where have we arrived? Only at some common characteristics of art and advertising. Both are rhetorical, and both literally false; both expound an emotional reality deeper than the "real"; both pretend to "higher" purposes, although different ones; and the excellence of each is judged by its effect on its audience—its persuasiveness, in short. I do not mean to imply that the two are fundamentally the same, but rather that they both represent a pervasive, and I believe *universal*, characteristic of human nature—the human audience *demands* symbolic interpretation in everything it sees and knows. If it doesn't get it, it will return a verdict of "no interest."

To get a clearer idea of the relation between the symbols of advertising and the products they glorify, something more must be said about the fiat the consumer gives to industry to "distort" its messages.

Symbol & substance

As we have seen, man seeks to transcend nature in the raw everywhere. Everywhere, and at all times, he has been attracted by the poetic imagery of some sort of art, literature, music, and mysticism. He obviously wants and needs the promises, the imagery, and the symbols of the poet and the priest. He refuses to live a life of primitive barbarism or sterile functionalism.

Consider a sardine can filled with scented powder. Even if the U.S. Bureau of Standards were to certify that the contents of this package are identical with the product sold in a beautiful paisley-printed container, it would not sell. The Boston matron, for example, who has built herself a deserved reputation for pinching every penny until it hurts, would unhesitatingly turn it down. While she may deny it, in self-assured

and neatly cadenced accents, she obviously desires and needs the promises, imagery, and symbols produced by hyperbolic advertisements, elaborate packages, and fetching fashions.

The need for embellishment is not confined to personal appearance. A few years ago, an electronics laboratory offered a $700 testing device for sale. The company ordered two different front panels to be designed, one by the engineers who developed the equipment and one by professional industrial designers. When the two models were shown to a sample of laboratory directors with Ph.D.'s, the professional design attracted twice the purchase intentions that the engineer's design did. Obviously, the laboratory director who has been baptized into science at M.I.T. is quite as responsive to the blandishments of packaging as the Boston matron.

And, obviously, both these customers define the products they buy in much more sophisticated terms than the engineer in the factory. For a woman, dusting powder in a sardine can is not the same product as the identical dusting powder in an exotic paisley package. For the laboratory director, the test equipment behind an engineer-designed panel just isn't as "good" as the identical equipment in a box designed with finesse.

Form follows the ideal function

The consumer refuses to settle for pure operating functionality. "Form follows function" is a resoundingly vacuous cliché which, like all clichés, depends for its memorability more on its alliteration and brevity than on its wisdom. If it has any truth, it is only in the elastic sense that function extends beyond strict mechanical use into the domain of imagination. We do not choose to buy a particular product; we choose to buy the functional expectations that we attach to it, and we buy these expectations as "tools" to help us solve a problem of life.

Under normal circumstances, furthermore, we must judge a product's "nonmechanical" utilities before we actually buy it. It is rare that we choose an object after we have experienced it; nearly always we must make the choice before the fact. We choose on the basis of promises, not experiences.

Whatever symbols convey and *sustain* these promises in our minds are therefore truly functional. The promises and images which imaginative ads and sculptured packages induce in us are as much the product as the physical materials themselves. To put this another way, these ads and packagings describe the product's fullness for us: in our minds, the product becomes a complex abstraction which is, as Immanuel Kant might have said, the conception of a perfection which has not yet been experienced.

But all promises and images, almost by their very nature, exceed their capacity to live up to themselves. As every eager lover has ever known, the consummation seldom equals the promises which produced the chase. To forestall and suppress the visceral expectation of disappointment that life has taught us must inevitably come, we use art, architecture, literature, and the rest, and advertising as well, to shield ourselves, in advance of experience, from the stark and plain reality in which we are fated to live. I agree that we wish for unobtainable unrealities, "dream castles." But why promise ourselves reality, which we already possess? What we want is what we do *not* possess!

Everyone in the world is trying in his special personal fashion to solve a primal problem of life—the problem of rising above his own negligibility, of escaping from nature's confining, hostile, and unpredictable reality, of finding significance, security, and comfort in the things he must do to survive. Many of the so-called distortions of advertising, product design, and packaging may be viewed as a paradigm of the many responses that man makes to the conditions of survival in the environment. Without distortion, embellishment, and elaboration, life would be drab, dull, anguished, and at its existential worst.

Symbolism useful & necessary

With*out* symbolism, furthermore, life would be even more confusing and anxiety-ridden than it is *with* it. The foot soldier must be able to recognize the general, good or bad, because the general is clothed with power. A general without his stars and suite of aides-de-camp to set him apart from the privates would suffer in authority and credibility as much as perfume packaged by Dracula or a computer designed by Rube Goldberg. Any ordinary soldier or civilian who has ever had the uncommon experience of being in the same shower with a general can testify from the visible unease of the latter how much clothes "make the man."

Similarly, verbal symbols help to make the product—they help us deal with the uncertainties of daily life. "You can be sure ... if it's

Westinghouse" is a decision rule as useful to the man buying a turbine generator as to the man buying an electric shaver. To label all the devices and embellishments companies employ to reassure the prospective customer about a product's quality with the pejorative term "gimmick," as critics tend to do, is simply silly. Worse, it denies, against massive evidence, man's honest needs and values. If religion must be architectured, packaged, lyricized, and musicized to attract and hold its audience, and if sex must be perfumed, powdered, sprayed, and shaped in order to command attention, it is ridiculous to deny the legitimacy of more modest, and similar, embellishments to the world of commerce.

But still, the critics may say, commercial communications tend to be aggressively deceptive. Perhaps, and perhaps not. The issue at stake here is more complex than the outraged critic believes. Man wants and needs the elevation of the spirit produced by attractive surroundings, by handsome packages, and by imaginative promises. He needs the assurances projected by well-known brand names, and the reliability suggested by salesmen who have been taught to dress by Oleg Cassini and to speak by Dale Carnegie. Of course, there are blatant, tasteless, and willfully deceiving salesmen and advertisers, just as there are blatant, tasteless, and willfully deceiving artists, preachers, and even professors. But, before talking blithely about deception, it is helpful to make a distinction between things and descriptions of things.

The question of deceit

Poetic descriptions of things make no pretense of being the things themselves. Nor do advertisements, even by the most elastic standards. Advertisements are the symbols of man's aspirations. They are not the real things, nor are they intended to be, nor are they accepted as such by the public. A study some years ago by the Center for Research in Marketing, Inc. concluded that deep down inside the consumer understands this perfectly well and has the attitude that an advertisement is an ad, not a factual news story.

Even Professor Galbraith grants the point when he says that "... because modern man is exposed to a large volume of information of varying degrees of unreliability ... he establishes a system of discounts which he applies to various sources almost without thought.... The discount becomes nearly total for all forms of advertising. The merest child watching television dismisses the health and status-giving claims of a breakfast cereal as 'a commercial.' " [2]

This is not to say, of course, that Galbraith also discounts advertising's effectiveness. Quite the opposite: "Failure to win belief does not impair the effectiveness of the management of demand for consumer products. Management involves the creation of a compelling image of the product in the mind of the consumer. To this he responds more or less automatically under circumstances where the purchase does not merit a great deal of thought. For building this image, palpable fantasy may be more valuable than circumstantial evidence." [3]

Linguists and other communications specialists will agree with the conclusion of the Center for Research in Marketing that "advertising is a symbol system existing in a world of symbols. Its reality depends upon the fact that it is a symbol ... the content of an ad can never be real, it can only say something about reality, or create a relationship between itself and an individual which has an effect on the reality life of an individual."

Consumer, know thyself!

Consumption is man's most constant activity. It is well that he understands himself as a consumer.

The object of consumption is to solve a problem. Even consumption that is viewed as the creation of an opportunity—like going to medi-

cal school or taking a singles-only Caribbean tour—has as its purpose the solving of a problem. At a minimum, the medical student seeks to solve the problem of how to lead a relevant and comfortable life, and the lady on the tour seeks to solve the problem of spinsterhood.

The "purpose" of the product is not what the engineer explicitly says it is, but what the consumer implicitly demands that it shall be. Thus the consumer consumes not things, but expected benefits—not cosmetics, but the satisfactions of the allurements they promise; not quarter-inch drills, but quarter-inch holes; not stock in companies, but capital gains; not numerically controlled milling machines, but trouble-free and accurately smooth metal parts; not low-cal whipped cream, but self-rewarding indulgence combined with sophisticated convenience.

The significance of these distinctions is anything but trivial. Nobody knows this better, for example, than the creators of automobile ads. It is not the generic virtues that they tout, but more likely the car's capacity to enhance its user's status and his access to female prey.

Whether we are aware of it or not, we in effect expect and demand that advertising create these symbols for us to show us what life *might* be, to bring the possibilities that we cannot see before our eyes and screen out the stark reality in which we must live. We insist, as Gilbert put it, that there be added a "touch of artistic verisimilitude to an otherwise bald and unconvincing narrative."

Understanding the difference

In a world where so many things are either commonplace or standardized, it makes no sense to refer to the rest as false, fraudulent, frivolous, or immaterial. The world works according to the aspirations and needs of its actors, not according to the arcane or moralizing logic of detached critics who pine for another age—an age which, in any case, seems different from today's largely because its observers are no longer children shielded by protective parents from life's implacable harshness.

To understand this is not to condone much of the vulgarity, purposeful duplicity, and scheming half-truths we see in advertising, promotion, packaging, and product design. But before we condemn, it is well to understand the differ-

2. John Kenneth Galbraith, *The New Industrial State* (Boston, Houghton Mifflin Company, 1967), pp. 325-326.

3. Ibid., p. 326.

ence between embellishment and duplicity and how extraordinarily uncommon the latter is in our times. The noisy visibility of promotion in our intensely communicating times need not be thoughtlessly equated with malevolence.

Thus the issue is not the prevention of distortion. It is, in the end, to know what kinds of distortions we actually want so that each of our lives is, without apology, duplicity, or rancor, made bearable. This does not mean we must accept out of hand all the commercial propaganda

to which we are each day so constantly exposed, or that we must accept out of hand the equation that effluence is the price of affluence, or the simple notion that business cannot and government should not try to alter and improve the position of the consumer vis-à-vis the producer. It takes a special kind of perversity to continue any longer our shameful failure to mount vigorous, meaningful programs to protect the consumer, to standardize product grades, labels, and packages, to improve the consumer's information-getting process, and to mitigate the

vulgarity and oppressiveness that is in so much of our advertising.

But the consumer suffers from an old dilemma. He wants "truth," but he also wants and needs the alleviating imagery and tantalizing promises of the advertiser and designer.

Business is caught in the middle. There is hardly a company that would not go down in ruin if it refused to provide fluff, because nobody will buy pure functionality. Yet, if it uses too much fluff and little else, business invites possibly ruinous legislation. The problem therefore is to find a middle way. And in this search, business can do a great deal more than it has been either accustomed or willing to do:

○ It can exert pressure to make sure that no single industry "finds reasons" why it should be exempt from legislative restrictions that are reasonable and popular.

○ It can work constructively with government to develop reasonable standards and effective sanctions that will assure a more amenable commercial environment.

○ It can support legislation to provide the consumer with the information he needs to make easy comparison between products, packages, and prices.

○ It can support and help draft improved legislation on quality stabilization.

○ It can support legislation that gives consumers easy access to strong legal remedies where justified.

○ It can support programs to make local legal aid easily available, especially to the poor and undereducated who know so little about their rights and how to assert them.

○ Finally, it can support efforts to moderate and clean up the advertising noise that dulls our senses and assaults our sensibilities.

It will not be the end of the world or of capitalism for business to sacrifice a few commercial freedoms so that we may more easily enjoy our own humanity. Business can and should, for its own good, work energetically to achieve this end. But it is also well to remember the limits of what is possible. Paradise was not a free-goods society. The forbidden fruit was gotten at a price.

Albert Z. Carr

Is business bluffing ethical?

*The ethics of business are not those of
society, but rather those of the poker game*

Foreword

"If the law as written gives a man a wide-open chance to make a killing, he'd be a fool not to take advantage of it. If he doesn't, somebody else will," remarked a friend of the author. Mr. Carr likens such behavior to the bluffing of the poker player who seizes every opportunity to win, as long as it does not involve outright cheating. "No one thinks any the worse of poker on that account," says the author. "And no one should think any the worse of the game of business because its standards of right and wrong differ from the prevailing traditions of morality in our society."

Mr. Carr became interested in this subject when he was a member of a New York firm of consultants to large corporations in many fields. The confidences of many stress-ridden executives made him aware of the extent to which tensions can arise from conflicts between an individual's ethical sense and the realities of business. He was struck also by the similarity of the special ethical attitude shown by many successful and stress-free businessmen in their work to that of good poker players.

Mr. Carr was Assistant to the Chairman of the War Production Board during World War II and later served on the White House staff and as a Special Consultant to President Truman. He is now writing full-time. Among his books is *John D. Rockefeller's Secret Weapon*, a study of corporate development. This article is adapted from a chapter in his book, *Business As a Game*, published by New American Library in 1968. *Reprint 68102*

A respected businessman with whom I discussed the theme of this article remarked with some heat, "You mean to say you're going to encourage men to bluff? Why, bluffing is nothing more than a form of lying! You're advising them to lie!"

I agreed that the basis of private morality is a respect for truth and that the closer a businessman comes to the truth, the more he deserves respect. At the same time, I suggested that most bluffing in business might be regarded simply as game strategy—much like bluffing in poker, which does not reflect on the morality of the bluffer.

I quoted Henry Taylor, the British statesman who pointed out that "falsehood ceases to be falsehood when it is understood on all sides that the truth is not expected to be spoken"—an exact description of bluffing in poker, diplomacy, and business. I cited the analogy of the criminal court, where the criminal is not expected to tell the truth when he pleads "not guilty." Everyone from the judge down takes it for granted that the job of the defendant's attorney is to get his client off, not to reveal the truth; and this is considered ethical practice. I mentioned Representative Omar Burleson, the Democrat from Texas, who was quoted as saying, in regard to the ethics of Congress, "Ethics is a barrel of worms" [1]—a pungent summing up of the problem of deciding who is ethical in politics.

I reminded my friend that millions of businessmen feel constrained every day to say *yes* to their bosses when they secretly believe *no* and that this is generally accepted as permissible strategy when the alternative might be the loss

1. *The New York Times*, March 9, 1967.

of a job. The essential point, I said, is that the ethics of business are game ethics, different from the ethics of religion.

He remained unconvinced. Referring to the company of which he is president, he declared: "Maybe that's good enough for some business-men, but I can tell you that we pride ourselves on our ethics. In 30 years not one customer has ever questioned my word or asked to check our figures. We're loyal to our customers and fair to our suppliers. I regard my handshake on a deal as a contract. I've never entered into price-fixing schemes with my competitors. I've never allowed my salesmen to spread injurious rumors about other companies. Our union contract is the best in our industry. And, if I do say so my-self, our ethical standards are of the highest!"

He really was saying, without realizing it, that he was living up to the ethical standards of the business game—which are a far cry from those of private life. Like a gentlemanly poker player, he did not play in cahoots with others at the table, try to smear their reputations, or hold back chips he owed them.

But this same fine man, at that very time, was allowing one of his products to be adver-tised in a way that made it sound a great deal better than it actually was. Another item in his product line was notorious among dealers for its "built-in obsolescence." He was holding back from the market a much-improved product be-cause he did not want it to interfere with sales of the inferior item it would have replaced. He had joined with certain of his competitors in hiring a lobbyist to push a state legislature, by methods that he preferred not to know too much about, into amending a bill then being enacted.

In his view these things had nothing to do with ethics; they were merely normal business practice. He himself undoubtedly avoided out-right falsehoods—never lied in so many words. But the entire organization that he ruled was deeply involved in numerous strategies of de-ception.

Pressure to deceive

Most executives from time to time are almost compelled, in the interests of their companies or themselves, to practice some form of decep-tion when negotiating with customers, dealers, labor unions, government officials, or even other departments of their companies. By con-scious misstatements, concealment of pertinent facts, or exaggeration—in short, by bluffing—they seek to persuade others to agree with them. I think it is fair to say that if the individual executive refuses to bluff from time to time—if he feels obligated to tell the truth, the whole truth, and nothing but the truth—he is ignoring opportunities permitted under the rules and is at a heavy disadvantage in his business dealings.

But here and there a businessman is unable to reconcile himself to the bluff in which he plays a part. His conscience, perhaps spurred by religious idealism, troubles him. He feels guilty; he may develop an ulcer or a nervous tic. Before any executive can make profitable use of the strategy of the bluff, he needs to make sure that in bluffing he will not lose self-respect or become emotionally disturbed. If he is to reconcile personal integrity and high standards of honesty with the practical requirements of business, he must feel that his bluffs are ethical-ly justified. The justification rests on the fact that business, as practiced by individuals as well as by corporations, has the impersonal character of a game—a game that demands both special strategy and an understanding of its spe-cial ethics.

The game is played at all levels of corporate life, from the highest to the lowest. At the very instant that a man decides to enter business, he may be forced into a game situation, as is shown by the recent experience of a Cornell honor graduate who applied for a job with a large company:

□ This applicant was given a psychological test which included the statement, "Of the fol-lowing magazines, check any that you have read either regularly or from time to time, and double-check those which interest you most. *Reader's Digest, Time, Fortune, Saturday Evening Post, The New Republic, Life, Look, Ramparts, Newsweek, Business Week, U.S. News & World Report, The Nation, Playboy, Esquire, Harper's, Sports Illustrated.*"

His tastes in reading were broad, and at one time or another he had read almost all of these magazines. He was a subscriber to *The New Re-public*, an enthusiast for *Ramparts*, and an avid student of the pictures in *Playboy*. He was not sure whether his interest in *Playboy* would be held against him, but he had a shrewd suspicion that if he confessed to an interest in *Ramparts* and *The New Republic*, he would be thought a liberal, a radical, or at least an intellectual, and his chances of getting the job, which he needed, would greatly diminish. He therefore checked five of the more conservative magazines. Apparently it was a sound decision, for he got the job.

He had made a game player's decision, consistent with business ethics.

A similar case is that of a magazine space salesman who, owing to a merger, suddenly found himself out of a job:

☐ This man was 58, and, in spite of a good record, his chance of getting a job elsewhere in a business where youth is favored in hiring practice was not good. He was a vigorous, healthy man, and only a considerable amount of gray in his hair suggested his age. Before beginning his job search he touched up his hair with a black dye to confine the gray to his temples. He knew that the truth about his age might well come out in time, but he calculated that he could deal with that situation when it arose. He and his wife decided that he could easily pass for 45, and he so stated his age on his résumé.

This was a lie; yet within the accepted rules of the business game, no moral culpability attaches to it.

The poker analogy

We can learn a good deal about the nature of business by comparing it with poker. While both have a large element of chance, in the long run the winner is the man who plays with steady skill. In both games ultimate victory requires intimate knowledge of the rules, insight into the psychology of the other players, a bold front, a considerable amount of self-discipline, and the ability to respond swiftly and effectively to opportunities provided by chance.

No one expects poker to be played on the ethical principles preached in churches. In poker it is right and proper to bluff a friend out of the rewards of being dealt a good hand. A player feels no more than a slight twinge of sympathy, if that, when—with nothing better than a single ace in his hand—he strips a heavy loser, who holds a pair, of the rest of his chips. It was up to the other fellow to protect himself. In the words of an excellent poker player, former President Harry Truman, "If you can't stand the heat, stay out of the kitchen." If one shows mercy to a loser in poker, it is a personal gesture, divorced from the rules of the game.

Poker has its special ethics, and here I am not referring to rules against cheating. The man who keeps an ace up his sleeve or who marks the cards is more than unethical; he is a crook, and can be punished as such—kicked out of the game or, in the Old West, shot.

In contrast to the cheat, the unethical poker player is one who, while abiding by the letter of the rules, finds ways to put the other players at an unfair disadvantage. Perhaps he unnerves them with loud talk. Or he tries to get them drunk. Or he plays in cahoots with someone else at the table. Ethical poker players frown on such tactics.

Poker's own brand of ethics is different from the ethical ideals of civilized human relationships. The game calls for distrust of the other fellow. It ignores the claim of friendship. Cunning deception and concealment of one's strength and intentions, not kindness and openheartedness, are vital in poker. No one thinks any the worse of poker on that account. And no one should think any the worse of the game of business because its standards of right and wrong differ from the prevailing traditions of morality in our society.

Discard the golden rule

This view of business is especially worrisome to people without much business experience. A minister of my acquaintance once protested that business cannot possibly function in our society unless it is based on the Judeo-Christian system of ethics. He told me:

"I know some businessmen have supplied call girls to customers, but there are always a few rotten apples in every barrel. That doesn't mean the rest of the fruit isn't sound. Surely the vast majority of businessmen are ethical. I myself am acquainted with many who adhere to strict codes of ethics based fundamentally on religious teachings. They contribute to good causes. They participate in community activities. They cooperate with other companies to improve working conditions in their industries. Certainly they are not indifferent to ethics."

That most businessmen are not indifferent to ethics in their private lives, everyone will agree. My point is that in their office lives they cease to be private citizens; they become game players who must be guided by a somewhat different set of ethical standards.

The point was forcefully made to me by a Midwestern executive who has given a good deal of thought to the question:

"So long as a businessman complies with the laws of the land and avoids telling malicious lies, he's ethical. If the law as written gives a man a wide-open chance to make a killing, he'd be a fool not to take advantage of it. If he doesn't, somebody else will. There's no obligation on him to stop and consider who is going to get hurt. If the law says he can do it, that's all the justification he needs. There's nothing unethical about that. It's just plain business sense."

This executive (call him Robbins) took the stand that even industrial espionage, which is frowned on by some businessmen, ought not to be considered unethical. He recalled a recent meeting of the National Industrial Conference Board where an authority on marketing made a speech in which he deplored the employment of spies by business organizations. More and more companies, he pointed out, find it cheaper to penetrate the secrets of competitors with concealed cameras and microphones or by bribing employees than to set up costly research and design departments of their own. A whole branch of the electronics industry has grown up with this trend, he continued, providing equipment to make industrial espionage easier.

Disturbing? The marketing expert found it so. But when it came to a remedy, he could only appeal to "respect for the golden rule." Robbins thought this a confession of defeat, believing that the golden rule, for all its value as an ideal for society, is simply not feasible as a guide for business. A good part of the time the businessman is trying to do unto others as he hopes others will *not* do unto him.[2] Robbins continued:

"Espionage of one kind or another has become so common in business that it's like taking a drink during Prohibition—it's not considered sinful. And we don't even have Prohibition where espionage is concerned; the law is very tolerant in this area. There's no more shame for a business that uses secret agents than there is for a nation. Bear in mind that there already

is at least one large corporation—you can buy its stock over the counter—that makes millions by providing counterespionage service to industrial firms. Espionage in business is not an ethical problem; it's an established technique of business competition."

'We don't make the laws'

Wherever we turn in business, we can perceive the sharp distinction between its ethical standards and those of the churches. Newspapers abound with sensational stories growing out of this distinction:

☐ We read one day that Senator Philip A. Hart of Michigan has attacked food processors for deceptive packaging of numerous products.[3]

☐ The next day there is a Congressional to-do over Ralph Nader's book, *Unsafe At Any Speed*, which demonstrates that automobile companies for years have neglected the safety of car-owning families.[4]

☐ Then another Senator, Lee Metcalf of Montana, and journalist Vic Reinemer show in their book, *Overcharge*, the methods by which utility companies elude regulating government bodies to extract unduly large payments from users of electricity.[5]

These are merely dramatic instances of a prevailing condition; there is hardly a major industry at which a similar attack could not be aimed. Critics of business regard such behavior as unethical, but the companies concerned know that they are merely playing the business game.

Among the most respected of our business institutions are the insurance companies. A group of insurance executives meeting recently in New England was startled when their guest speaker, social critic Daniel Patrick Moynihan, roundly berated them for "unethical" practices. They had been guilty, Moynihan alleged, of using outdated actuarial tables to obtain unfairly high premiums. They habitually delayed the hearings of lawsuits against them in order to tire out the plaintiffs and win cheap settlements. In their employment policies they used ingenious devices to discriminate against certain minority groups.[6]

It was difficult for the audience to deny the validity of these charges. But these men were business game players. Their reaction to Moynihan's attack was much the same as that of the automobile manufacturers to Nader, of the utili-

2. See Bruce D. Henderson, "Brinkmanship in Business," HBR March-April 1967, p. 49.

3. *The New York Times*, November 21, 1966.

4. New York, Grossman Publishers, Inc., 1965.

5. New York, David McKay Company, Inc., 1967.

6. *The New York Times*, January 17, 1967.

ties to Senator Metcalf, and of the food processors to Senator Hart. If the laws governing their businesses change, or if public opinion becomes clamorous, they will make the necessary adjustments. But morally they have in their view done nothing wrong. As long as they comply with the letter of the law, they are within their rights to operate their businesses as they see fit.

The small business is in the same position as the great corporation in this respect. For example:

☐ In 1967 a key manufacturer was accused of providing master keys for automobiles to mail-order customers, although it was obvious that some of the purchasers might be automobile thieves. His defense was plain and straightforward. If there was nothing in the law to prevent him from selling his keys to anyone who ordered them, it was not up to him to inquire as to his customers' motives. Why was it any worse, he insisted, for him to sell car keys by mail, than for mail-order houses to sell guns that might be used for murder? Until the law was changed, the key manufacturer could regard himself as being just as ethical as any other businessman by the rules of the business game.[7]

Violations of the ethical ideals of society are common in business, but they are not necessarily violations of business principles. Each year the Federal Trade Commission orders hundreds of companies, many of them of the first magnitude, to "cease and desist" from practices which, judged by ordinary standards, are of questionable morality but which are stoutly defended by the companies concerned.

In one case, a firm manufacturing a well-known mouthwash was accused of using a cheap form of alcohol possibly deleterious to health. The company's chief executive, after testifying in Washington, made this comment privately:

"We broke no law. We're in a highly competitive industry. If we're going to stay in business, we have to look for profit wherever the law permits. We don't make the laws. We obey them. Then why do we have to put up with this 'holier than thou' talk about ethics? It's sheer hypocrisy. We're not in business to promote ethics. Look at the cigarette companies, for God's sake! If the ethics aren't embodied in the laws by the men who made them, you can't expect businessmen to fill the lack. Why, a sudden submission to Christian ethics by businessmen would bring about the greatest economic upheaval in history!"

It may be noted that the government failed to prove its case against him.

Cast illusions aside

Talk about ethics by businessmen is often a thin decorative coating over the hard realities of the game:

☐ Once I listened to a speech by a young executive who pointed to a new industry code as proof that his company and its competitors were deeply aware of their responsibilities to society. It was a code of ethics, he said. The industry was going to police itself, to dissuade constituent companies from wrongdoing. His eyes shone with conviction and enthusiasm.

The same day there was a meeting in a hotel room where the industry's top executives met with the "czar" who was to administer the new code, a man of high repute. No one who was present could doubt their common attitude. In their eyes the code was designed primarily to forestall a move by the federal government to impose stern restrictions on the industry. They felt that the code would hamper them a good deal less than new federal laws would. It was, in other words, conceived as a protection for the industry, not for the public.

The young executive accepted the surface explanation of the code; these leaders, all experienced game players, did not deceive themselves for a moment about its purpose.

The illusion that business can afford to be guided by ethics as conceived in private life is often fostered by speeches and articles containing such phrases as, "It pays to be ethical," or, "Sound ethics is good business." Actually this is not an ethical position at all; it is a self-serving calculation in disguise. The speaker is really saying that in the long run a company can make more money if it does not antagonize competitors, suppliers, employees, and customers by squeezing them too hard. He is saying that oversharp policies reduce ultimate gains. That is true, but it has nothing to do with ethics. The underlying attitude is much like that in the familiar story of the shopkeeper who finds an extra $20 bill in the cash register, debates with himself the ethical problem—should he tell his partner?—and finally decides to share the money because the gesture will give him an edge over the s.o.b. the next time they quarrel.

7. Cited by Ralph Nader in "Business Crime," *The New Republic*, July 1, 1967, p. 7.

I think it is fair to sum up the prevailing attitude of businessmen on ethics as follows:

We live in what is probably the most competitive of the world's civilized societies. Our customs encourage a high degree of aggression in the individual's striving for success. Business is our main area of competition, and it has been ritualized into a game of strategy. The basic rules of the game have been set by the government, which attempts to detect and punish business frauds. But as long as a company does not transgress the rules of the game set by law, it has the legal right to shape its strategy without reference to anything but its profits. If it takes a long-term view of its profits, it will preserve amicable relations, so far as possible, with those with whom it deals. A wise businessman will not seek advantage to the point where he generates dangerous hostility among employees, competitors, customers, government, or the public at large. But decisions in this area are, in the final test, decisions of strategy, not of ethics.

The individual & the game

An individual within a company often finds it difficult to adjust to the requirements of the business game. He tries to preserve his private ethical standards in situations that call for game strategy. When he is obliged to carry out company policies that challenge his conception of himself as an ethical man, he suffers.

It disturbs him when he is ordered, for instance, to deny a raise to a man who deserves it, to fire an employee of long standing, to prepare advertising that he believes to be misleading, to conceal facts that he feels customers are entitled to know, to cheapen the quality of materials used in the manufacture of an established product, to sell as new a product that he knows to be rebuilt, to exaggerate the curative powers of a medicinal preparation, or to coerce dealers.

There are some fortunate executives who, by the nature of their work and circumstances, never have to face problems of this kind. But in one form or another the ethical dilemma is felt sooner or later by most businessmen. Possibly the dilemma is most painful not when the company forces the action on the executive but when he originates it himself—that is, when he has taken or is contemplating a step which is in his own interest but which runs counter to his early moral conditioning. To illustrate:

□ The manager of an export department, eager to show rising sales, is pressed by a big customer to provide invoices which, while containing no overt falsehood that would violate a U.S. law, are so worded that the customer may be able to evade certain taxes in his homeland.

□ A company president finds that an aging executive, within a few years of retirement and his pension, is not as productive as formerly. Should he be kept on?

□ The produce manager of a supermarket debates with himself whether to get rid of a lot of half-rotten tomatoes by including one, with its good side exposed, in every tomato six-pack.

□ An accountant discovers that he has taken an improper deduction on his company's tax return and fears the consequences if he calls the matter to the president's attention, though he himself has done nothing illegal. Perhaps if he says nothing, no one will notice the error.

□ A chief executive officer is asked by his directors to comment on a rumor that he owns stock in another company with which he has placed large orders. He could deny it, for the stock is in the name of his son-in-law and he has earlier formally instructed his son-in-law to sell the holding.

Temptations of this kind constantly arise in business. If an executive allows himself to be torn between a decision based on business considerations and one based on his private ethical code, he exposes himself to a grave psychological strain.

This is not to say that sound business strategy necessarily runs counter to ethical ideals. They may frequently coincide; and when they do, everyone is gratified. But the major tests of every move in business, as in all games of strategy, are legality and profit. A man who intends to be a winner in the business game must have a game player's attitude.

The business strategist's decisions must be as impersonal as those of a surgeon performing an operation—concentrating on objective and technique, and subordinating personal feelings. If the chief executive admits that his son-in-law owns the stock, it is because he stands to lose more if the fact comes out later than if he states it boldly and at once. If the supermarket manager orders the rotten tomatoes to be discarded, he does so to avoid an increase in consumer complaints and a loss of goodwill. The company president decides not to fire the elderly executive in the belief that the negative reaction of other employees would in the long run cost the company more than it would lose in keeping him and paying his pension.

All sensible businessmen prefer to be truthful, but they seldom feel inclined to tell the *whole* truth. In the business game truth-telling usually has to be kept within narrow limits if trouble is to be avoided. The point was neatly made a long time ago (in 1888) by one of John D. Rockefeller's associates, Paul Babcock, to Standard Oil Company executives who were about to testify before a government investigating committee: "Parry every question with answers which, while perfectly truthful, are evasive of *bottom* facts." [8] This was, is, and probably always will be regarded as wise and permissible business strategy.

For office use only

An executive's family life can easily be dislocated if he fails to make a sharp distinction between the ethical systems of the home and the office—or if his wife does not grasp that distinction. Many a businessman who has remarked to his wife, "I had to let Jones go today" or "I had to admit to the boss that Jim has been goofing off lately," has been met with an indignant protest. "How could you do a thing like that? You know Jones is over 50 and will have a lot of trouble getting another job." Or, "You did that to Jim? With his wife ill and all the worry she's been having with the kids?"

If the executive insists that he had no choice because the profits of the company and his own security were involved, he may see a certain cool and ominous reappraisal in his wife's eyes. Many wives are not prepared to accept the fact that business operates with a special code of ethics. An illuminating illustration of this comes from a Southern sales executive who related a conversation he had had with his wife at a time when a hotly contested political campaign was being waged in their state:

"I made the mistake of telling her that I had had lunch with Colby, who gives me about half my business. Colby mentioned that his company had a stake in the election. Then he said, 'By the way, I'm treasurer of the citizens' committee for Lang. I'm collecting contributions. Can I count on you for a hundred dollars?'

"Well, there I was. I was opposed to Lang, but I knew Colby. If he withdrew his business I could be in a bad spot. So I just smiled and wrote out a check then and there. He thanked me, and we started to talk about his next order. Maybe he thought I shared his political views. If so, I wasn't going to lose any sleep over it.

"I should have had sense enough not to tell Mary about it. She hit the ceiling. She said she was disappointed in me. She said I hadn't acted like a man, that I should have stood up to Colby.

"I said, 'Look, it was an either-or situation. I had to do it or risk losing the business.'

"She came back at me with, 'I don't believe it. You could have been honest with him. You could have said that you didn't feel you ought to contribute to a campaign for a man you weren't going to vote for. I'm sure he would have understood.'

"I said, 'Mary, you're a wonderful woman, but you're way off the track. Do you know what would have happened if I had said that? Colby would have smiled and said, "Oh, I didn't realize. Forget it." But in his eyes from that moment I would be an oddball, maybe a bit of a radical. He would have listened to me talk about his order and would have promised to give it consideration. After that I wouldn't hear from him for a week. Then I would telephone and learn from his secretary that he wasn't yet ready to place the order. And in about a month I would hear through the grapevine that he was giving his business to another company. A month after that I'd be out of a job.'

"She was silent for a while. Then she said, 'Tom, something is wrong with business when a man is forced to choose between his family's security and his moral obligation to himself. It's easy for me to say you should have stood up to him—but if you had, you might have felt you were betraying me and the kids. I'm sorry that you did it, Tom, but I can't blame you. Something is wrong with business!' "

This wife saw the problem in terms of moral obligation as conceived in private life; her husband saw it as a matter of game strategy. As a player in a weak position, he felt that he could not afford to indulge an ethical sentiment that might have cost him his seat at the table.

Playing to win

Some men might challenge the Colbys of business—might accept serious setbacks to their business careers rather than risk a feeling of

8. Babcock in a memorandum to Rockefeller (Rockefeller Archives).

moral cowardice. They merit our respect—but as private individuals, not businessmen. When the skillful player of the business game is compelled to submit to unfair pressure, he does not castigate himself for moral weakness. Instead, he strives to put himself into a strong position where he can defend himself against such pressures in the future without loss.

If a man plans to take a seat in the business game, he owes it to himself to master the principles by which the game is played, including its special ethical outlook. He can then hardly fail to recognize that an occasional bluff may well be justified in terms of the game's ethics and warranted in terms of economic necessity. Once he clears his mind on this point, he is in a good position to match his strategy against that of the other players. He can then determine objectively whether a bluff in a given situation has a good chance of succeeding and can decide when and how to bluff, without a feeling of ethical transgression.

To be a winner, a man must play to win. This does not mean that he must be ruthless, cruel, harsh, or treacherous. On the contrary, the better his reputation for integrity, honesty, and decency, the better his chances of victory will be in the long run. But from time to time every businessman, like every poker player, is offered a choice between certain loss or bluffing within the legal rules of the game. If he is not resigned to losing, if he wants to rise in his company and industry, then in such a crisis he will bluff—and bluff hard.

Every now and then one meets a successful businessman who has conveniently forgotten the small or large deceptions that he practiced on his way to fortune. "God gave me my money," old John D. Rockefeller once piously told a Sunday school class. It would be a rare tycoon in our time who would risk the horse laugh with which such a remark would be greeted.

In the last third of the twentieth century even children are aware that if a man has become prosperous in business, he has sometimes departed from the strict truth in order to overcome obstacles or has practiced the more subtle deceptions of the half-truth or the misleading omission. Whatever the form of the bluff, it is an integral part of the game, and the executive who does not master its techniques is not likely to accumulate much money or power.

The executive's conscience

It must be admitted...that not all ethical questions in business can be sharply divided between black and white. Often there is a gray area within which honorable men may differ. When the question falls in that category the junior may properly accept the judgment of his superior, and carry out his instruction. But where the action required is unqualifiedly repugnant to his own conscience he has no alternative. He must quit rather than go ahead. The consequences may be devastating in his own life. The threat to his financial security, and to the welfare of his family, may be almost beyond his power to cope with. Nevertheless the answer is clear. He must walk off the job and preserve his honor, no matter what the sacrifice.

The key...is the executive's personal sensitivity to ethical problems. Few men who are able and mature enough to carry significant responsibility in the business world transgress the general code of morality with the conscious intention of doing wrong. The difficulty is that the warning bell of their conscience does not ring as they take their decisions. They plunge into action without pausing to reflect upon the moral implications of the course to which they are committing themselves and their corporations. They have been carefully trained in engineering, cost accounting, pricing, human relations, and other phases of management, but not in ethics.

What industry needs to offset the growing atmosphere of public suspicion is new emphasis on conscience, new discussion of ethical problems at all levels, and greater awareness of the importance of moral considerations in the formation of management policy.

Clarence B. Randall,
The Executive in Transition,
New York,
McGraw-Hill Book Company,
1967, pp. 137-138.

Are corporate executives overpaid?

John C. Baker

Supplements to their spectacular salaries make some executives resemble 'present-day royalty'

The system by which top executives of large, publicly owned U.S. corporations are rewarded has got out of hand, a long-time observer of compensation practices charges in this article. While maintaining that capable managers should be well compensated, the author criticizes such aspects of the system as inordinately high salaries and payments based on corporate earnings. (The notion that such bonuses have incentive value is unproved, he asserts.) The responsibility for the current situation lies mainly with the board of directors, and a remedy for it lies principally with the board, too—particularly with the outside directors. The author proposes independence for the board's compensation committee, with the obligation of reporting its activities regularly to the public and the stockholders.

John C. Baker is a pioneer in the study of executive compensation and boards of directors, having conducted the first systematic examinations of each subject and written books in the 1930s and 1940s about his findings. For many years, he acted in research and administrative capacities at the Harvard Business School, and he served as president of Ohio University from 1945 to 1962. He has been connected with many companies as a director, compensation committee member, and consultant on compensation.

Reprint 77402

As everyone knows, public and stockholder mistrust of large corporations is widespread and appears to be growing. Among the reasons for this mistrust are fear of corporate size and power, danger from monopolies, illegal political contributions, scandals, bribery, and even dishonesty by a few. Corporate abuses make news and when exposed are rightly featured in the press.

A more subtle cause of unrest than these stems from stockholders' and the public's suspicions of top-level salaries, contracts, consulting fees, fringe benefits, and other payment policies.

Sensational headlines from newspapers and magazines feed and reflect their suspicions: "Bonuses Not Linked to Profits"; "Shareholders Question Chrysler Executive Benefits"; "Sweet Deal: Little Work Required by Ex-officers Named Consultants"; "Lockheed to Pay $750,000 Over 10 Years to Each of Two Officers Who Quit Recently."

These two excerpts are typical of the news stories under these headlines:

"In the company's proxy statement for its annual meeting May 3, Chrysler said that Chairman John Riccardo earned $691,733 last year, [including] a $445,900 bonus tied to earnings. President E.A. Cafiero's salary and bonuses totaled $620,000, [including] $401,300 in bonuses.... Three stockholder proposals are included on the meeting agenda and all would restrict in one way or another the amounts and methods of determining and distributing incentive bonus pay and the granting of stock options to corporate officials. All are opposed by Chrysler directors."[1]

"Judge Milton Pollock approved an amended settlement of a stockholders' suit in Federal District Court in Manhattan after two top officials of the Simplicity Pattern Company agreed to relinquish stock options worth more than $1 million...."[2]

Even a cursory examination of annual meeting proxy statements from year to year exposes an ever-increasing flood of complex—sometimes bizarre—plans exceptionally favorable to top officers. In fashioning their program, they can choose from a compensation bill of fare that includes cash salaries and bonuses, retirement plans, stock options (a variety), profit-sharing plans, savings and investment plans, long-term incentive plans, performance shares, stock purchase plans, low-interest loans, special contracts, consulting arrangements, "phantom" stock, and "stock appreciation rights." In addition, they can obtain lush fringe benefits ranging from medical care, legal and financial counseling, and airplanes and yachts to free travel for spouses, vacation allowances, personal use of hotel suites, and a variety of other perquisites.

Consider the employment contract of Robert F. Six, chairman of Continental Air Lines. Signed in 1975, the contract guarantees his services as chairman and chief executive at $300,000 annually until mid-1978 and then as chairman of the executive committee at $175,000 annually until mid-1981, when he will have reached the age of 74. During the next decade, his "retirement period," he will receive $100,000 annually. Supplementing these stipends are formula adjustments for inflation, incentive and deferred compensation, retirement benefits, and other "perks" such as use of company-paid apartments.[3]

A study I made of 50 successful industrial companies indicates that besides paying substantial competitive cash salaries in 1975, they offered the following supplementary compensation arrangements: all 50 had retirement plans; 46 had bonus (incentive) payments; 47 had stock option plans; 29, savings and investment plans; 22, deferred compensation; 22, special executive employment contracts. A comparison of these companies with a slightly smaller group in 1965 revealed over the decade large regular salary increases, as well as a doubling in the number of bonus plans, a large increase in savings and invest-

ment plans, and a modest increase in deferred compensation arrangements.

Stockholders and the knowledgeable public agree that sound, honest, and imaginative management should be well rewarded. Substantial salaries, fringe benefits, savings and investment plans, and profit-sharing plans covering large groups of employees, including executives, are quite acceptable.

Stockholders and the public resent, however, the prospect that key executives are becoming a privileged class, receiving special contracts or bonuses along with their extensive perquisites and often spectacular salaries—regardless of the performance of their companies. The rewards should not be, as a judge once termed them, "a misuse or waste of corporate funds, or a gift to a favored few."[4] Executive compensation practices that undermine public trust must be changed, or capitalists themselves will become a major force undermining capitalism.

Causes & reasons

One fundamental question of course is: What conditions led to the development of this chaotic situation? A simple answer is: neglect by directors who, following tradition, assume but do not *exercise* their proper responsibility. This answer—to some extent true—ignores, however, the great variety of ordinarily overlooked forces operating in this area. Five clearly discernible elements I shall discuss in detail are (a) the corporate power structure, (b) company directors, (c) the widely accepted fictions about executive motivation, (d) the character of executives, and (e) government and taxes.

Corporate power structure

The corporate power structure includes not only senior executives but also directors and certain junior officers as well as the infrastructure of accountants, lawyers, economists, consultants, com-

1. *Wall Street Journal*, March 21, 1977.

2. *Wall Street Journal*, September 16, 1976.

3. Details can be found in the Continental Air Lines 10-K statement for fiscal 1975.

4. Gallin v. National City Bank, 273 NYS 113-114, Affirmed 281 NYS 800.

"This is my executive suite and this is my executive vice-president, Ralph Anderson, and my executive secretary, Adele Eades, and my executive desk and my executive carpet and my executive wastebasket and my executive ashtray and my executive pen set and my ..."

Drawing by H. Martin; ©1974 The New Yorker Magazine, Inc.

mercial bankers, and others. But the very limited number of senior executives dominate the scene. "What does top management want?" is a question always in the minds of other members of the power structure.

Although approval by the board of directors and stockholders may be required, the final agreement on executive rewards lies with the senior management echelon. No group in the power structure is more influential in deciding their rewards than the involved executives themselves. This highly centralized decision making creates conflicts of interest, with opportunities for great personal gain and for public misunderstanding.

Public opinion, tax rulings, the Internal Revenue Service, and the courts are the main external countervailing forces moderating this centralized power. The misconception persists, however, that corporate directors and stockholders independently exercise final power over the adoption of compensation programs. But outside directors are usually selected by

senior officers and recommended to the full board for election—and thus are to a degree beholden to top management. Outside directors are busy people and therefore may not take the time to scrutinize compensation plans proposed by the infrastructure and supported by the senior executives. As for stockholders, in most listed corporations they are numerous, own individually only a few shares in relation to the total outstanding, are widely scattered, and are ignorant of the nuances in complicated compensation plans.

Consultants, accounting firms, lawyers, and others play a far more important role than is generally recognized. The work of these groups receives little public attention; nevertheless, these specialists originate compensation plans as well as develop ideas submitted to them by their clients. Of course, they depend on senior executive approval for their substantial fees and their continuing employment.

These comments about those in the corporate power structure are in no way meant as criticism of their integrity or ability but rather as explanation of why mistrust of the current procedures exists. Human nature being what it is, the belief that "he who pays the piper calls the tune" is widely held. It is not the individuals involved but the system that breeds concern.

Boards of directors

The days are rapidly passing when boards of directors can be complacent about compensation responsibilities. Government agencies, stockholders, and the public will not tolerate much longer their uncritical attitude about these vital management issues.

The boards of most large companies have a mix of inside and outside directors. Insiders, as employees, can be rewarded or penalized by senior officers and understandably tend to agree with the senior officers' wishes on compensation issues. Outside directors are supposed to be knowledgeable and independent, especially on compensation questions. But like the insiders, they are selected by management and for the most part support management. Moreover, the outside director may very well be a personal friend of the top corporate officers of the company on whose board he or she serves.

Directors, who are frequently busy corporate officers themselves, instinctively shy from criticizing management unless serious abuses are uncovered. Generally they take the position, "We've elected him to run things. We won't interfere." And many chief executives welcome this attitude, as one of them has been quoted as saying:

"I think the outside directors on a compensation committee do serve as a conscience. It doesn't go much beyond the conscience role though, because if outside directors tend to interfere they dilute my responsibility and authority." [5]

Far from interfering, at times outside directors (who are supposed to represent stockholders) are the very ones to urge the top officers to demand *more* in the way of salary, bonus, contracts, and fringe benefits than the historical pattern in the particular company or industry warrants. Such director back scratching has probably been observed on every board.

Usually, the strongest influence of outside directors on compensation policies is indirect. Astute executives ordinarily submit to the compensation committee of directors only those proposals that they think will meet with director approval.

Fictions about motivation

Senior executives' incentive payment plans, direct descendants of the discredited bonus plans of the late 1920s, are described and justified as "incentives to increase earnings." There is little solid evidence, however, that they result in greater earnings or even make executives more effective.

There is nothing new about incentives. In 500 B.C., Xenophon explained the payment and incentive system for Greek mercenaries of all ranks: "A stater of Cyzicus every month with double pay for captains and four times as much for generals: also as much land as they wanted; yokes of oxen; a fortified town on the coast." [6] Fortunately for mankind, the military have become professionals and are paid as such. How long will it take for our corporate officials to be paid on a rational basis?

The fictions about the incentive value of such payments are hoary with age—and hallowed by wide acceptance. Cynically stated, this policy is simply the "carrot before the donkey" idea. If you question this, you are told, "Look how successful General Motors has been by using such payments." The defenders of this thesis never mention, however, that other great companies with similar incentive plans have not enjoyed similar success. There are other, more powerful explanations for success and failure than the executive bonus payment plans in use in these companies.

Until recently, the notion was widely promoted and accepted that large, almost unlimited chances for monetary rewards of top executives—not just incentive plans—lead invariably to corporate success. In the early 1970s that fiction should have been destroyed when such prestigious, well-established companies as RCA, United Technology, Gulf Oil, Singer, NCR, and General Foods took write-downs of millions of dollars. At this time their senior officers were being liberally rewarded in a variety of ways.

Forces over which executives in our great corporations have little or no control, such as business conditions, government intervention, international eco-

5. Myles L. Mace, *Directors: Myth and Reality* (Boston: Division of Research, Harvard Business School, 1971), p. 27.

6. Xenophon, *The Persian Expedition* (Edinburgh: Penguin Books, 1975), p. 261.

nomics, and strikes, can affect earnings—and negate bonuses. On the other hand, fortuitous events may lead to windfall profits instead of disastrous losses to the company.

Bonus-paying companies do not necessarily outperform nonbonus-paying companies. In 1969, I made a study of 42 "growth" companies—24 bonus-paying and 18 nonbonus-paying companies whose average price-earnings ratio was 25 to 1. The median net income in percentages related to stockholders' equity for the bonus-paying companies was 12.4% and for the nonbonus-paying companies, 14.5%.

Many of today's incentive compensation programs are tied closely to corporate net income, which supposedly is a sound basis for supplementary compensation payments. As the events of 1974 clearly revealed, however, this may be an unsatisfactory figure on which to base supplementary compensation. Few corporate statistics are so complicated as net earnings and so exposed to interpretation. Even sophisticated defenders of bonus payments have trouble with this base.

Many discerning executives have deep reservations about the effectiveness of incentive payments. They admit that such payments are soon taken for granted and lose their leverage. Their relationship to earnings and the difficulties of awarding them equitably disturb these executives. They know that bonuses may produce destructive, not constructive, results.

In the last decade much attention has been given to the psychological or behavioral aspects of management incentive plans. Studies indicate that many highly successful executives are not motivated by exceptionally large monetary incentives. Rather, pride in title, position, achievements, and power are more important.

Executive character

An important, but too often ignored, intangible force in executive rewards is the character and temperament of the few dominant senior executives. Whatever their motivations are—desire for achievement, for public recognition, for power, money, show, prestige—they sooner or later are reflected in the philosophy behind the compensation policies and plans of the company. The spirit of the top officer permeates the entire executive group; nowhere is it likely to be more pervasive than in his attitudes toward executive rewards.

Revealing examples of upper-level influence on payment policies are legion. There is the fair-minded executive who believes in incentive payments but excludes himself from them so that he can control them and keep his judgment unclouded by personal gain. In contrast is the arrogant executive who feels that, being indispensable to his company's success, he is underpaid—even though his financial rewards may be very high for his industry. This type demands the lion's share.

Another executive, dubious about the equities of incentive payments, favors liberal cash salaries with full fringe benefits because he ardently believes in cooperation and teamwork. He is convinced that executives work harder and contribute more to the company when times are bad, earnings limited, and supplementary payments low or nonexistent. Finally, there is the emulative executive who, when he learns that a competitor has adopted what sounds to him like an advantageous plan, directs his staff to adapt it.

Government & taxes

By means of high income taxes the federal government has been one of the most compelling forces shaping compensation plans. Taxes have both directly and indirectly increased the variety and complexity of these compensation plans. As personal income taxes have at times risen to the confiscatory level, executives have properly demanded relief. With great ingenuity, consultants, lawyers, accountants, and others have found ways to reduce legally the tax bite, such as wider use of stock options, deferred compensation, and special contracts.

Some of these plans have proved to be a real boon to executives. When their effectiveness has failed for economic, legal, or other reasons, new plans have been devised. The result of their success and the tax advantages, of course, has been to confer on executives extraordinary privileges and to isolate them from other employees, stockholders, and the public.

The 1969 Tax Reform Act phased in the maximum tax on earned income at 60% for 1970 and 50% for 1971 and later years. The stated purpose was to reduce the pressure on high-income individuals to seek out tax shelters and various tax-avoidance gimmicks. How successful this significant change has been is still unclear, but I fear that the gimmicks are still increasing.

Restoring a balance

As long as corporate directors retain their present-day responsibilities, they must play a decisive role in devising and administering compensation programs. To enable outside directors to function properly on a compensation committee in this sensitive area, many long-accepted corporate procedures must be drastically changed. Deep-rooted customs, however wrong, are never easily altered. New policies must be developed at board meetings, and compensation committees must be strengthened.

A corporation's bylaws should require an independent, top-level compensation or salary committee, elected by the board and approved by stockholder vote—just as the auditors must be. This committee should have a knowledgeable, experienced chairman (an outsider) interested as much in the welfare of stockholders as in the well-being of the executives.

The committee should operate on its own budget so that its chairman could, as necessary, employ consultants, accountants, lawyers, and any staff required to furnish annually (or more frequently) the data needed for intelligent and fair committee decisions. These groups would work for and report to the committee chairman. He would report to shareholders at the annual meeting and publicly explain and defend committee policies and decisions.

In certain companies this proposal, I recognize, would lead to great changes in the relationship between directors and senior executives. Outside directors may be obliged to say "no" to top management more often, when they contemplate the prospect of publicly defending a particular compensation plan. But the changes in practice are essential to ensure acceptance by stockholders and the public.

Executive rewards, however, are too serious a problem to be left to boards of directors or individual advisers to solve without guiding principles. A fundamental, widely accepted philosophy for payments and other rewards—laid down by top management and the board—is essential.

'On top of responsibilities'

Executives, a key group in our free enterprise society, must be adequately and properly rewarded.

They are also vulnerable to the charge that with their unusual advantages they are present-day royalty. Unfortunately, no individual, no consultants, no group of directors have a reassuring answer as to how they should be paid.

We do know, however, that many compensation policies engender suspicion of and enmity against our corporations and accord, or appear to accord, special privileges to the top few. Many detached observers believe that these practices are unfair to stockholders, are heavily weighted with potential conflicts of interest, and ignore moral and public issues. These conditions create grave suspicions of abused executive power and set an unfortunate example for payments to employees at all levels of the corporation.

Boards of directors are being seriously criticized for failure to get on top of their responsibilities. In the area of executive rewards, their failure could derive both from ignorance—not knowing what sound policies are—and from the equivocal relationship between them and senior officers. In view of the complexities in this area, it is certainly unfair to assume that abuses arise simply from director complacency or venality. Whatever the causes, however, directors carry the burden of all grievances.

The establishment of independent, properly staffed, outsider-dominated salary committees would be an important first step in restoring public and stockholder confidence in top management and our great corporations. Such committees might well become an informed "police force" and bring some balance and order generally into the compensation field.

This article is not an indictment of executives but rather an exposure of a system of payment practices that needs to be changed. The mounting abuses and misunderstandings must be corrected to forestall harassment by stockholder suits and increasing control of executive compensation policies by government regulation. Fifty years ago Owen D. Young, chairman of the General Electric Company, issued a warning to unresponsive corporate executives that has not lost its pertinence:

"Too frequently businessmen have acquiesced, even if they did not participate, in objectionable practices until an outraged society compelled amateurs to interfere. The amateurs were frequently in the legislature and unwise laws were enacted." [7]

7. Address at the Harvard Business School, June 4, 1927.

Printed in U.S.A. by
Harvard University
Office of the University Publisher,
Boston, Massachusetts 02134